THE TRADER'S GUIDE TO THE EURO AREA

Since 1996, Bloomberg Press has published books for financial professionals on investing, economics, and policy affecting investors. Titles are written by leading practitioners and authorities, and have been translated into more than 20 languages.

The Bloomberg Financial Series provides both core reference knowledge and actionable information for financial professionals. The books are written by experts familiar with the work flows, challenges, and demands of investment professionals who trade the markets, manage money, and analyze investments in their capacity of growing and protecting wealth, hedging risk, and generating revenue.

For a list of available titles, please visit our website at www.wiley.com/go/bloombergpress.

THE TRADER'S GUIDE TO THE EURO AREA

Economic Indicators, the ECB and the Euro Crisis

David J. Powell

WILEY | Bloomberg PRESS

© 2013 John Wiley & Sons Ltd

Registered office
John Wiley & Sons Ltd, The Atrium, Southern Gate, Chichester, West Sussex, PO19 8SQ, United Kingdom

For details of our global editorial offices, for customer services and for information about how to apply for permission to reuse the copyright material in this book please visit our website at www.wiley.com.

All rights reserved. No part of this publication may be reproduced, stored in a retrieval system, or transmitted, in any form or by any means, electronic, mechanical, photocopying, recording or otherwise, except as permitted by the UK Copyright, Designs and Patents Act 1988, without the prior permission of the publisher.

Wiley publishes in a variety of print and electronic formats and by print-on-demand. Some material included with standard print versions of this book may not be included in e-books or in print-on-demand. If this book refers to media such as a CD or DVD that is not included in the version you purchased, you may download this material at http://booksupport.wiley.com. For more information about Wiley products, visit www.wiley.com.

Designations used by companies to distinguish their products are often claimed as trademarks. All brand names and product names used in this book are trade names, service marks, trademarks or registered trademarks of their respective owners. The publisher is not associated with any product or vendor mentioned in this book.

Limit of Liability/Disclaimer of Warranty: While the publisher and author have used their best efforts in preparing this book, they make no representations or warranties with respect to the accuracy or completeness of the contents of this book and specifically disclaim any implied warranties of merchantability or fitness for a particular purpose. It is sold on the understanding that the publisher is not engaged in rendering professional services and neither the publisher nor the author shall be liable for damages arising herefrom. If professional advice or other expert assistance is required, the services of a competent professional should be sought.

Library of Congress Cataloging-in-Publication Data

Powell, David J., 1980-
 The trader's guide to the euro area : economic indicators, the ECB and the euro crisis / David J. Powell.
   pages cm
 Includes bibliographical references and index.
 ISBN 978-1-118-44005-6 (cloth)
  1. Investments—European Union countries. 2. Eurozone. 3. Finance—European Union countries. 4. Financial crises—European Union countries. 5. Economic indicators—European Union countries. 6. European Union countries—Economic conditions. I. Title.
 HG5430.5.A3P69 2013
 330.94—dc23
                                                                                      2013022398

A catalogue record for this book is available from the British Library.

ISBN 978-1-118-44005-6 (hbk) ISBN 978-1-118-44003-2 (ebk)
ISBN 978-1-118-44002-5 (ebk) ISBN 978-1-118-44004-9 (ebk)

Set in 11/13 AGaramondPro by MPS Limited, Chennai, India
Printed in Great Britain by TJ International Ltd, Padstow, Cornwall, UK

Contents

Acknowledgements	ix
CHAPTER 1	
Introduction	1
CHAPTER 2	
Gross Domestic Product	5
The Expenditure Approach	5
The Output Method	10
The Income Method	11
GNP vs. GDP	11
Release Schedule	12
Trend Growth	15
The Business Cycle	16
Monetary Conditions Index	19
Effects of Monetary Policy on GDP	19
Effects of the Exchange Rate on GDP	21
Exchange-Rate Deflators	23
CHAPTER 3	
Coincident Indicators	27
PMI Surveys	27
Industrial Production	31
CHAPTER 4	
Leading Indicators	35
Financial Conditions Index	35
The U.S. Business Cycle	38
ZEW Survey	39
Ifo Survey	41
M1 Money Supply Growth	52

v

CHAPTER 5
Inflation Measures — 57
Consumer Price Index — 57
Producer Price Index — 63
Labor Costs — 65
Money Supply — 68
Inflation Expectations — 76

CHAPTER 6
The European Central Bank — 83
Traffic Light System — 86
Mandate — 88
Two-Pillar Strategy — 90
Monetary Policy Implementation — 91
Intervention in the Currency Markets — 93
Taylor Rule — 95

CHAPTER 7
Other Institutions — 101
Council of the European Union — 101
European Parliament — 102
European Commission — 102
Ecofin — 103
Eurogroup — 103
European Council — 104

CHAPTER 8
Euro Crisis — 105
Origins — 105
Optimal Currency Area Theory — 109
Fiscal Consolidation — 111
Quantitative and Qualitative Easing — 112
Government Bond Purchases — 115
Measures of National Solvency — 117
Target2 Balances — 121
Resolution — 123
Departure from the Euro Area — 127
Tools for Analyzing Debt Sustainability — 127

CHAPTER 9
Germany — 133
Labor Market — 133
Political Institutions — 137
Political Parties — 139

CHAPTER 10
  France   **143**

CHAPTER 11
  United Kingdom   **145**
  The Bank of England   145
  Quantitative Easing   153
  GDP   155
  Inflation Measures   157
  House Prices   158
  Political Institutions   164

CHAPTER 12
  Switzerland   **167**
  The Swiss National Bank   167
  KOF Leading Indicator   168

CHAPTER 13
  Sweden   **171**

CHAPTER 14
  Norway   **175**

Bibliography   **179**

Index   **197**

Acknowledgements

Few goals in life can be achieved without the support of other people. This book is no exception.

I am indebted to David Hauner. He always found time to share his expertise. His wife, Manuela Doeller-Hauner, was responsible for the most enjoyable of these discussions through her gracious hospitality.

The book also greatly benefited from the generosity and intellect of Holger Schmieding. He thoroughly read the manuscript, provided detailed feedback and pointed out many inaccuracies.

Mike Rosenberg provided valuable comments as well. I read Mike's classic book, *Exchange-Rate Determination*, the year I finished graduate school and at the time never thought I would have the honor of him editing my own.

I would like to thank a few colleagues at Bloomberg. This book would never have come to fruition without the support and approval of Ted Merz, Brian Rooney and JP Zammitt. In addition, I am grateful to Rich Yamarone for having introduced me to the editors at Wiley and to Chris Kirkham for his help in the editing process.

I am also grateful to many acquaintances, colleagues – former and present – and friends who provided hours of useful discussion in the years before I started working on this book and during the writing process. The list includes Landé Abisogun, Colin Asher, Riccardo Barbieri, Kurt Bayer, Joe Brusuelas, Marc Chandler, Bob Lawrie, Mike McDonough, Niraj Shah and Bob Sinche.

I would also like to thank the people who granted permission to reproduce some of their work or quotes. The list includes Willem Buiter, Paul De Grauwe, Thomas Mayer, Gilles Moec, Jim O'Neill, Erik Nielsen, Lucrezia Reichlin and Huw Worthington.

I am grateful to the staff of the Ifo Institute as well. Hans-Werner Sinn provided some helpful remarks on the section on the euro crisis. Klaus Wohlrabe kindly reviewed the section on the Ifo Survey. Wolfgang Nierhaus and Wolfgang Ruppert granted permission to reproduce some of their work. I also appreciate the assistance of Sigrid Stallhofer.

I would like to express appreciation to my parents, Carol Powell and Michael Powell. Their commitment to my education provided the foundation for this book.

I would like to acknowledge a few friends from my hometown of Cold Spring, New York. Alix, Bob, Juliette and Marie-Claude Morgan kindly hosted me at their summer home in France when I was completing the research for this book. Greg Highlen provided helpful comments during the writing process.

Lastly, I would also like to acknowledge a few individuals who provided support during my formative years and were crucial to my intellectual development. They are: the late John Mills, his wife, Margaret Mills, and the late Margaret Mudd.

CHAPTER 1

Introduction

The euro area remains in a state of flux and appears to be unsustainable in its present form. The outcome of the crisis may be unknown for years and a judgment on the project's success or failure may be out of reach for decades.

In the meantime, analysts, portfolio managers and traders will still have daily, weekly, quarterly and annual benchmarks. They will have to analyze economic developments in the euro area and their impacts on financial assets. The objective of this book is to provide a framework for that analysis that is comprehensible to most financial market participants.

The book begins with a focus on coincident and leading economic indicators for the euro area. The former furnish information on the state of the economy and the latter signal the future directions of those coincident indicators. Leading indicators, therefore, often attract the most attention in the financial markets.

Klaus Abberger and Wolfgang Nierhaus, economists at the Ifo Institute in Munich, have defined the characteristics of a good leading indicator. They have written, "The characteristic of a good indicator is that it signals turning points in economic activity in a timely and clear fashion (i.e. without false alarms). In addition the lead of the indicator should be stable so that a relatively reliable estimate can be made as to how early the signal of the indicator occurs. Finally, the results should be available in a timely manner and not subject to any major revisions after publication."[1]

Unfortunately, no indicator exists that perfectly fits that description and an analyst should therefore have a broad-based view and needs to watch a

---

[1]Abberger, Klaus and Nierhaus, Wolfgang *The Ifo Business Cycle Clock: Circular Correlation with the Real GDP*. CESIfo Working Paper No. 3179, Ifo Institute, 2010.

variety of indicators. That's the method of most economists. Alan Blinder, former vice chairman of the Board of Governors of the Federal Reserve System, said his approach while at the central bank was relatively simple: "Use a wide variety of models and don't ever trust any one of them too much."[2]

Mervyn King, former governor of the Bank of England, delivered a similar message: "The wealth and diversity of published labour statistics means it is rare for them all to point in the same direction. The MPC's analysis of the labour market is like the construction of a jigsaw puzzle. The pieces of data are assessed alongside each other in order to build up as clear a picture as possible. No single piece of data is interpreted in isolation. And no single piece of data is, in itself, decisive."[3] One could easily say the same thing about the economy as a whole.

Subsequent chapters attempt to provide an explanation of euro-area institutions. The region, with 17 central bank governors, 17 finance ministers and 17 heads of government as well as countless policy makers in Brussels, has become increasingly difficult to understand without knowledge of the roles of those bodies.

Chapter 8 focuses on the euro crisis. It attempts to provide an explanation of its origins and a glimpse of the potential outcomes. In addition, the tools needed to analyze the crisis as it evolves are presented. No one knows exactly how the crisis will end and financial market participants need to be armed with the appropriate instruments to understand the latest developments.

The views of some of the most widely-quoted economists – Willem Buiter, David Blanchflower, Paul De Grauwe, Barry Eichengreen, Milton Friedman, Paul Krugman, Thomas Mayer, Carmen Reinhart, Kenneth Rogoff and Hans-Werner Sinn – are frequently cited. Their insights into the debacle have been unparalleled, though some of the arguments may have shifted with time. The views of most economists are constantly evolving along with the events of the debt crisis. As John Maynard Keynes quipped, "When the facts change, I change my mind. What do you do, sir?"

The remaining chapters provide information unique to the economies of Germany, France, the U.K., Switzerland, Sweden and Norway. These countries have many of the same economic indicators – gross domestic product, industrial production, purchasing manager indices, etc. – as the euro area.

---

[2]Blinder, Alan *Central Banking in Theory and Practice*. Cambridge, Mass.: MIT Press, 1998.

[3]King, Mervyn "Employment Policy Institute's Fourth Annual Lecture." Bank of England, December 1, 1998. {http://www.bankofengland.co.uk/publications/Pages/speeches/1998/speech 29.aspx}

These data points are basically the same for those countries as for the euro area as a whole, though some details may differ. A second review of the indicators for the individual countries is avoided.

The reality is no one – not even the best economists – can see into the future. All anyone can do is make the best decisions possible based on a set of incomplete information. The best way to be armed for that decision-making process, despite its flaws and incompleteness, may be to understand the present state of the economy and the political debate as fully as possible.

CHAPTER 2

Gross Domestic Product

GDP is the most commonly cited comprehensive indicator of economic activity. It is the total market value of the goods and services produced within a nation or, in the case of the euro area, a monetary union. It can also be described as the total income of the geographic area.

The first word of the term – gross – indicates that depreciation of equipment and factories used in the production process is excluded from the calculation.[1] For example, the decline in the value of an aging computer is ignored in this measure of national output.

The second word of the term – domestic – indicates the inclusion of all production within the region's borders irrespective of the country of origin of the producer.[2] For example, if a Mercedes is produced in a plant constructed by the German company in the U.S., the car is included in U.S. GDP and excluded from German GDP. If the car is produced in Germany and shipped to the U.S., it is included in German GDP and excluded from U.S. GDP.

Three methods of measuring GDP exist: expenditure, output and income. In theory, all three methods should produce the same figure. In practice, measurement problems normally lead to discrepancies.

The Expenditure Approach

The expenditure approach is based on the final or end use of the produced goods and services. This method has historically been used most frequently by national statistical agencies. In a report from 1996 of 18 member countries, the OECD calculated that all of them reported GDP using the expenditure

---

[1] *Principal European Economic Indicators: A Statistical Guide*. Eurostat, 2009.
[2] *Ibid.*

approach. Sixteen of them also tallied the figure using the output method and 10 used the income approach as well.[3] These numbers have since risen to 18, 17 and 16, respectively.[4]

The accounting identity used to calculate GDP under the expenditure approach states that GDP equals consumption plus investment plus net exports. Consumption is broken down into private consumption and government consumption and investment consists of gross fixed capital investment and the change in inventories. The sum of consumption and investment equals domestic demand. Net exports equals exports minus imports.

Consumption (= Private Consumption + Government Consumption)
+ Investment (= Gross Fixed Capital Investment
+ Change in Inventories)
= Domestic Demand
+ Net Exports (= Exports − Imports)
= Gross Domestic Product

Private consumption is spending on goods and services by non-governmental entities such as individuals and households. It is the largest category of GDP for most developed economies. For example, it was about 71% of GDP of the U.S.; 64% of that of the U.K. and 57% of that of Germany in 2011.

Eurostat also includes a group called NPISH in its calculation of private consumption (Table 2.1). It is an acronym for non-profit institutions serving households. It includes charities, churches, political parties and trade unions.

Government consumption represents the purchase of goods and services by general government. It made up about 20% of GDP of the U.S.; 20% of that of Germany; and 22% of that of the U.K. in 2011.

Investment is the spending used to increase future consumption. The category breaks down into gross fixed capital formation and inventories.

Gross fixed capital formation represents the acquisition of fixed assets minus the disposal of those items. In this case, "gross" refers to the exclusion of depreciation costs. Fixed assets are defined by Eurostat as "tangible or intangible assets produced as outputs from the processes of production that are themselves used repeatedly, or continuously, in processes of production for more than one year."[5] An example of a tangible asset from this category is a factory and one of an intangible asset is a patent.

---

[3] *Quarterly National Accounts: Sources and Methods Used by OECD Member Countries*. OECD, 1996. {http://www.oecd.org/std/na/1909562.pdf}

[4] E-mail to David Powell from the OECD, March 18, 2013.

[5] *Gross Fixed Capital Formation*. Eurostat. {http://circa.europa.eu/irc/dsis/nfaccount/info/data/esa95/en/een00137.htm}

TABLE 2.1 Euro-Area GDP and Expenditure Components

T1																													
GDP AND EXPENDITURE COMPONENTS																													
t/t-1	PERCENTAGE CHANGE OVER THE PREVIOUS QUARTER – SEASONALLY ADJUSTED – CHAIN-LINKED VOLUMES																												

	GDP						Household & NPISH final consumption expenditure						Government final consumption expenditure						Gross Fixed Capital Formation						Exports						Imports					
	2011			2012			2011			2012			2011			2012			2011			2012			2011			2012			2011			2012		
	Q3	Q4		Q1	Q2		Q3	Q4		Q1	Q2		Q3	Q4		Q1	Q2		Q3	Q4		Q1	Q2		Q3	Q4		Q1	Q2		Q3	Q4		Q1	Q2	
EA17	0.1	−0.3		0.0	**−0.2**		0.2	−0.5		−0.2	**−0.2**		−0.2	0.0		0.2	**0.1**		−0.4	−0.5		−1.3	**−0.8**		1.5	−0.2		0.7	**1.3**		0.5	−1.4		−0.2	**0.9**	
EU27	0.2	−0.3		0.0	**−0.1**		0.0	−0.3		−0.1	**−0.2**		−0.3	0.1		0.4	**0.2**		−0.1	−0.3		−0.7	**−0.9**		1.4	0.1		0.5	**1.0**		0.6	−1.0		−0.2	**0.9**	
US	0.3	1.0		0.5	**0.4**		0.4	0.5		0.6	**0.4**		−0.6	−0.7		−0.3	**−0.3**		2.6	2.0		1.3	**1.1**		1.5	0.4		1.1	**1.5**		1.1	1.2		0.8	**0.7**	
JP	1.8	0.1		1.3	**0.3**		1.1	0.7		1.2	**0.1**		0.2	0.4		1.0	**0.3**		0.6	3.3		−0.4	**1.5**		7.9	−3.6		3.4	**1.2**		3.4	1.0		2.2	**1.6**	

Source: Eurostat

The remainder of investment spending consists of inventory accumulation. Inventories are used to meet future demand.

Investment, under the framework of national accounting, is undertaken mostly by businesses. The purchase of new homes is the only part of personal spending that falls into this category. Government spending generally falls into the category of consumption.[6]

The category of net exports is the difference between exports and imports. It represents the portion of aggregate domestic production that is beyond the goods and services needed for domestic consumption.

The breakdown by category of expenditure allows for an analysis of the type of spending that drives economic growth. Investment – gross fixed capital formation and inventories – tends to be the most cyclical category of spending. That is because businesses will likely delay plans for expansion or reduce their stocks of inventories as long as their managers perceive the outlook for demand to be uncertain or weak.

The recession in the euro area from 2008 to 2009 provided a good example. GDP contracted for five quarters – from the second quarter of 2008 through the second quarter of 2009. The economy contracted by 1.2% per quarter, on average, during that period. The contraction in investment spending was responsible for 1 percentage point of that average quarterly decline. Specifically, 0.7 of a percentage point was due to the decline in gross fixed capital formation and 0.3 of a percentage point to the change in inventories.

The subsequent recovery provided a similar picture. The economy expanded for nine consecutive quarters – from the third quarter of 2009 through the third quarter of 2011 – after the recession ended. The contribution to economic growth from investment spending was greater than that of any other source of domestic demand (Figure 2.1).

On average, the economy expanded by 0.4% per quarter during that period. Half of that growth – 0.2 of a percentage point – came from investment spending. The contribution to growth from household consumption was 0.1 of a percentage point and that from government spending was close to flat as austerity programs were implemented. The contribution from net exports – 0.2 of a percentage point – explains the other major source of growth. The figures fail to add up perfectly due to rounding.

During the recovery, the majority of the growth in investment spending came from inventory accumulation, though the decline in inventories played a smaller role than the decline of gross fixed capital formation during

---

[6]The Economist *Guide to Economic Indicators: Making Sense of Economics*, seventh edition. Hoboken, NJ: John Wiley & Sons, Inc., 2011.

FIGURE 2.1 Contributions to euro-area GDP growth from Q3 2009 to Q3 2011.

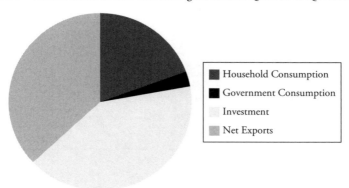

Source: Bloomberg, Eurostat

the recession. "Recessions and recoveries are (mostly) inventory cycles. While inventory investment typically only accounts for a tiny fraction of GDP, swings in inventories account for a large share of the cyclical swing in GDP," according to Ethan Harris, co-head of economic research at Bank of America–Merrill Lynch.[7]

He contends "inventories do not cause cycles in the economy, rather they amplify or 'accelerate' swings in the economy." They tend to lower output during recessions and increase output in the early stages of recoveries.

An outlook for inventory growth can be formed by looking at the monthly economic sentiment indicator of the European Commission in conjunction with the state of the economy. The industry and the retail trade surveys both contain questions about stocks (Figures 2.2 and 2.3). Respectively, they are:

Q4 Do you consider your current stock of finished products to be . . . ?
   + too large (above normal)
   = adequate (normal for the season)
   − too small (below normal)

Q2 Do you consider the volume of stock currently held to be . . . ?
   + too large (above normal)
   = adequate (normal for the season)
   − too small (below normal)

---

[7]Harris, Ethan "The Opposite of 'Stagflation'." *The Market Economist*. Bank of America–Merrill Lynch, September 18, 2009.

FIGURE 2.2 Inventory component of industrial confidence indicator.

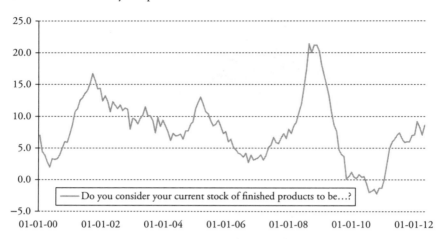

Source: Bloomberg

FIGURE 2.3 Inventory component of retail trade confidence indicator.

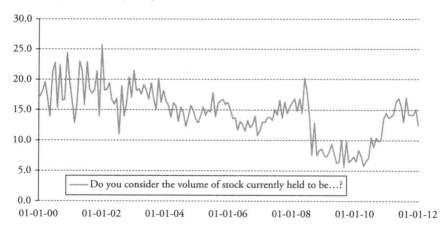

Source: Bloomberg

The Output Method

The output method measures the gross value added in an economy. In other words, it measures the value of all goods and services produced minus the value of all goods and services used in their production. The second category is subtracted from the first to avoid double accounting.

The reading is normally broken down by industry of the economy. For example, Eurostat provides a breakdown into the following industries (Table 2.2):

1. Agriculture, Fishing and Forestry.
2. Industry (Mining, Manufacturing, Electricity, Water and Waste).
3. Manufacturing.
4. Construction.
5. Trade, Transport, Accommodation, and Food Service Activities.
6. Information and Communication.

The Income Method

The third method of GDP calculation is based on income earned through the production of all the goods and services in an economy. It measures the incomes obtained from wages and salaries, rent, interest, corporate profits and proprietors' income.[8] GDP excludes transfer payments such as government benefits.

GNP vs. GDP

Gross national product measures the incomes of the residents of a country, regardless of where they were earned. For example, the net income that is transferred to its German owners from a Mercedes factory in the U.S. would be included in the GNP of Germany and excluded from that of the U.S.

Central bankers and economic policy makers tend to focus on GDP, though private economists refer to GNP on occasion. For example, Paul Krugman has often argued that economists should focus on GNP in the case of Ireland.[9]

Ireland is an exception to the rule that the difference between GNP and GDP is normally negligible.[10] The difference between these two figures

---

[8]Auerbach, Alan J. and Kotlikoff, Laurence J. *Macroeconomics: An Integrated Approach*, second edition. Cambridge, MA: The MIT Press, 1998.

[9]Krugman, Paul "Ireland Triumphs!" *The New York Times*, September 30, 2011.

[10]The Economist *Guide to Economic Indicators: Making Sense of Economics,* seventh edition. Hoboken, NJ: John Wiley & Sons, Inc., 2011.

TABLE 2.2 Euro-Area GDP and Gross Value Added by Industry

T4a												
t/t-1	\multicolumn{12}{c}{PERCENTAGE CHANGE OVER THE PREVIOUS QUARTER –}											
NACE Rev.2 Description:	\multicolumn{4}{c}{GDP}	\multicolumn{4}{c}{Agriculture, forestry and fishing}	\multicolumn{4}{c}{Industry (mining, manufacturing, electricity, water and waste)}											
Division:					\multicolumn{4}{c}{A}	\multicolumn{4}{c}{B, C, D and E}									
	2011		2012		2011		2012		2011		2012	
	Q3	Q4	Q1	Q2	Q3	Q4	Q1	Q2	Q3	Q4	Q1	Q2
EA17	0.1	−0.3	0.0	**−0.2**	0.7	−0.1	1.7	**−0.4**	0.0	−1.6	0.1	**−0.3**
EU27	0.2	−0.3	0.0	**−0.1**	0.3	−0.8	0.8	**−0.4**	0.0	−1.3	0.2	**−0.3**

Source: Eurostat

is about 25% for Ireland, 2% for the U.S. and 2% for Germany.[11] This is probably due to the large number of multinational corporations operating in Ireland as a result of its low level of corporate taxation.

Release Schedule

Eurostat publishes three releases for GDP. The first two GDP releases are accompanied by a press statement. The third release is only a database update.

All three releases publish the data in the form of growth over the previous quarter and over the previous year. They are normally referred to as quarter-over-quarter and year-over-year rates of growth. The latter is a smoothing technique, which removes short-term influences on the quarterly numbers and is a good measure of the recent trend.

---

[11] The figure for Germany is calculated using Gross National Income (GNI). The glossary of statistical terms of the OECD indicates that GNI and GNP are the same. It says, "Gross national income is identical to gross national product as previously used in national accounts generally." Some countries report small differences. For example, the Central Statistics Office of Ireland indicates that GNP totaled 130,202 million euros and GNI totaled 131,295 million euros in 2010.

ADDED BY INDUSTRY

SEASONALLY ADJUSTED – CHAIN-LINKED VOLUMES

of which: Manufacturing				Construction				Trade, transport, accommodation and food service activities				Information and communication			
C				F				G, H and I				J			
2011		2012		2011		2012		2011		2012		2011		2012	
Q3	Q4	Q1	Q2	Q3	Q4	Q1	Q2	Q3	Q4	Q1	Q2	Q3	Q4	Q1	Q2
−0.2	−1.4	0.0	**−0.5**	−0.7	−0.1	−1.0	**−0.7**	0.1	−0.2	0.0	**−0.4**	0.3	0.1	−0.1	−0.1
−0.2	−1.1	0.1	**−0.5**	−0.3	−0.1	−2.4	**−1.2**	0.1	−0.2	0.2	**−0.2**	0.6	0.1	−0.1	−0.3

The first release, which is called the flash estimate, is published about 45 days after the end of the reporting period (Table 2.3). It only provides headline figures for the euro area, the EU and individual countries of those regions for the latest quarter.

The second estimate appears about 65 days after the reporting period. It provides a breakdown from the expenditure and from the value-added points of view.

A third and final release appears about 100 days after the end of the reporting period. All current and past figures are open to revision, starting with the second release.

The first release only contains the GDP data with the effect of inflation removed. The broad term "real growth" is used to describe that adjustment. It can be applied to all aggregates, including those for income, which do not have directly observable volumes.[12] Specifically, the first release of GDP is expressed in terms of chain-linked volumes with a reference year of 2000. "Volume growth," which is a narrower term than "real growth," is used for items with a physical quantity that can theoretically be measured directly.

---

[12] *National Accounts Frequently Asked Questions.* Eurostat. {http://epp.eurostat.ec.europa.eu/portal/page/portal/national_accounts/documents/FAQ_NA_1.pdf}

TABLE 2.3 Quarterly National Accounts Release Policy

In the current release policy for the calculation of European aggregates there are four releases during a quarter Q. The three first releases (T + 45, T + 65 and T + 75) are database releases that are combined with a news release. The T + 100 release is only a database release. The following table summarises the release coverage:

	ESA	T + 45	T + 65	T + 75	T + 100
Flash GDP volume		Q* only	--	--	--
GDP (+)		--	Up to Q	--	Up to Q
Output A6 (+)	0101	--	Up to Q*	--	Up to Q
Main expenditure (+)	0102	--	Up to Q*	--	Up to Q
GFCF AN_F6 (+)	0102	--	--	Up to Q*	Up to Q
Exports/imports (+)	0102	--	--	Up to Q*	Up to Q
Income	0103	--	--	Up to Q*	Up to Q
Compensation A6	0103	--	--	Up to Q-1	Up to Q*
National income	0107	--	--	Up to Q-1	Up to Q*
Employment A6	0111	--	--	Up to Q*	Up to Q

+ estimation includes current prices, chain-linked volumes and previous year's prices.
* and bold: first release of figures for the new quarter.
Up to Q: whole time series up to the new quarter is revised.
Up to Q-1: whole time series up to the previous quarter is revised (aligned with higher level data), data for Q not available yet.
Shaded: Data is included and commented on in the news release.
Note that all "Up to" releases include also revisions of the underlying annual figures.
Source: Eurostat

The releases after the flash estimate contain data on nominal GDP as well. That figure is GDP expressed at current prices.

The first GDP release for the euro area is published much later than that for the U.K. or the U.S. As mentioned previously, it is announced 45 days after the end of the reporting period. In the latter two countries, the figures are published 25 days after the end of the quarter. Countries that delay the publication of economic statistics often argue that a trade-off exists between timing and accuracy.

The difference in accuracy between the GDP statistics for the euro area and those of the U.S. appears small. The flash GDP estimate for the euro area was unchanged relative to the second estimate for 40 of the last 46 quarters, as of August 2012, according to Eurostat, which began reporting a flash estimate in May 2003. In the other six of those 46 quarters, the two figures differed by plus or minus 0.1 of a percentage point.[13] The absolute difference

---

[13] *Eurostat News Release: Flash Estimate for the Second Quarter of 2012.* Eurostat, August 14, 2012.

between the advance (first) and the preliminary (second) estimates of U.S. GDP has been 0.5 of a percentage point on an annualized basis from 1983 to 2008, according to the Bureau of Economic Analysis of the U.S. Department of Commerce.[14] That equals about 0.125 of a percentage point on a quarter-over-quarter basis.

Trend Growth

The long-term path of GDP growth is normally assumed to be in line with the historic trend rate of growth. The easiest way of determining that figure is by taking a long-term average of output growth. Recent data may be most useful for the euro area as a result of the structural changes that have taken place since the birth of the monetary union. The 10-year average for the euro area is 1.1%, using data from 2002 to 2011. It is 1.6% for the U.K. and for the U.S.

These figures are below the long-term potential growth estimates of policy makers. The ECB has cited 2% to 2.5% as the trend rate of growth for the euro-area economy.[15] The Federal Reserve has estimated 2.2% to 3% as the equivalent figure for the U.S.[16] These figures are likely to be revised down as the level of economic growth experiences a structural decline in the aftermath of the global financial crisis.

The ECB has attributed the higher rate of potential growth in the U.S. – relative to the euro area – to demographic developments and the rate of productivity growth.[17] These demographic developments refer to the growth in the population, which is the pool of labor for production. Annual population growth in the euro area has averaged 0.5% over the 10-year period from 2002 to 2011. That figure for the U.S. has been 1.1%.

---

[14] *National Income and Product Accounts: Gross Domestic Product, 2nd Quarter 2012 (Advance Estimate)*. Bureau of Economic Analysis, July 27, 2012.
[15] "Output, Demand and the Labour Market." *ECB Monthly Bulletin*. Frankfurt: European Central Bank, July 2009.
[16] *Economic Projections of Federal Reserve Board Members and Federal Reserve Bank Presidents, September 2012*. Board of Governors of the Federal Reserve System, September 13, 2012.
[17] "Patterns of Euro Area and U.S. Macroeconomic Cycles – What Has Been Different This Time?" *ECB Monthly Bulletin*. Frankfurt: European Central Bank, May 2011.

The Business Cycle

Deviations in GDP growth from that long-term trend occur as part of the business cycle. Arthur Burns, former chairman of the Board of Governors of the Federal Reserve System and president of the National Bureau of Economic Research, and Wesley Mitchell, a founder of the NBER, proposed a definition for the business cycle:

> "Business cycles are a type of fluctuation found in the aggregate economic activity of nations that organize their work mainly in business enterprises: a cycle consists of expansions occurring at about the same time in many economic activities, followed by similarly general recessions, contractions, and revivals which merge into the expansion phase of the next cycle; this sequence of changes is recurrent but not periodic; in duration business cycles vary from more than one year to ten or twelve years; they are not divisible into shorter cycles of similar character with amplitudes approximating their own."[18]

The NBER in Cambridge, Massachusetts is the official arbitrator of recessions in the U.S. It defines a recession as a "significant decline in economic activity spread across the economy, lasting more than a few months, normally visible in real GDP, real income, employment, industrial production, and wholesale-retail sales."[19] It doesn't use the popular definition of recession – two consecutive quarters of negative GDP growth. The NBER has identified 33 recessions in the U.S. since the middle of the 19th century (Table 2.4).

The Centre for Economic Policy Research in London is the European equivalent of the NBER. In 2002, the CEPR created a Business Cycle Dating Committee for the euro area. It has established four recessions for the euro area since 1970 (Table 2.5).

The CEPR, like the NBER, announces the end of a recession long after it occurs. For example, it declared the ending point of the 2008–2009 downturn to be in the second quarter of the latter year more than a year later – on October 4, 2010.

---

[18]Burns, Arthur F. and Mitchell, Wesley C. *Measuring Business Cycles*. Cambridge, Mass.: NBER, 1946.

[19]*US Business Cycle Expansions and Contractions*. The National Bureau of Economic Research. {http://www.nber.org/cycles.html}

Gross Domestic Product

TABLE 2.4 U.S. Business Cycle Expansions and Contractions

BUSINESS CYCLE REFERENCE DATES		DURATION IN MONTHS			
Peak	Trough	Contraction	Expansion	Cycle	
Quarterly dates are in parentheses		Peak to trough	Previous trough to this peak	Trough from previous trough	Peak from previous peak
	December 1854 (IV)	--	--	--	--
June 1857 (II)	December 1858 (IV)	18	30	48	--
October 1860 (III)	June 1861 (III)	8	22	30	40
April 1865 (I)	December 1867 (I)	32	46	78	54
June 1869 (II)	December 1870 (IV)	18	18	36	50
October 1873 (III)	March 1879 (I)	65	34	99	52
March 1882 (I)	May 1885 (II)	38	36	74	101
March 1887 (II)	April 1888 (I)	13	22	35	60
July 1890 (III)	May 1891 (II)	10	27	37	40
January 1893 (I)	June 1894 (II)	17	20	37	30
December 1895 (IV)	June 1897 (II)	18	18	36	35
June 1899 (III)	December 1900 (IV)	18	24	42	42
September 1902 (IV)	August 1904 (III)	23	21	44	39
May 1907 (II)	June 1908 (II)	13	33	46	56
January 1910 (I)	January 1912 (IV)	24	19	43	32
January 1913 (I)	December 1914 (IV)	23	12	35	36
August 1918 (III)	March 1919 (I)	7	44	57	67
January 1920 (I)	July 1921 (III)	18	10	28	17
May 1923 (II)	July 1924 (III)	14	22	36	40
October 1926 (III)	November 1927 (IV)	13	27	40	41
August 1929 (III)	March 1933 (I)	43	21	64	34
May 1937 (II)	June 1938 (II)	13	50	63	93

(*Continued*)

TABLE 2.4 *Continued*

BUSINESS CYCLE REFERENCE DATES		DURATION IN MONTHS			
Peak	Trough	Contraction	Expansion	Cycle	
Quarterly dates are in parentheses		Peak to trough	Previous trough to this peak	Trough from previous trough	Peak from previous peak
February 1945 (I)	October 1945 (IV)	8	80	88	93
November 1948 (IV)	October 1949 (IV)	11	37	48	45
July 1953 (II)	May 1954 (II)	10	45	55	56
August 1957 (III)	April 1958 (II)	8	39	47	49
April 1960 (II)	February 1961 (I)	10	24	34	32
December 1969 (IV)	November 1970 (IV)	11	106	117	116
November 1973 (IV)	March 1975 (I)	16	36	52	47
January 1980 (I)	July 1980 (III)	6	58	64	74
July 1981 (III)	November 1982 (IV)	16	12	28	18
July 1990 (III)	March 1991(I)	8	92	100	108
March 2001 (I)	November 2001 (IV)	8	120	128	128
December 2007 (IV)	June 2009 (II)	18	73	91	81

Source: NBER

TABLE 2.5 Peaks and Troughs of Euro-Area Business Cycles

PEAK	TROUGH
1974Q3	1975Q1
1980Q1	1982Q3
1992Q1	1993Q3
2008Q1	2009Q2
2011Q3	-

Source: CEPR Business Cycle Dating Committee {www.cepr.org}. Reproduced by permission of the CEPR.

Policy makers have normally responded to deviations in GDP growth from the long-term trend. They attempt to slow the rate of growth if inflationary pressures start to build and to stimulate the economy during periods of recession.

The economy can be stimulated or restricted through three primary channels: the exchange rate, fiscal policy and monetary policy. Central banks have historically only controlled monetary policy directly through changes in short-term policy rates and indirectly through changes of the exchange rate, though some of the unconventional measures implemented by monetary authorities in recent years have been used to influence longer-term interest rates and could be interpreted as measures of fiscal policy.

Monetary Conditions Index

A monetary conditions index can provide a reading of the level of stimulus provided by the main policy rate and the exchange rate relative to the past. The effects of these variables can be gauged by measuring changes in the real three-month interest rate and the real effective exchange rate, an inflation-adjusted and trade-weighted measure of a country's currency. The weighting of each component should be a function of the openness of the economy to imports and exports.

The weightings of the exchange and interest rates can be determined by calculating the openness of the economy to trade.[20] Mathematically, the indices can be expressed as

$$MCI_1 = \alpha(r_1 - r_0) + \beta((e_1/e_0) - 1) + 100$$

where r is the three-month interest rate deflated by the consumer price index; e is the real effective exchange rate as calculated by the International Monetary Fund; $\beta = ((\text{imports plus exports})/2)/\text{nominal GDP}$; and $\alpha = 1 - \beta$.

Effects of Monetary Policy on GDP

Monetary policy works with long and variable lags, as Milton Friedman famously said. The OECD's global macroeconomic model signals that the effect of a change in monetary policy may be felt over about five years. The

---

[20]Verdelhan, Adrien "Construction d'un indicateur des conditions monétaires pour la zone euro." *Bulletin de la Banque de France*, No. 58, October 1998.

TABLE 2.6 Sustained Increase in Euro-Area Interest Rates (100 Basis Points)

	Percentage Deviations from Baseline				
	Years after Shock				
	Year 1	Year 2	Year 3	Year 4	Year 5
UNITED STATES					
GDP level	0.0	0.0	0.0	−0.1	−0.1
Inflation	0.0	0.0	0.0	0.0	0.0
Current account (% GDP)	0.1	0.1	0.1	0.1	0.1
Government net lending (% GDP)	0.0	0.0	0.0	0.0	0.0
Japan					
GDP level	0.0	0.0	0.0	−0.1	−0.1
Inflation	0.0	0.0	0.0	0.0	0.0
Current account (% GDP)	0.0	0.0	−0.1	−0.1	−0.1
Government net lending (% GDP)	0.0	0.0	0.0	0.0	0.0
Euro					
GDP level	0.0	−0.1	−0.3	−0.5	−0.7
Inflation	0.0	0.0	−0.1	−0.1	−0.2
Current account (% GDP)	0.1	0.2	0.3	0.4	0.5
Government net lending (% GDP)	0.0	−0.1	−0.2	−0.2	−0.2
GDP level					
Other OECD Europe	0.0	0.0	−0.1	−0.2	−0.3
Other OECD	0.0	0.0	0.0	−0.1	−0.1
Total OECD	*0.0*	*0.0*	*−0.1*	*−0.2*	*−0.3*
China	0.0	0.0	−0.1	−0.1	−0.1
Other non-OECD Asia	0.0	0.0	−0.1	−0.1	0.0
Non-OECD Europe	0.0	0.0	−0.1	−0.1	−0.1
Other non-OECD	0.0	0.0	0.0	0.0	0.0
Total non-OECD	*0.0*	*0.0*	*−0.1*	*−0.1*	*−0.1*
World	*0.0*	*0.0*	*−0.1*	*−0.2*	*−0.2*

Source: OECD. Reproduced by permission of the OECD.

model suggests that a sustained increase in "policy determined nominal short-term interest rates" of the euro area by 100 basis points has no effect on the level of GDP during the first year after the shock (Table 2.6). It then estimates that the policy change will reduce the level of output by a cumulative 0.1% during the second year, 0.3% during the third year, 0.5% during the fourth year and 0.7% during the fifth year.[21]

The ECB supports the view that monetary policy has no effect on long-term real GDP growth. In other words, the central bank states that its actions

---

[21]Hervé, K. *et al.* "The OECD's New Global Model", OECD Economics Department Working Papers, No. 768, OECD Publishing, 2010. {http://dx.doi.org/10.1787/5kmftp85kr8p-en}

can only amplify or dampen the effects of the business cycle without affecting trend growth. The staff economists claim that this is consistent with the "large body of theoretical and empirical literature on money neutrality."[22] Their view is not held universally by economists.

Effects of the Exchange Rate on GDP

A change in the exchange rate, often induced by monetary policy developments, also has an effect on GDP. The OECD's global macroeconomic model suggests that a 10% depreciation of the nominal effective exchange rate of the euro boosts the level of GDP of the euro area by a cumulative 0.7% in the first year after the drop, 1.3% by the second year, 1.7% by the third year, 1.8% by the fourth year and 1.6% by the fifth year (Table 2.7).

In other words, after five years, a 10% decline in the trade-weighted currency would have an effect on GDP that is close to reducing short-term interest rates by 200 basis points. The model assumes that the exchange rate stays at the new level throughout the simulation period. The OECD's economists state that the effects of currency appreciation are broadly symmetric to those of currency depreciation.

The stimulus to GDP growth would likely be greater for the euro area during the debt crisis, as pointed out by Laurence Boone and Huw Worthington.[23] That's because the OECD assumes the central bank will raise interest rates in response to the currency depreciation to counteract the inflationary pressures. By contrast, the ECB eventually reduced its main policy rate to a record low level.

The effect of a depreciation of the euro is also likely to vary from country to country. Céline Allard, Mario Catalan, Luc Everaert and Silvia Sgherri of the IMF found that the goods exports of Germany are the least sensitive to changes in the country's real effective exchange rate out of those from the monetary union's four largest national economies.

The estimated exchange rate elasticity for goods – the ratio of the percentage change of goods exports to the percentage change of the exchange rate – for Germany stands at minus 0.32. In other words, as the country's real

---

[22] "Recent Findings on Monetary Policy Transmission in the Euro Area." *ECB Monthly Bulletin*. Frankfurt: European Central Bank, October 2002.
[23] Boone, Laurence and Worthington, Huw *European Government Monitor: Is Further Tightening Desirable?* Barclays Capital, September 1, 2010.

TABLE 2.7 10% Euro Depreciation

	Percentage Deviations from Baseline				
	Years after Shock				
	Year 1	Year 2	Year 3	Year 4	Year 5
UNITED STATES					
GDP level	−0.1	−0.2	−0.2	−0.3	−0.3
Inflation	−0.1	−0.1	−0.1	−0.2	−0.3
Interest rates (basis points)	−10	−20	−30	−45	−50
Current account (% GDP)	0.1	0.0	0.0	0.0	−0.1
Japan					
GDP level	0.0	−0.1	−0.2	−0.3	−0.4
Inflation	−0.1	−0.1	−0.1	−0.1	−0.2
Interest rates (basis points)	−10	−20	−20	−35	−50
Current accout (% GDP)	−0.1	−0.2	−0.3	−0.4	−0.4
Euro					
GDP level	0.7	1.3	1.7	1.8	1.6
Inflation	0.3	0.7	1.0	0.9	0.9
Interest rates (basis points)	85	165	220	210	200
Current account (% GDP)	0.3	0.2	0.5	0.8	1.0
GDP level					
Other OECD Europe	−0.2	−03	−0.4	−0.5	−0.5
Other OECD	−0.3	−0.4	−0.4	−0.4	−0.3
Total OECD	*0.1*	*0.2*	*0.2*	*0.2*	*0.1*
China	−0.1	−0.1	−0.2	−0.4	−0.4
Other non-OECD Asia	0.2	0.0	−0.2	−0.2	−0.2
Non-OECD Europe	0.7	0.7	0.5	0.2	−0.1
Other non-OECD	0.5	0.5	0.2	0.1	0.0
Total non-OECD	*0.3*	*0.3*	*0.1*	*−0.1*	*−0.1*
World	*0.2*	*0.2*	*0.2*	*0.1*	*0.1*

Source: OECD. Reproduced by permission of the OECD.

effective exchange rate – based on unit labor costs in the manufacturing sector – increases by 1%, the export of goods declines by 0.32%. The equivalent figure is minus 0.7 for Italy, minus 0.8 for France and minus 1.5 for Spain.[24]

Economists from the Bundesbank attribute the muted effect of currency movements on the volume of German exports to their price inelasticity. This implies that German exports – probably as a result of their high quality – are

---

[24]Allard, Céline, Catalan, Mario, Everaert, Luc and Sgherri, Silvia *Explaining Differences in External Sector Performance Among Large Euro Area Countries.* International Monetary Fund, October 12, 2005.

not easily substituted with other products. They wrote, "this relatively small influence is due partly to the fact that the share of relatively price-inelastic goods in the range of German exports is quite high. Exports to non-euro-area countries, in particular, respond relatively weakly to price competitiveness."

They concluded, "the German economy's export activity fundamentally depends much more on the growth of export markets and attractiveness of exporters' product profile than merely on exchange rate changes."[25] As a general rule, economists believe the level of growth of a country's export activity is more highly dependent on the rate of GDP growth in the economies of a country's largest trading partners than the value of the domestic currency vis à vis the currencies of those trading partners.

In addition, the composition of German exports creates a natural hedge, the Bundesbank study concluded. Because many of the country's products are manufactured goods, which require imported materials for production, the appreciation of the euro reduces the price of those intermediate inputs, cushioning the bottom line of corporate balance sheets. That natural hedge probably exists to a lesser extent for other euro-area countries with different export compositions.

Exchange-Rate Deflators

Economists look mostly at the real effective exchange rate of a country rather than the nominal effective exchange rate as a measure of price competitiveness in international markets. The use of that inflation-adjusted measure requires a measure of inflation as a deflator.

Most economists seem to agree that unit labor costs are the best deflator, at least in theory. That is because they are the most relevant costs for international trade. The debate assumes that goods are priced by adding a mark-up to the cost of production.[26] The higher unit labor costs, the higher the final price of the product and the higher the real exchange rate. The appreciation of the real exchange rate lowers international demand for a country's goods.

---

[25] "Macroeconomic Effects of Changes in Real Exchange Rates." *Deutsche Bundesbank Monthly Report*. Deutsche Bundesbank, March 2008.
[26] Chinn, Menzie D. "Effective Exchange Rates" in *The Princeton Encyclopaedia of the World Economy*. Editors in chief, Kenneth A. Reinert and Ramkishen S. Rajan; Associate editors, Amy Jocelyn Glass and Lewis S. Davis. Princeton: Princeton University Press, 2009.

The major disadvantage of using unit labor costs as a deflator is that neither a consistent nor a timely measure of those costs is available for many countries.[27] Another disadvantage of this deflator is that it ignores all input costs apart from labor. Other deflators also have advantages and disadvantages.

The advantage of the CPI is the inclusion of the prices of both goods and services. The disadvantages of this measure are the inclusion of the impacts of subsidies and taxes and the prices of non-traded goods and services and the exclusion of non-consumer goods.

The advantage of the producer price index is the exclusion of many services that are non-traded. The disadvantage of this measure is that comparable figures across a wide variety of countries are unavailable.

The advantage of the wholesale price index is that it may be less affected by subsidies and taxes than the CPI because it tracks prices in various stages of the production process. The disadvantages are that it includes non-traded goods and excludes the costs of services.[28]

The CPI has become the most commonly used deflator. These indices are often comparable around the world and are published on a timely basis.[29]

The IMF tends to use the CPI as a deflator for real effective exchange rates. The staff economists have also primarily used CPI-based measures of the real effective exchange rate in their reports on the bailouts of the euro-area countries.[30]

The choice of a deflator can significantly affect the level of the real effective exchange rate. In a 2005 study, Menzie Chinn found that, "after accounting for productivity changes, the (U.S.) dollar at the end of 2001 is less than 20 percent weaker than its 1985 peak using the CPI deflated rate, while the unit labor deflated series is 40 percent weaker."[31]

Similarly, in a 2011 study, IMF economists Tamim Bayoumi, Richard Harmsen and Jarkko Turunen stated, "While Italy's competitiveness does

---

[27] *Ibid.*

[28] This list is drawn mostly from an IMF paper by Tamim Bayoumi, Richard Harmsen and Jarkko Turunen titled "Euro Area Export Performance and Competitiveness." It covers some of the major advantages and disadvantages of the various price indices, though it is not comprehensive.

[29] Ellis, Luci *Measuring the Real Exchange Rate: Pitfalls and Practicalities.* Reserve Bank of Australia, August 2001.

[30] See: *Greece: IMF Country Report No. 12/57: Request for Extended Arrangement Under the Extended Fund Facility – Staff Report.* International Monetary Fund, March 2012.

[31] Chinn, Menzie D. *A Primer on Real Effective Exchange Rates: Determinants, Overvaluation, Trade Flows and Competitive Devaluation.* National Bureau of Economic Research, July 2005.

appear to have eroded, the size of this effect is, frankly, anyone's guess – while the CPI- and WPI-based measures (of the real effective exchange rate) show only modest appreciation since 1995, the ULC- and XUV- (export unit valued) based indicators have appreciated by about 50 to 110 percent, respectively."[32]

The long lag between the end of a particular month or quarter and the publication of the GDP data leads economists, market participants and policy makers to watch other data releases that are coincident indicators closely. They provide a more timely reading of the state of the economy.

---

[32] Bayoumi, Tamim, Harmsen, Richard and Turunen, Jarkko *Euro Area Export Performance and Competitiveness*. International Monetary Fund, June 2011. Reproduced by permission of the International Monetary Fund.

CHAPTER 3

Coincident Indicators

PMI Surveys

The purchasing manager indices are based on surveys conducted by Markit Economics, a London-based data provider. They fall in between the categories of coincident and leading indicators. They are the timeliest indicators of the present state of the economy and among the first monthly economic indicators released. This means that they report on current – not future – economic performance with a large publishing lead, though some components have leading qualities.

The PMI surveys show a strong relationship with economic activity (Figure 3.1). For example, the correlation between the quarterly average of the euro-area composite PMI survey and quarter-over-quarter GDP growth from the third quarter of 2005 to the fourth quarter of 2012 stands at 0.9. The figure falls to 0.84 when year-over-year GDP growth is used.

Markit collects data from about 5000 firms in the manufacturing and service sectors. About 3000 of these firms participate in the survey for the former sector and about 2000 for that of the latter sector.

The PMI publishes three indices for the euro area: the composite, the manufacturing and the services readings.

The composite index is close to a representation of the overall economy. The manufacturing and services measures only cover those sectors. The manufacturing sector represents 17.8% of the euro-area economy and the service sector produces 74.2% of total output. The remainder consists of the construction industry at 6.3% and the agricultural, hunting, forestry and fishing industries at 1.6%.[1] These PMI readings correspond to the categories of GDP published under the output method.

---

[1] *Europe in Figures: Eurostat Yearbook 2011*. Eurostat, 2011.

FIGURE 3.1 Euro-area composite PMI and GDP growth.

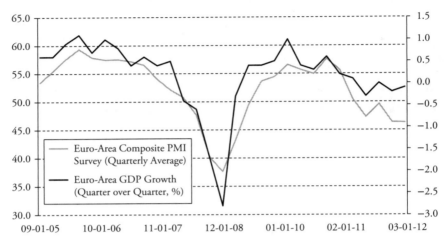

Source: Bloomberg

Two readings are published for each index. The flash readings are released about three weeks into the period in question. They are based on about 75–85% of the total responses for each month.[2] The final readings are delivered just a couple of days after the end of the month. The latter are not revised apart from minor seasonal adjustments on occasion.[3]

The difference between the two readings has historically been small, suggesting that the flash estimate provides a reliable reading. For the composite survey, the average difference has been 0.0 and the average difference in absolute terms has been 0.2. These figures for the manufacturing survey have been 0.0 and 0.2, respectively. The numbers for the services survey have been 0.0 and 0.4, respectively. The average difference is an indicator of any bias that may exist and the average difference in absolute terms gives a signal of overall variation.[4]

All three surveys have a headline reading. It is an output index for the composite and manufacturing measures and a business activity index for the services measure.

---

[2]*News Release: Markit Eurozone Composite PMI – Final Data.* Markit, August 3, 2012.
[3]*Markit Economics: About PMI Data.* Markit. {http://www.markiteconomics.com/Survey/Page.mvc/AboutPMIData}
[4]*News Release: Markit Eurozone Composite PMI – Final Data.* Markit, August 3, 2012.

Coincident Indicators 29

The manufacturing and services surveys have sub-categories as well. Those for the manufacturing survey are new orders, export orders, backlogs of work, employment, quantity of purchases, input costs, output prices, suppliers' delivery times, stocks of purchases and stocks of finished goods. Those for the services survey are incoming new business, business outstanding, employment, input costs and prices charged.

A diffusion index is calculated for the headline and each category. It measures the extent to which a change of sentiment from one month to the next is widespread or "diffused."[5] A respondent is asked a question that has three possible responses: increase, no change or decrease. For example: "Was output over the last month increased, unchanged or decreased?"

The index is calculated as the percentage of responses indicating an increase plus half of the responses indicating no change.[6] For example, if 60% of the respondents to a survey reported an increase, 20% reported a decrease and 10% reported no change, the diffusion index would be 65. It would be calculated as: $60 + (.5 \times 10) = 65$.

A reading of 50 indicates no change from the previous month, in theory. It would show an equal number of firms reporting an increase and a decrease in activity. For example, if 30% signaled an increase, 30% signaled a decrease and 40% signaled no change, the calculation would be: $30 + (.5 \times 40) = 50$.

The threshold that corresponds to a breakeven rate of GDP appears to be below that figure. The reason for the difference may relate to the pool of firms surveyed. New firms, which can have the highest levels of growth in an economy, may be excluded from the sample because they are too small and/or new to have been involved.

Markit provides separate surveys for several of the individual member countries. Manufacturing PMI surveys are produced for Austria, France, Germany, Greece, Ireland, Italy, the Netherlands and Spain (Table 3.1). Services PMI surveys are produced for France, Germany, Ireland, Italy and Spain.

These national breakdowns allow for international comparisons. This applies to countries within the euro area as well as countries outside the euro area. Markit reports that the statistics are compiled using an internationally compatible methodology, facilitating those comparisons. Markit publishes PMI surveys for more than 30 countries. A widely-watched PMI survey for the U.S. is also published by the Institute for Supply Management.

---

[5] ISM Report on Business Frequently Asked Questions. "What is a Diffusion Index?" {http://www.ism.ws/ISMReport/content.cfm?ItemNumber=10706}
[6] *News Release: Markit/CIPS UK Manufacturing PMI*. Markit, June 1, 2012.

TABLE 3.1 PMI Reports by Geography and Broad Sector

	Manufacturing	Services	Construction	Retail
Global	☐	☐	-	-
Eurozone	☐	☐	-	☐
Austria	☐	-	-	-
Brazil	☐	☐	-	-
Canada	☐	-	-	-
China	☐	☐	-	-
Czech Republic	☐	-	-	-
France	☐	☐	☐	☐
Germany	☐	☐	☐	☐
Greece	☐	-	-	-
Hong Kong*	☐	☐	☐	☐
India	☐	☐	-	-
Indonesia	☐	-	-	-
Ireland	☐	☐	☐	-
Italy	☐	☐	☐	☐
Japan	☐	☐	-	-
Mexico	☐	-	-	-
Netherlands	☐	-	-	-
Poland	☐	-	-	-
Russia	☐	☐	-	-
Saudi Arabia**	☐	☐	☐	☐
Spain	☐	☐	-	-
South Korea	☐	-	-	-
Taiwan	☐	-	-	-
Turkey	☐	-	-	-
United Arab Emirates**	☐	☐	☐	☐
United Kingdom	☐	☐	☐	-
United States	☐	-	-	-
Vietnam	☐	-	-	-

*total private sector
**non-oil private sector
Source: Markit. Reproduced by permission of Markit.

Ethan Harris and Neil Dutta have suggested that cross-border comparisons require some caution. They calculated the levels of the manufacturing PMI surveys that correspond with the breakeven levels for GDP. The level for the euro area stands at 47.7. The figure for France is 47, that for Germany is 48.6, that for Greece is 46.5, that for Italy is 49.3 and that for Spain is 43.3. The study noted that some of the standard errors – the standard deviations of the residuals — were high, suggesting that one needs to take the numbers with a grain of salt.[7]

In a separate study, Harris's team noted, "a simple time series regression exercise of annualized quarterly real GDP growth against the quarterly average of the manufacturing PMI for a set of 26 countries finds that systematic over- or under-prediction of growth is quite common." For example, in that 26-country sample, the mean absolute error from the estimated ISM relationship was 1.6 percentage points in the fourth quarter of 2011.[8]

Analysts tend to view the ratio of the orders component to the inventory component as a leading indicator. If orders are high relative to inventories, output will naturally have to be increased in the near future to satisfy the net increase in demand coming from firms' order books. By contrast, if orders are low relative to the size of inventories, a company can decrease output in the weeks ahead.

Industrial Production

The industrial production index provides a good indicator of overall GDP (Figure 3.2). That is the case even though the manufacturing sector is small in most developed economies relative to the size of the service sector. For example, in the euro area, the former makes up only 17.8% of the economy and the latter represents about 74.2% of total output.

A regression of industrial production on a year-over-year basis on GDP data in the same form suggests that it explains 77% of the variation in overall output using data from the first quarter of 1995 to the second quarter of 2012. Using quarter-over-quarter data, the equivalent figure is 65%. These results are probably due to businesses and consumers increasing their purchases of big-ticket items, such as computers, and durable consumer goods, such as cars and televisions, during expansionary periods for the overall economy and then doing the opposite during downturns.

In a 2010 study of short-term economic indicators for the euro area, the U.S. and the U.K., James Ashley and Simon Hayes of Barclays Capital's Global Research Division found that industrial production was the best

---

[7]Dutta, Neil and Harris, Ethan S. *Europe Sneezes, the US Catches a Cold*. Bank of America–Merrill Lynch, August 6, 2010.

[8]*Morning Market Tidbits: PMIs Not Good Predictors of GDP*. Bank of America–Merrill Lynch, May 8, 2012.

FIGURE 3.2 Euro-area industrial production growth and GDP growth.

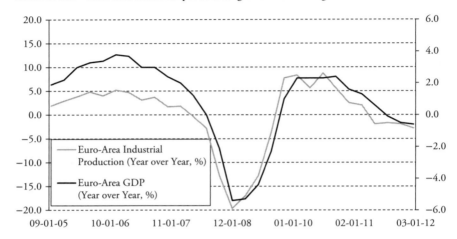

Source: Bloomberg

"stand-alone indicator" of contemporaneous activity. They concluded, "this presumably reflects the sensitivity of the industrial sector to shifts in aggregate demand, both domestically and internationally."[9]

Data on industrial production are published by Eurostat on a monthly basis about six weeks after the end of the reporting period. The statistics are reported for the first month of the quarter about two months before the official GDP data. For example, in 2012, the industrial output data for January were released on March 14, the figure for February on April 12 and the number for March on May 14. The GDP report for that three-month period was published on May 15. It is working-day and seasonally adjusted.

The industrial production index, which is price adjusted, measures the value added by industry. In other words, it reports the value of the output of a country's factories, mines and utilities minus the cost of goods and services used to create that output and taxes (Figure 3.3). Eurostat officially defines value added as "turnover (excluding VAT and other similar deductible taxes directly linked to turnover), plus capitalised production, plus other operating income, plus or minus changes in stocks, minus the purchases of goods and services, minus taxes on products linked to turnover but not deductible, plus any subsidies on products received."[10]

---

[9]Ashley, James and Hayes, Simon "Clearing the Fog: How Useful Are Short-Term Economic Indicators?" *World Economics*, Volume 11, No. 2, April–June 2010.
[10]*Principal European Economic Indicators: A Statistical Guide.* Eurostat, 2009.

FIGURE 3.3 Industrial production data compilation.

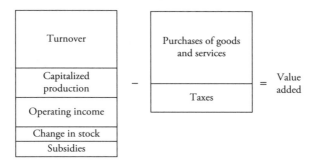

Source: Eurostat

The Eurostat data for the monetary union cover mining and quarrying, manufacturing and electricity, gas and water supply. They exclude construction, though some countries, such as Germany, include construction in their measures of industrial production.[11] The statistical agency provides a breakdown into the categories of: intermediate goods, energy, capital goods, durable consumer goods and non-durable consumer goods.

Caution is still required when using the national industrial output data to forecast euro-area GDP as a result of seasonal adjustments. "Eurostat applies its own seasonal adjustment method to raw [industrial production] data from the national statistics institutes. This can lead to large divergences," according to Gilles Moec, Co-Chief European Economist at Deutsche Bank and a former Banque de France economist.

He calculated that, in January and February of 2010, industrial production excluding construction increased by 3% from the end of the previous year. The aggregation of the seasonally adjusted national data from the five biggest members of the euro area, accounting for more than 80% of EMU's GDP, pointed to a gain of only 1% for the same period. The seasonal adjustments matter because the national seasonally-adjusted data – not Eurostat's – are used to calculate euro-area GDP, according to the research report.[12]

Economists, market participants and policy makers watch leading indicators for insight into the future direction of coincident indicators such as

---

[11] *The Economist*, 2011.
[12] Moec, Gilles *Euroland IP: Statistical Issues Matter*. Deutsche Bank, April 14, 2010.

industrial production and, ultimately, GDP. These indicators are used mostly for determining the turning points and the trend of GDP rather than the precise rate of growth. Jürg Lindlbauer, an economist at the Ifo Institute, has argued, "precise quantitative forecasting is not the actual task of an indicator; its main objective is to provide early indications of the future trend of the reference series and especially to forecast cyclical turning points."[13]

---

[13]Lindlbauer, Jürg "Evaluation and Development of Composite Leading Indicators Based on Harmonised Business and Consumer Surveys." *Handbook of Survey-Based Business Cycle Analysis*. Cheltenham: Edward Elgar Publishing Limited, 2007. Reproduced by permission of Edward Elgar Publishing Limited.

CHAPTER 4

Leading Indicators

Financial Conditions Index

The Bloomberg Euro-Area Financial Conditions Index has become a leading indicator of GDP growth in the monetary union (Figure 4.1). It has a lead time of two quarters. The quarterly correlation between the index – with a two-quarter lead – and year-over-year GDP growth from the first quarter of 1999 to the fourth quarter of 2010 stands at 0.86. The index is continuously updated on an intraday basis and is available on the Bloomberg Professional Service. Using a five-day moving average provides a reading of the short-term trend.

A wide variety of institutions – public and private – have recently created financial conditions indices to monitor the impact of financial conditions on economic growth, particularly since the onset of the global financial crisis. The list of institutions includes the Bank of Canada, the Federal Reserve Banks of Chicago, Kansas City and St. Louis, the IMF, the OECD and the Riksbank.[1]

Financial conditions play an important role in the decision processes that lead to the generation or curtailment of many types of economic activity (Figure 4.2).[2] They drive borrowing decisions of businesses, lending decisions of banks and spending decisions of households. If corporate debt yields rise to levels that make investing in additional production capacity unprofitable, capital formation will likely come to a halt. Banks become less likely to lend during such periods of stress. In addition, if equity markets decline precipitously, consumers are likely to feel less wealthy and reduce their consumption.

---

[1] Rosenberg, Michael R. *Financial Conditions Watch*. Bloomberg, October 26, 2011.
[2] Rosenberg, 2011.

FIGURE 4.1 Bloomberg euro-area financial conditions index and GDP growth.

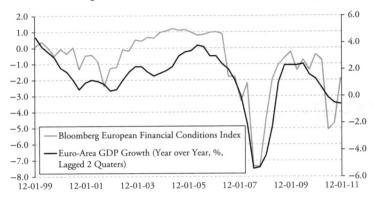

Source: Bloomberg

FIGURE 4.2 Financial conditions drive real economic activity.

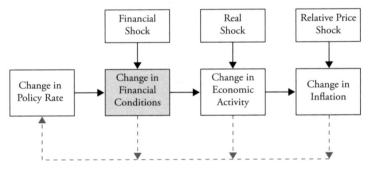

Source: Bloomberg. Reproduced by permission of Bloomberg.

Financial conditions are the first variables normally impacted by changes in monetary policy. In March 2007, Ben Bernanke, chairman of the Board of Governors of the Federal Reserve System, stated, "Monetary policy works in the first instance by affecting financial conditions, including the levels of interest rates and asset prices. Changes in financial conditions in turn influence a variety of decisions by households and firms, including choices about how much to consume, to produce, and to invest."[3]

The Bloomberg Euro-Area Financial Conditions Index combines yield spreads from the bond and money markets and readings on the performance

---

[3]Bernanke, Ben S. "Globalization and Monetary Policy." Speech to the Stanford Institute for Economic Policy Research. Board of Governors of the Federal Reserve System, March 2, 2007.

of equity markets into a normalized index. Specifically, it includes the J.P. Morgan High Yield Europe Index, which is a measure of the return on high-yield euro-denominated corporate debt, a 10-year swap rate for the euro area, the euro TED spread (three-month Euribor minus the three-month German sovereign yield), the three-month Euribor – overnight indexed swap spread, the ratio of the EuroStoxx to its five-year average, and the ratio of the VDAX (a measure of volatility of the German DAX Index) to its five-year average. They each have a weight of 16.7%.

The index is expressed in terms of a z-score, which is a measure of the number of standard deviations from the long-term average. The period of the mean for the Bloomberg Euro-Area Financial Conditions Index is from 1999 to 2008. Each of the six components is expressed in terms of its distance from that long-term average. The headline reading is an average of those six components.

Box 4.1   Euribor vs. EUR LIBOR

Euribor and EUR LIBOR have historically been close. They are both measures of interest rates on short-term loans from one bank to another, denominated in euros. Selected banks submit the rates they charge to an organization to determine the average rate at the time of fixing. The major difference between Euribor and EUR LIBOR is the members of the panel of banks that contribute.

The panel for Euribor has 39 banks.[4] Thirty-three of these banks are from countries that belong to the euro area. Their interest rates for loans to be settled in two days within the euro area are submitted to the Brussels-based European Banking Federation at 11:00 a.m. Central European Time.[5] The highest and the lowest 15% of bids are excluded from the calculation.[6]

The panel for EUR LIBOR has 15 banks.[7] Only three of these banks are from countries that belong to the euro area. The interest rates for loans to be settled in two days in London are submitted to Thomson Reuters between 12:00 p.m. and 12:10 p.m. Central European Time. The highest and the lowest 25% of bids are excluded from the calculation.[8]

(*Continued*)

---

[4]For a full list of the contributing banks, see: *Euribor Panel Banks*. European Banking Federation. {http://www.euribor-ebf.eu/euribor-org/panel-banks.html}
[5]*Euribor Rates*. European Banking Federation. {http://www.euribor-ebf.eu/euribor-org/euribor-rates.html}
[6]*What is Euribor?* Triami Media. {http://www.euribor-rates.eu/what-is-euribor.asp}
[7]For a full list of the contributing banks, see: *Euro Panel*. Bbalibor. {http://www.bbalibor.com/panels/eur}
[8]*The Basics*. Bbalibor. {http://www.bbalibor.com/bbalibor-explained/the-basics}

The difference between these two interest rates can be measured as an indication of risk in the respective banking industry. For example, from the start of 2008 to November 1, 2012, the spread between three-month Euribor and three-month EUR LIBOR averaged 4 basis points. From the start of 1999 to the start of 2008, the spread between three-month Euribor and three-month EUR LIBOR averaged 0 basis points.

This suggests a higher risk premium was being charged to banks within the euro area borrowing in euros relative to those banks in London borrowing in euros. That may have been a reflection of the inability of many euro-area nations to provide additional bailouts to their own banks as a result of the perilous state of national finances and the inability to print money.

The U.S. Business Cycle

Economic developments in the U.S. can be viewed as a leading indicator for those of the euro area. Researchers from the ECB have confirmed that the business cycle of the euro area is highly correlated with that of the U.S. and that the former lags the latter (Figure 4.3).

The period of lag differs for recessions and recoveries. The staff economists of the ECB have found that downturns in the U.S. take about two quarters to be transmitted to the euro area and that upturns are transmitted in about six quarters.[9]

The ECB suggests that this phenomenon can be attributed to the flexibility of the U.S. economy, which is plagued by fewer legal restrictions than its European counterparts. If companies can quickly shed workers during a downturn, they can return to profitability more quickly in the U.S. than in Europe, increase investment and thereby help push the economy out of recession.

Mingyi Kang of the University of Minnesota produced findings with his empirical research in line with those of the ECB. He concluded, "In the U.S. the labor market is flexible and the effects of shocks on economic activity are immediate. However, in the other countries hit by the same shock hitting the U.S., the effects of the shock manifest only through time since their labor markets are rigid. Therefore, statistically the U.S. appears to be the leader."[10]

---

[9]"Patterns of Euro Area and U.S. Macroeconomic Cycles – What Has Been Different This Time?" *ECB Monthly Bulletin*. Frankfurt: European Central Bank, May 2011.

[10]Kang, Mingyi *Leading and Lagging Relationships in International Business Cycles*. University of Minnesota, January 1, 2010.

FIGURE 4.3 Output gaps (as a percentage of estimated potential).

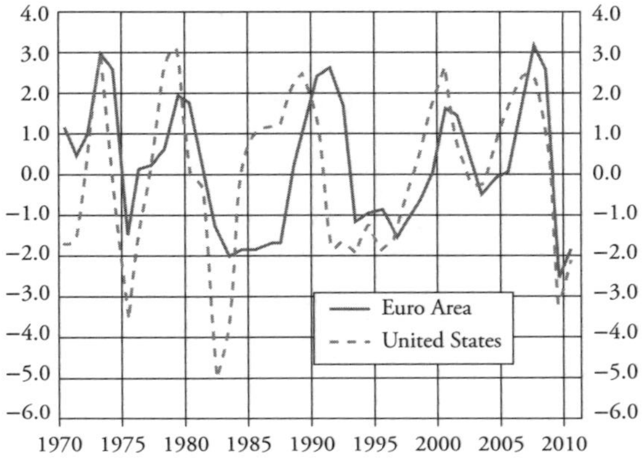

Source: European Commission, ECB. Copyright European Central Bank, Frankfurt am Main, Germany. This information may be obtained free of charge from {www.ecb.int}.

By contrast, the U.S. economy has historically – though the period of the European sovereign debt crisis may prove to be an exception – been unaffected by economic developments across the Atlantic. Domenico Giannone, Michele Lenza and Lucrezia Reichlin, staff economists of the ECB, concluded, "Euro area–U.S. dynamics can be characterized as the euro area rate of growth adjusting itself to the U.S. growth while the U.S. not responding to shocks specific to the euro area."[11]

ZEW Survey

The ZEW Survey is one of the most widely watched business surveys in Europe. It has been a good indicator of the euro-area economy as a whole, though the survey is only based on feedback, with a few exceptions, from financial analysts in Germany, the continent's largest economy.

The ZEW Indicator of Economic Sentiment for Germany has two main components. The most important is the figure on economic expectations. It is comparable to the expectations reading of the Ifo Survey. The ZEW Survey also has a component on the current economic situation, like the Ifo Survey,

---

[11]Giannone, Domenico, Lenza, Michele and Reichlin, Lucrezia *Business Cycles in the Euro Area*. Working Papers Series, No. 1010. Frankfurt: European Central Bank, February 2009.

TABLE 4.1 Correlations of ZEW and Ifo Readings with Euro-Area GDP

Correlation	Euro-Area GDP						
	No Advance	1 Quarter Lag	2 Quarter Lag	3 Quarter Lag	4 Quarter Lag	5 Quarter Lag	6 Quarter Lag
Ifo Headline	0.62	0.60	0.44	0.16	−0.13	−0.35	−0.48
Ifo Current	0.53	0.41	0.19	−0.07	−0.31	−0.47	−0.55
Ifo Expectations	0.59	0.74	0.69	0.48	0.17	−0.09	−0.26
ZEW Current	0.54	0.40	0.18	−0.08	−0.32	−0.48	−0.58
ZEW Expectations	0.17	0.42	0.60	0.68	0.63	0.53	0.43

	2002–2012
Ifo Current	0.58
ZEW Current	0.45

though it lacks a headline number that combines the two figures similar to that of the Ifo Survey.

The quarterly average of the expectations component of the ZEW Survey is most highly correlated with year-over-year euro-area GDP with a lead of three quarters and the quarterly average of the current situation reading is most highly correlated with year-over-year euro-area GDP with no lead. These correlations stand at 0.68 and 0.54, respectively, using data from the first quarter of 1995 to the second quarter of 2011 (Table 4.1).

Business surveys, including the ZEW data, should be compared with their 10-year averages, which should strip out the effects of the business cycle. Comparing the number of standard deviations – or z-score – of the latest reading from that long-term mean provides historic context.

The survey is normally released during the third week of the month by the Centre for European Economic Research (Zentrum für Europäische Wirtschaftsforschung or ZEW) in Mannheim, Germany. It is conducted during the first two weeks of the month.

The ZEW Institute surveys about 350 financial analysts located in Germany. They come from banks, insurance companies and large industrial enterprises. Within those firms, they hold positions in the finance and economic and research departments or as fund managers, investment consultants or traders.[12]

---

[12]Köhler, Matthias and Schmidt, Sandra *ZEW Financial Market Survey*. Zentrum für Europäische Wirtschaftsforschung. {http://www.zew.de/en/publikationen/Kurzinfo_English.pdf}

The respondents are asked a wide variety of questions. The answers to them are available on the webpage of the ZEW Institute, though they are not reflected in the headline reading. The questions ask respondents about their perceptions of the current economic situation and their economic expectations for the euro area, Germany, the U.S., Japan, the U.K., France and Italy (Table 4.2). They also ask about their expectations for inflation rates, short-term interest rates, long-term interest rates and stock market indices for those regions. The remaining questions focus on their expectations for major exchange rates, oil and the profitability of 13 industries in Germany.

The headline figures, as well as the balances for the other questions, are calculated by subtracting the percentage of respondents that are optimistic from the percentage of those that are pessimistic.[13] Those who look for no change are ignored. All of the possible responses are qualitative. For example, if 40% of respondents expect the German economy to improve in six months, 30% look for no change and 30% call for it to get worse, the headline reading will be 10.

Ifo Survey

The Ifo Business Climate Index may be the most watched economic indicator in the euro area. Like the ZEW Survey, it has been a good indicator of the euro-area economy as a whole, though the survey is only based on feedback from companies in Germany.

The data are normally released around the 23rd of the month of the reporting period by the Ifo Institute in Munich, Germany. The survey has three main numbers: the headline reading, which is called the Business Climate Index, a current situation component and an expectations component. The Ifo Survey has about 7000 participants from firms in construction, manufacturing, retailing and wholesaling. It excludes respondents from the finance industry.[14]

The largest category of firms is manufacturing. It represents about 56% of the firms to which surveys are sent by the Ifo Institute. The remainder of

---

[13]*ZEW Indicator of Economic Sentiment: A Leading Indicator for the German Economy.* {http://www.zew.de/en/publikationen/Konjunkturerwartungen/konjunkturerwartungenberechnung.php3}

[14]*Ifo Business Climate Germany: Results of the Ifo Business Survey for August 2012.* Ifo Institute, August 27, 2012.

TABLE 4.2 Detailed Results for the October 2012 ZEW Survey

ZEW - Financial Market Survey: Results October 2012

Current Economic Situation	Good		Normal		Bad		Balance	
Eurozone	0.0	(+/−0.0)	20.6	(−3.1)	79.4	(+3.1)	−79.4	(−3.1)
Germany	18.7	(−2.7)	72.6	(+2.8)	8.7	(−0.1)	10.0	(−2.6)
USA	3.8	(+1.2)	72.4	(+1.1)	23.8	(−2.3)	−20.0	(+3.5)
Japan	1.1	(−0.5)	50.9	(−4.8)	48.0	(+5.3)	−46.9	(−5.8)
United Kingdom	0.7	(+0.7)	26.3	(−6.1)	73.0	(+5.4)	−72.3	(−4.7)
France	1.1	(+0.7)	28.7	(−3.3)	70.2	(+2.6)	−69.1	(−1.9)
Italy	0.0	(+/−0.0)	10.5	(−1.2)	89.5	(+1.2)	−89.5	(−1.2)

Economic Expectations	Improve		No Change		Get Worse		Balance	
Eurozone	24.3	(+ 3.6)	50.0	(− 4.8)	25.7	(+ 1.2)	−1.4	(+2.4)
Germany (**ZEW Indicator**)	21.5	(+ 3.1)	45.5	(+ 0.5)	33.0	(− 3.6)	−11.5	(+6.7)
USA	24.7	(−1.7)	56.8	(+0.1)	18.5	(+1.6)	6.2	(−3.3)
Japan	13.7	(−1.7)	69.0	(+1.1)	17.3	(+0.6)	−3.6	(−2.3)
United Kingdom	14.0	(−4.0)	65.1	(+2.2)	20.9	(+1.8)	−6.9	(−5.8)
France	14.5	(−1.0)	53.4	(−4.8)	32.1	(+5.8)	−17.6	(−6.8)
Italy	19.7	(−0.5)	52.9	(+0.9)	27.4	(−0.4)	−7.7	(−0.1)

Inflation Rate	Increase		No Change		Decrease		Balance	
Eurozone	28.1	(−3.4)	50.5	(+2.0)	21.4	(+1.4)	6.7	(−4.8)
Germany	30.5	(−4.1)	54.4	(+4.0)	15.1	(+0.1)	15.4	(−4.2)
USA	28.2	(−3.6)	64.7	(+4.6)	7.1	(−1.0)	21.1	(−2.6)
Japan	13.8	(+0.6)	78.4	(−1.8)	7.8	(+1.2)	6.0	(−0.6)
United Kingdom	25.7	(−0.3)	60.2	(+2.1)	14.1	(−1.8)	11.6	(+1.5)
France	27.5	(−1.0)	54.3	(+0.4)	18.2	(+0.6)	9.3	(−1.6)
Italy	27.7	(−1.4)	49.8	(−0.8)	22.5	(+2.2)	5.2	(−3.6)

Short-term Interest Rates	Increase		No Change		Decrease		Balance	
Eurozone	7.7	(+1.9)	78.4	(+11.6)	13.9	(−3.5)	−6.2	(+15.4)
USA	5.9	(+3.5)	90.6	(−1.6)	3.5	(−1.9)	2.4	(+5.4)
Japan	1.9	(−0.5)	95.9	(+0.8)	2.2	(−0.3)	−0.3	(−0.2)
United Kingdom	4.8	(+1.5)	86.4	(+1.5)	8.8	(−3.0)	−4.0	(+4.5)

Long-term Interest Rates	Increase		No Change		Decrease		Balance	
Germany	58.2	(+0.1)	37.9	(−0.2)	3.9	(+0.1)	54.3	(+/−0.0)
USA	44.7	(+4.5)	52.5	(−4.6)	2.8	(+0.1)	41.9	(+4.4)
Japan	19.2	(−5.2)	78.9	(+4.5)	1.9	(+0.7)	17.3	(−5.9)
United Kingdom	37.7	(−3.7)	57.9	(+3.0)	4.4	(+0.7)	33.3	(−4.4)

Stock Market Indices	Increase		No Change		Decrease		Balance	
STOXX 50 (Eurozone)	44.8	(+4.3)	33.3	(−4.3)	21.9	(+/−0.0)	22.9	(+4.3)

Leading Indicators

ZEW - Financial Market Survey: Results October 2012

Stock Market Indices	Increase		No Change		Decrease		Balance	
DAX (Germany)	46.3	(+4.8)	30.9	(−3.7)	22.8	(−1.1)	23.5	(+5.9)
TecDax (Germany)	42.7	(+3.0)	35.3	(−4.3)	22.0	(+1.3)	20.7	(+1.7)
Dow Jones Industrial (USA)	44.2	(+1.7)	35.8	(−4.5)	20.0	(+2.8)	24.2	(−1.1)
Nikkei 225 (Japan)	33.2	(+2.9)	50.6	(−5.7)	16.2	(+2.8)	17.0	(+0.1)
FT-SE-100 (UK)	33.0	(+0.1)	45.2	(−3.4)	21.8	(+3.3)	11.2	(−3.2)
CAC-40 (France)	33.7	(+2.6)	42.1	(−0.6)	24.2	(−2.0)	9.5	(+4.6)
MIBtel (Italy)	35.3	(+3.2)	38.6	(−3.4)	26.1	(+0.2)	9.2	(+3.0)

Exchange Rates (vs. Euro)	Appreciate		No Change		Depreciate		Balance	
Dollar	32.2	(+1.4)	41.4	(+6.6)	26.4	(−8.0)	5.8	(+9.4)
Yen	14.3	(−1.5)	57.8	(+3.6)	27.9	(−2.1)	−13.6	(+0.6)
UK Pound	16.3	(−1.1)	51.9	(+4.2)	31.8	(−3.1)	−15.5	(+2.0)
Swiss Franc	9.3	(+0.8)	75.3	(+1.5)	15.4	(−2.3)	−6.1	(+3.1)

Commodities	Increase		No Change		Decrease		Balance	
Oil (Brent Crude)	29.1	(−3.1)	49.8	(+6.3)	21.1	(−3.2)	8.0	(+0.1)

Sectors	Improve		No Change		Get Worse		Balance	
Banks	11.0	(−4.1)	32.0	(−2.2)	57.0	(+6.3)	−46.0	(−10.4)
Insurance companies	8.7	(−3.3)	39.9	(+0.8)	51.4	(+2.5)	−42.7	(−5.8)
Automobile	4.5	(−4.9)	32.9	(−7.7)	62.6	(+12.6)	−58.1	(−17.5)
Chemicals/Pharmaceuticals	16.9	(−2.4)	64.5	(+4.9)	18.6	(−2.5)	−1.7	(+0.1)
Steel	9.6	(−3.4)	44.8	(−0.9)	45.6	(+4.3)	−36.0	(−7.7)
Electronics	11.6	(−2.9)	64.3	(+5.9)	24.1	(−3.0)	−12.5	(+0.1)
Mechanical engineering	14.9	(+2.2)	44.6	(−3.1)	40.5	(+0.9)	−25.6	(+1.3)
Retail/Consumer goods	19.1	(+0.8)	66.9	(+0.8)	14.0	(−1.6)	5.1	(+2.4)
Construction	24.3	(+1.6)	55.0	(+2.3)	20.7	(−3.9)	3.6	(+5.5)
Utilities	15.4	(−2.2)	68.0	(+2.8)	16.6	(−0.6)	−1.2	(−1.6)
Services	24.9	(−0.2)	62.7	(−3.1)	12.4	(+3.3)	12.5	(−3.5)
Telecommunications	11.6	(+2.1)	70.1	(−5.1)	18.3	(+3.0)	−6.7	(−0.9)
Information technology	27.4	(+1.3)	61.3	(−0.9)	11.3	(−0.4)	16.1	(+1.7)

Note: 288 analysts participated in the October-survey which was conducted during the period 10/1-10/15/2012. Analysts were asked about their expectations for the next 6 months. Numbers displayed are percentages (month-over-month percentage point changes in parentheses). Balances refer to the difference between positive and negative assessments.

Source: ZEW Institute. For more information, please see: {http://www.zew.de/en//index.php3}. Reproduced by permission of the ZEW Institute.

the surveys is split between construction (14%), retailing (14%) and wholesaling (16%), according to the think tank.[15] The responses are weighted to account for the importance of the industry.[16]

The business climate is the geometric mean of the figures on the current situation and expectations. The use of the geometric mean – as opposed to an arithmetic mean – dampens the impact of extreme values.[17] Specifically, the formula is:[18]

$$\text{Business Climate} = \sqrt{(situation + 200)(expectations + 200)} - 200$$

The figure on the current business situation is a diffusion index. The firms surveyed can characterize their situations as "good," "satisfactory" or "poor." The balance is the difference between the percentages of the number of responses indicating the situation is "good" and those stating it as "poor." The respondents who judge their situations as "satisfactory" are considered to be "neutral" and have no effect on the index.

The component on expectations is also a diffusion index. The firms surveyed indicate their expectations for the business environment in six months as "more favorable," "unchanged" or "more unfavorable." The balance is the difference between the percentages of the number of responses indicating the situation is "more favorable" and those stating it as "more unfavorable." Once again, the respondents who judge their situations as "unchanged" are considered to be "neutral" and have no effect on the index.

To calculate the readings of the current business situation and expectations, these balances are increased by 200 and normalized to the average of a base year, which is currently 2005.[19] Specifically, the formula is:

$$\text{Index Value} = ((\text{balance in the current month} + 200)/(\text{average balance in the base year} + 200)) \times 100$$

---

[15]E-mail from Ifo Institute to David Powell, August 31, 2012.

[16]*Calculating the Ifo Business Climate.* {http://www.cesifo-group.de/ifoHome/facts/Survey-Results/Business-Climate/Calculating-the-Ifo-Business-Climate.html}

[17]Abberger, Klaus and Nierhaus, Wolfgang *The Ifo Business Cycle Clock: Circular Correlation with the Real GDP.* CESIfo Working Paper No. 3179. Ifo Institute, 2010.

[18]*Calculating the Ifo Business Climate.* {http://www.cesifo-group.de/ifoHome/facts/Survey-Results/Business-Climate/Calculating-the-Ifo-Business-Climate.html}

[19]*Ibid.*

The two questions mentioned above serve as bookends for a set of 12 that are asked on a monthly basis. The complete list of questions is as follows, with XY referring to the company's product:

Current Situation

1. We evaluate our business situation with respect to XY as
   Good
   Satisfactory
   Unsatisfactory
2. We feel that at present our stocks of unsold finished goods of XY are
   Too small
   Adequate (normal for the time of year)
   Too large
   We do not normally maintain stocks
3. We feel that at present our backlogs of orders on hand of XY are
   Relatively large
   Adequate (normal for the time of year) or not customary
   Too small
   We don't export XY

Tendencies in the Past Month

4. The demand situation with respect to XY has
   Improved
   Remained unchanged
   Got worse
5. Our backlog of orders for XY (home and foreign, in terms of value) has
   Increased
   Remained the same (or not applicable)
   Declined
6. Our domestic production activity (without taking into account differences in the length of months of seasonal fluctuations) with respect to XY has
   Increased
   Remained virtually unchanged
   Gone down
   No noteworthy domestic production
7. Taking into account changes in the condition of selling transactions, our net domestic sales prices for XY have
   Increased
   Remained about the same
   Gone down

Expectations for the Coming Three Months

8. Our domestic production activity (without taking into account differences in the length of months or seasonal fluctuations) with respect to XY will probably
   Increase
   Remain virtually unchanged
   Decline
   No noteworthy domestic production
9. Taking into account changes in the conditions agreed upon in selling transactions, our net domestic sales prices will probably
   Increase
   Remain about the same
   Decline
10. Taking into account the foreign orders received to date and the sales negotiations being conducted, the volume of our exports of XY will probably
    Increase
    Remain about the same
    Go down
    We don't export XY
11. Employment related to the production of XY in domestic production unit(s) will probably
    Increase
    Remain about the same
    Go down

Expectations for the Next Six Months

12. Our business situation with respect to XY will, in a cyclical view,
    Improve
    Remain about the same
    Develop unfavorably

The survey period covers the first three weeks of each month, though it can vary from month to month. The paper questionnaires are sent out at the beginning of the month and a few days later the online survey is opened. Reminders are sent one week before the publication date. The Ifo Institute tries to include as many questionnaires as possible.[20]

---

[20] E-mail from Ifo Institute to David Powell, August 31, 2012.

Exhibit 4.1 Ifo business survey on manufacturing

ifo Institute

Department of Business Cycle Analyses and Surveys
P.O.B. 86 04 60 81831 Munich
e-mail: Internet:http://www.ifo.de
Telephone: (089) 9224-0   In case of questions:
Telefax: (089)

ifo Business Survey Manufacturing

The questions refer to the denoted product group and referred hereafter as XY. Please mark the appropriate boxes.
All information supplied will be treated as **strictly confidential**.
Legal protection of data applies with full force.

Manufacturing Western Germany

Branch Code:

(reflecting your current information stand)

Product group (XY):

Current Situation

1) We evaluate our **business situation** with respect to XY as
   - good
   - satisfactory
   - unsatisfactory

2) We feel that at present our stocks of unsold **finished goods** of XY are
   - too small
   - adequate (normal for the time of year)
   - too large
   - we do not normally maintain stocks

3) We feel that at present our **backlogs of orders** on hand of XY are over-all / export
   - relatively large
   - adequate (normal for the time of year) or not customary
   - too small
   - we don't export XY

Tendencies in the past month

4) The **demand situation** with respect to XY has
   - improved
   - remained unchanged
   - got worse

5) Our **backlog of orders** for XY (home and foreign, *in terms of value*) has
   - increased
   - remained the same (or not applicable)
   - declined

6) Our domestic **production activity***) with respect to XY has
   - increased
   - remained virtually unchanged
   - gone down
   - no noteworthy domestic production

*) Without taking into account differences in the length of months or seasonal fluctuations

7) Taking into account changes in the condition of selling transactions, our net **domestic sales prices** for XY have
   - increased
   - remained about the same
   - gone down

Expectations for the next 3 months

8) Our domestic **production activity***) with respect to XY will probably
   - increase
   - remain virtually unchanged
   - decline
   - no noteworthy domestic production

9) Taking into account changes in the conditions agreed upon in selling transactions, our net **domestic sales prices** for XY will probably
   - increase
   - remain about the same
   - decline

10) Taking into account the foreign orders received to date and the sales negotiations being conducted, the volume of our **exports** of XY will probably
    - increase
    - remain about the same
    - go down
    - we don't export XY

11) **Employment** related to the production of XY in domestic production unit(s) will probably
    - increase
    - remain about the same
    - go down

Expectations for the next 6 months

12) Our **business situation** with respect to XY will in a cyclical view
    - improve
    - remain about the same
    - develop unfavourably

Supplementary questions

A) How many months of production are assured by your **current** overall **order books**?
   order books   for .... months   If more than 10 months please indicate number
   ½ 1 2 3 4 5 6 7 8 9 10   more than 100%

B) The **capacity utilisation** of our equipment for the production of XY (as a percentage of full capacity = 100%) is currently ..... %
   30 40 50 60 70 75 80 85 90 95 100   more than 100% and i.e.

C) Considering your *current* order books and the *expected* change in demand over the coming next 12 months, how do you assess your current **production capacity** for XY. It is...
   - more than sufficient
   - sufficient
   - not sufficient

D1) Our current domestic **production** is limited
    yes / no

D2) **if yes**, which are the main factors:
    - insufficient demand
    - shortage of labourforce
    - shortage of material and/or equipment
    - insufficient technical capacity
    - financial constraints
    - others

E) How has your **comptitive position** developed over the last 3 months compared to the previous 3 months? It has ....
   on the domestic market / on the foreign markets inside / outside of the EU
   - improved
   - remained unchanged
   - deteriorated
   - we don't export XY

Source: Ifo Institute. Reproduced by permission of the Ifo Institute.

The survey also has supplementary questions, which appear on a quarterly basis. According to an article by Wolfgang Ruppert, in a book published by the Ifo Institute, they cover the following areas:[21]

1. The thematic area of backlog of orders, capacity utilization, obstacles to production activity and competitive position (January, April, July and October) with the following questions:
    a. Production months covered by the existing backlog of orders;
    b. Degree of capacity utilization expressed as a percentage of the production unit's normal full utilization;
    c. Evaluation of currently available technical production capacity with reference to the backlog of orders on books and to orders expected in the next 12 months;
    d. Obstacles to production activity (lack of orders, difficulties in finding skilled labor, lack of raw materials, inadequate technical production capacity, lack of finance, other factors).
2. The thematic area of stocks held (February, May, August and November) with questions on:
    e. Extent of stocks of raw materials and intermediary inputs (expressed in weeks of production);
    f. Extent of stocks of finished goods (expressed in weeks of production).
3. The thematic area of employment and labor market (March, June, September and December) with questions on:
    g. Overtime (in terms of normal or above normal for the production unit);
    h. Short-time work (at the present time, expected in the course of the coming three months);
    i. Evaluation of the current staffing level in view of the turnover expected in the coming 12 months.
4. In addition, at longer intervals supplementary questions are asked referring to:
    j. Profitability and profit developments of the enterprise (May, September);
    k. The readiness of banks to extend credit to enterprises (March, August);
    l. Innovation (December).

Additional supplementary questions are posed on an ad hoc basis.

---

[21]Ruppert, Wolfgang "Business Survey in Manufacturing." *Handbook of Survey-Based Business Cycle Analysis*. Cheltenham: Edward Elgar Publishing Limited, 2007. Reproduced by permission of Edward Elgar Publishing Limited.

Lead

The quarterly average of the expectations component of the Ifo Survey tends to lead the year-over-year rate-of-change of euro-area GDP by three to six months. The correlations with the latter lagged by one and two quarters stand at 0.74 and 0.69, respectively, using data from the first quarter of 1995 to the second quarter of 2011. When the publishing lag is included, the lead is about four to seven months. Comparisons between the levels of the Ifo Survey and the year-over-year rate-of-change of euro-area GDP are easiest, though the most accurate comparisons are between the rate of change of GDP and that of the Ifo Business Climate Index.[22]

The reading on current expectations provides only a publishing lead. Georg Goldrian of the Ifo Institute has confirmed, "only the business expectations transmit really early signals of the cyclical development."[23]

The relationship of the headline reading – the Ifo Business Climate Index – with GDP falls in between those of the figures on the current situation and expectations, as logic implies. The quarterly average of the headline reading is most highly correlated with the year-over-year rate-of-change of euro-area GDP by zero to three months. The correlations with the latter lagged by zero and one quarter stand at 0.62 and 0.60, respectively, using data from the first quarter of 1995 to the second quarter of 2011.

Trend

Three consecutive readings in a new direction are required before a change in the trend can be confirmed, according to Christian Hott of the Swiss National Bank and André Kunkel and Gernot Nerb of the Ifo Institute.[24] In other words, a peak is predicted if the Business Climate Index falls three times consecutively within an upswing and a trough is predicted if it rises three times consecutively within a downturn.

---

[22] Hott, Christian, Kunkel, André and Nerb, Gernot "The Accuracy of Turning Point Predictions with the Ifo Business Climate." *Handbook of Survey-Based Business Cycle Analysis.* Cheltenham: Edward Elgar Publishing Limited, 2007.

[23] Goldrian, Georg "A Leading Indicator Composed of Survey Data: Appropriate Construction and Prognostic Significance." *Handbook of Survey-Based Business Cycle Analysis.* Cheltenham: Edward Elgar Publishing Limited, 2007. Reproduced by permission of Edward Elgar Publishing Limited.

[24] Hott, Kunkel and Nerb, 2007.

These three economists applied the "three-times rule" to the German economy. They found that all eight peaks in industrial production and seven troughs between 1969 and 2001 were flagged by the rule. In addition, three false cycles were signaled. They defined a peak using the rules set by the Bundesbank. A peak was declared when a local maximum of the trend-adjusted industrial production was hit and then it fell below its trend. The rule for a trough was symmetrical.

Business Cycle Clock

The Ifo Institute has developed a framework – a business cycle clock – to translate the readings from the Ifo Survey into stages of the business cycle. It is a four-quadrant graph (Figure 4.4). The sections are categorized as the territories of "upswing," "boom," "downswing" and "recession." In theory, the cycle should move in a clockwise direction.

The framework has been described in detail by Klaus Abberger and Wolfgang Nierhaus of the Ifo Institute.[25] The time series of the present situation should be placed on the *x*-axis of the business cycle clock and that of the expectations should be placed on the *y*-axis. The axes of the graph divide it into four parts.

FIGURE 4.4 Ifo business cycle clock.

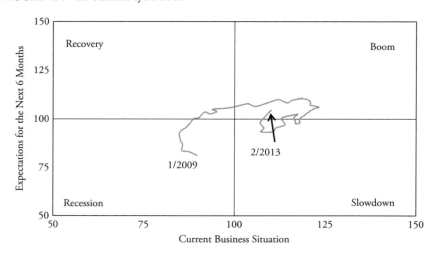

Source: Bloomberg, Ifo Institute

---

[25]Abberger and Nierhaus, September 2010.

Leading Indicators

The upswing phase is reached when the expectations component climbs above 100, while the present situation remains below 100. When both of these indicators are above 100, the business cycle clock indicates a boom. When the expectations component drops below 100 and the present situation remains above 100, a downturn is signaled. When both time series are below 100, a recession is flagged. Because the index is normalized to 100, that level signals the divide between positive and negative readings.

The readings on the present situation and expectations can also be combined in a simple format by subtracting the latter from the former (Figure 4.5). If the difference between the two is positive, businesses are more optimistic about the present than the future. That is likely to bode poorly for business spending and economic growth. By contrast, if the difference between the two is negative, businesses are more optimistic about the future than the present. That should be positive for those two variables.

Richard Yamarone has applied this framework to the Conference Board's measure of consumer confidence in the U.S. He summed the interpretation of the figure as, "The wider the spread in either direction, the drearier or dreamier future conditions are expected to be relative to the present."[26]

FIGURE 4.5 Spread between expectations component and current assessment component of Ifo Survey.

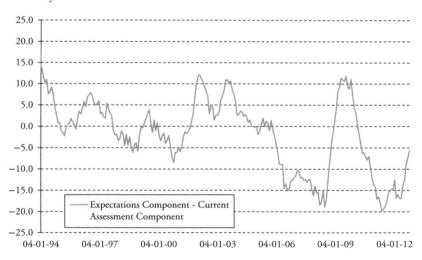

Source: Bloomberg

---

[26]Yamarone, Richard *The Trader's Guide to Key Economic Indicators*. New York: Bloomberg Press, 2004.

The quarterly average of the current assessment component of the Ifo Survey has recently been more highly correlated with the year-over-year growth of euro-area GDP than the quarterly average of the current situation component of the ZEW Survey. The two correlations stand at 0.58 and 0.45, using quarterly data from the fourth quarter of 2002 to the fourth quarter of 2012. That is likely due to the higher number of respondents for the former relative to the latter and to the closer link to the real economy of the former than the latter.

The difference in correlations in favor of the Ifo Survey disappears when examining a longer period of time. The correlations with GDP for the Ifo Survey and the ZEW Survey stand at 0.53 and 0.54, using quarterly data from the first quarter of 1995 to the fourth quarter of 2012.

M1 Money Supply Growth

Real M1 money supply growth is the indicator of economic growth that provides the longest lead. It leads GDP growth by about four quarters (Figure 4.6). The correlation between the year-over-year rate of growth of real M1 money supply with a four-quarter lead and the year-over-year GDP reading from the first quarter of 1995 to the fourth quarter of 2011 stands at 0.75.

The central bank publishes data on nominal M1 money supply growth on a monthly basis about 25 days after the end of the reporting period along with the figures for M3 money supply growth, which is mainly monitored as an indicator of medium- to long-term inflationary pressures (see page 68). The HICP inflation reading used as a deflator is published about 15 days after the reporting period. Real M1 money supply growth is calculated by subtracting the year-over-year growth rate of the headline reading of the CPI from the year-over-year growth rate of nominal M1 money supply.

This indicator of economic growth has been endorsed by Jürgen Stark, former Member of the Executive Board of the ECB. At the ECB and Its Watchers Conference in 2009, he said, "While developments in M3 contain relevant information about future inflation over medium to longer horizons, developments in M1 typically have good leading indicator properties for turning points in real GDP growth in the euro area."[27]

---

[27]Stark, Jürgen "The ECB's Monetary Policy: Preserving Price Stability in Time of Financial Distress." Speech at the conference "The ECB and Its Watchers XI", Center for Financial Studies, Frankfurt am Main, September 4, 2009.

FIGURE 4.6 Real M1 money supply growth and real GDP growth.

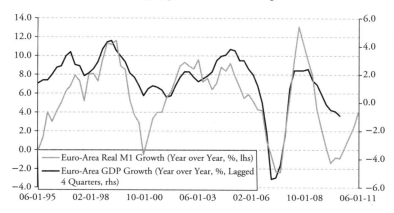

Source: Bloomberg

M1 money supply growth is the narrowest of the monetary aggregates apart from the monetary base. This aggregate may be related closely to growth because it is composed primarily of funds that can be accessed quickly by businesses and consumers for spending. It mostly includes cash and assets that can be converted easily into cash such as demand deposits.

Quantity Theory of Money

The principle that relates money supply to GDP growth is called the "quantity theory of money." It was stated in its modern version by Irving Fisher in his book, *The Purchasing Power of Money*, in 1911, though the theory can be traced back to the mid-16th century.[28] Fisher stated the following equation:

$$M \times V = T \times P$$

where M = money supply, V = the velocity of money, T = volume of trade and P = inflation. T – the volume of trade – can also be stated as real GDP. The equation can be restated as:

$$M \times V = Y \times P$$

---

[28]Belke, Ansgar and Polleit, Thorsten *Monetary Economics in Globalised Financial Markets.* Heidelberg: Springer, 2009.

where Y = real output. The right side of the equation equals nominal GDP. The expression can be condensed to:

$$M \times V = PY$$

where PY = nominal GDP.

Nominal money supply growth would have a direct relationship to nominal GDP, if velocity were assumed to be constant. This suggests that real money supply growth should have a direct relationship with real output, if both sides of the equation are deflated. Velocity can exhibit some stability over short periods of time, though that assumption fails to hold over the long term, especially for the U.S. economy.

M1 vs. M3 Money Supply

Real M1 money supply growth is a better indicator of the increase in economic output than real M3 money supply growth. As already stated, the correlation between the year-over-year rate of real M1 money supply growth with a four-quarter lead and real GDP growth on a year-over-year basis from the first quarter of 1995 to the fourth quarter of 2011 stands at 0.75. The equivalent figure for real M3 money supply growth and real GDP growth over the same period stands at minus 0.02.

The ECB still monitors M3 money supply growth as a guide to medium- to long-term risks to price stability. The central bank argues that the relationship between the broad monetary aggregate and inflation is more robust than those between the other monetary aggregates and inflation.

That phenomenon – M1 money supply being the best indicator of economic growth and M3 being the best indicator for inflationary pressures – seems logical. The ECB contends that businesses use their internal funds during the first part of an economic recovery and then later seek external financing.[29] Consumers may react in a similar fashion. They may initially use their savings and then apply for credit for big-ticket items as their confidence in the economic outlook increases. As the business cycle advances, aggregate demand will rise and unemployment will decline, putting upward pressure on wages and the overall price level.

Loan Growth

One of the counterparts of M3 money supply acts as a leading indicator. The growth of loans to households tends to lead that of GDP by one quarter, and

---

[29]"Loans to the Non-Financial Private Sector Over the Business Cycle in the Euro Area." *ECB Monthly Bulletin*. Frankfurt: European Central Bank, October 2009.

TABLE 4.3 Cyclical Correlation with Leads and Lags of Industrial Production

	Leads (+) and Lags (−)								
	−12	−9	−6	−3	0	3	6	9	12
Loans to non-financial corporations up to 1 year	0.56	0.78	0.68	0.29	−0.22	−0.60	−0.73	−0.61	−0.27
	(0.15)	(0.09)	(0.10)	(0.13)	(0.11)	(0.08)	(0.11)	(0.15)	(0.14)
	0.65	*0.79*	*0.65*	*0.26*	*−0.32*	*−0.77*	*−0.90*	*−0.64*	*−0.17*
Loans to non-financial corporations over 1 year	−0.17	−0.06	0.17	0.29	0.26	0.08	−0.08	−0.18	−0.19
	(0.23)	(0.30)	(0.22)	(0.18)	(0.21)	(0.18)	(0.15)	(0.16)	(0.15)
	−0.06	*−0.07*	*0.20*	*0.39*	*0.20*	*−0.27*	*−0.51*	*−0.29*	*0.07*
Consumer loans	−0.08	−0.10	−0.08	−0.09	−0.09	−0.03	0.10	0.15	0.12
	(0.26)	(0.24)	(0.24)	(0.20)	(0.23)	(0.23)	(0.15)	(0.17)	(0.17)
	0.09	*−0.05*	*−0.20*	*−0.41*	*−0.48*	*−0.25*	*−0.01*	*0.37*	*0.45*
Loans for house purchases	−0.54	−0.46	−0.14	0.29	0.55	0.55	0.33	0.05	−0.18
	(0.11)	(0.16)	(0.21)	(0.18)	(0.18)	(0.15)	(0.19)	(0.21)	(0.16)
	−0.68	*−0.73*	*−0.46*	*0.07*	*0.63*	*0.83*	*0.66*	*0.26*	*−0.16*
Other loans	0.20	0.47	0.55	0.42	0.09	−0.23	−0.42	−0.45	−0.35
	(0.16)	(0.18)	(0.20)	(0.16)	(0.16)	(0.12)	(0.15)	(0.18)	(0.19)
	0.28	*0.60*	*0.77*	*0.65*	*0.18*	*−0.35*	*−0.70*	*−0.73*	*−0.46*

Source: Giannone, Lenza and Reichlin. Reproduced by permission of Lucrezia Reichlin.

turning points in the former tend to lead turning points of the latter by two quarters, according to ECB research.[30] The correlation coefficient between real GDP growth and real loan growth to households for the last few decades stands at 0.67. The staff economists noted that this relationship holds on average and the relationship has, at times, deviated from average developments.

Specifically, the lead emanates from the sub-component of loans for house purchases. The sub-components of consumer credit and other lending tend to lag real GDP growth slightly.

The ECB states that the lead provided by loans for house purchases may be due to households increasing their demand for credit when their expectations for a recovery increase after house prices and interest rates have declined during a slowdown. In addition, the staff of the central bank says that this may be due to a preference of banks to supply credit for houses, which can be highly collateralized, over lending to firms, which may demand uncollateralized borrowing.

By contrast, loans to non-financial corporations act as a lagging indicator. The correlation coefficient is highest – at 0.7 – when real loan growth to non-financial corporations is lagged by three quarters. The staff economists of the ECB say that this may be due to companies first drawing down on internal funds during the beginning of a recovery before turning to banks for financing.

More specifically, Domenico Giannone, Michele Lenza and Lucrezia Reichlin found short-term loans (with a maturity up to one year) to non-financial corporations are the most cyclical, with a correlation with industrial production of about 0.8 using a lag of nine months (Table 4.3). By contrast, long-term loans to non-financial corporations are close to coincident with industrial production.[31]

---

[30]*Ibid.*
[31]Giannone, Domenico, Lenza, Michele and Reichlin, Lucrezia *Money, Credit, Monetary Policy and the Business Cycle in the Euro Area.* CEPR Discussion Paper 8944. Centre for Economic Policy Research, September 24, 2009.

CHAPTER 5

Inflation Measures

The ECB – and most central banks – aims to achieve price stability. This includes avoiding a continuous rise or decline of the general price level. The former is referred to as inflation and the latter as deflation. Disinflation refers to a deceleration in the rate of price increases. Economists generally believe that price stability contributes to increasing the level of economic output and employment in the medium to long term.

Economists break down inflation into two different types. The categories are referred to as cost push and demand pull. The former refers to a rise in prices that is caused by an increase in input costs such as commodities and wages. The latter refers to a rise in prices caused by demand outstripping supply.

Consumer Price Index

The most closely watched indicator of inflation for the euro area and most countries around the world is the CPI. The measure for the euro area is specifically called the harmonized index of consumer prices (HICP).

The data are released in two parts. Eurostat publishes a flash estimate on the last working day of the reference period. It is calculated by using energy prices, early HICP data from those member states that publish their own flash estimates (Germany, Italy, Spain and Slovenia) and "early estimates provided by some member states to Eurostat on a confidential basis."[1] The core measure, which excludes energy, food, alcohol and tobacco, is included with this release.

The readings from the individual countries are omitted from this announcement. The full report is published about 15 days after the end of

---
[1] E-mail from Eurostat Media & Institutional Support to David Powell, July 7, 2012.

the reporting month and provides a breakdown by category and figures for each country of the monetary union.

Eurostat makes no seasonal adjustments of the HICP time series. The month-over-month readings may therefore be influenced by holidays and the weather. For example, clothing prices may decline every year in January as retailers attempt to clear unsold inventories from the Christmas shopping period and fresh fruits may be more expensive in winter, when they are out of season, than in summer. Market participants focus on the year-over-year measure because it provides the underlying trend, though it may be distorted by base effects. The data series begins with figures from 1996, though they have been rebased to 2005.

The ECB uses this measure of inflation to evaluate price stability in the euro area. It measures the changes over time of the prices of consumer goods and services. The rise in prices is measured by analyzing the cost of a consumer basket, which is meant to be representative of the items purchased by the average consumer (Table 5.1).

TABLE 5.1 Euro-Area HICP Weights

Euro-Area HICP Weights	%
All Items	100
Food	15.24
Alcohol & Tobacco	3.83
Clothing	6.8
Housing	16.28
Household Equipment	6.65
Health	4.43
Transport	15.43
Communications	3.13
Recreation & Culture	9.26
Education	1.04
Hotels & Restaurants	9.18
Miscellaneous	8.74
All Items	
Excluding Energy	89.01
Excluding Energy, Food, Alcohol & Tobacco	69.94
Excluding Energy & Unprocessed Food	81.79
Excluding Energy & Seasonal Food	85.37
Excluding Tobacco	97.66
Energy	10.99
Food, Alcohol & Tobacco	19.07

Source: Eurostat

The EU has created consumer price indices based on a harmonized approach and a single set of definitions to facilitate cross-border comparisons throughout the region, though even the harmonized measures may have a different selection of goods and services in the consumer baskets of the various countries. A "European basket" does not exist. Adjustments are made each year for any "especially large changes in expenditure patterns."[2] Many member states still retain their old measures of national CPIs and they coexist with the harmonized measures.

One of the three primary differences identified by Eurostat between the harmonized CPI measures and the national figures is the treatment of owner-occupied housing.[3] The harmonized measure excludes this cost of housing. Some of the national CPIs contain a measure for it, and those that do include it may measure it differently.

Homes used by their owners are referred to as owner-occupied housing. An estimate of the rent – if the house were rented as opposed to being owned – can be calculated by observing rents for similar homes. That figure is often referred to as "owner's equivalent rent."

A second difference is the treatment of taxes and services such as health insurance. The harmonized measure includes the prices actually paid by consumers, including all taxes, and excluding reimbursements for such items as prescription medicines. The measurement of these items can vary in the national CPI numbers.

The third main difference is the coverage of households. The harmonized measure includes all expenditures for persons in a country regardless of whether they live in the country or are visiting and those for persons living in institutions such as patients in hospitals and soldiers in barracks. Some of the national CPIs record the prices paid by residents regardless of whether those goods were purchased in the country or abroad and may exclude costs faced by persons living in institutions.

Headline vs. Core Inflation

The ECB has historically been more focused on controlling headline inflation than the core reading. That is because the former is the rate of inflation actually experienced by consumers. The latter is an academic concept. Jürgen Stark once quipped that core inflation is "well suited for central bankers who don't eat or drive."[4]

---

[2] *Principal European Economic Indicators: A Statistical Guide*. Eurostat, 2009.
[3] *Ibid.*
[4] Atkins, Ralph "Hawkish ECB Treads Fine Line on Growth." *Financial Times*, January 27, 2011.

Paul Krugman has challenged that thinking. In a 2012 book, he wrote, "And people who say things like '. . . (Core inflation is) a stupid concept – people have to spend money on food and gas, so they should be in your inflation measures' are missing the point. Core inflation isn't supposed to measure the cost of living; it's supposed to measure something else: inflation inertia."[5]

Research from ECB staff members, Juan Angel Garcia and Thomas Werner, also suggests that core inflation – and not headline inflation – drives the level of inflation uncertainty in the euro area. That increased uncertainty can lead to a higher inflation risk premium in bond yields, raising borrowing costs and lowering investment in the long run. They define inflation uncertainty as the variance of the forecasts of individual economists who contributed to the ECB's survey of professional forecasters.

They found: "Only average uncertainty shows some significant correlation with core inflation (0.7 at the two year and 0.5 at the five year horizons), but not to headline inflation (0.4 and 0.1 respectively). To the extent that core inflation can be interpreted as an underlying trend of inflationary pressures, these correlations suggest that it is not the (noisy) monthly movements in inflation but the smoother, underlying trend of inflation which drives inflation uncertainty."[6]

Core inflation is likely to provide a measure of inflation inertia even more in the euro area than the U.S. In a report published in 2009, Holger Schmieding, chief economist of Berenberg Bank and former head of European economics at Bank of America–Merrill Lynch, and his team pointed out that, "In the institutional setting [a reference to the continent's relatively inflexible labor markets] of the Eurozone, core inflation tends to be somewhat sticky, partly because wage costs in labour-intensive services react less strongly to the business cycle than in the U.S. and the U.K."[7]

In contrast to the ECB, the Federal Reserve has tended to focus on core inflation, though it ultimately aspires to stabilize the headline measure just like the ECB. Chairman Ben Bernanke has explained this approach in saying:

---

[5]Krugman, Paul *End This Depression Now*. New York: W.W. Norton & Company Ltd., 2012.

[6]Garcia, Juan Angel and Werner, Thomas "Inflation Risks and Inflation Risk Premia." ECB Working Paper Series, No. 1162. Frankfurt: European Central Bank, March 2010. Copyright European Central Bank, Frankfurt am Main, Germany. This information may be obtained free of charge from {www.ecb.int}.

[7]Menuet, Guillaume, Schmieding, Holger and Sharratt, Matthew *Eurozone Quarterly Economic Update: A Stronger Recovery*. Bank of America–Merrill Lynch, October 20, 2009.

"Policymakers attempt to infer the 'true' underlying rate of inflation. In other words, policymakers must read the incoming data in real time to judge which changes in inflation are likely to be transitory and which may prove more persistent. Getting this distinction right has first-order implications for monetary policy: Because monetary policy works with a lag, policy should be calibrated based on forecasts of medium-term inflation, which may be different from the current inflation rate."[8]

The ECB's insistence on headline inflation may have led to some errors in the conduct of its monetary policy in the past. The Governing Council increased its main policy rate in July 2008 after the flash HICP estimate for June revealed a rise of the headline reading to 4% year over year from 3.7% year over year in May. The core reading for the latter month – the latest data available at that meeting – measured 1.7% year over year. That rate increase occurred just months before the deepest recession in Europe since the Second World War. The downturn was already evident in July, though it was greatly exacerbated by the bankruptcy of Lehman Brothers in September.

A similar situation arose in 2011. ECB President Jean-Claude Trichet announced a rate increase to 1.25% from 1% in April as the continent was trying to cope with banking and debt crises. A second 25-basis-point increase followed in July. The first tightening occurred after the flash estimate revealed a headline HICP reading of 2.6% year over year in March versus 2.4% in February. The core reading for the latter month stood at 1%. The intensification of the debt crisis forced Trichet's successor, Mario Draghi, to reverse those increases during his first two months in office.

Trichet appeared eager to tighten monetary policy long before underlying inflationary pressures began seriously to threaten price stability. As Paul Krugman wrote in the *New York Times*, the ECB had "been tightening money, trying to head off inflation risks that exist only in its imagination."[9]

GDP Deflator vs. CPI

In contrast to the ECB, the Federal Reserve has tended to place more weight on the GDP deflator than the CPI. The deflator is calculated by dividing nominal GDP by real GDP. Greg Mankiw, an economics professor at Harvard

---

[8]Bernanke, Ben S. "Outstanding Issues in the Analysis of Inflation." Speech at the Federal Reserve Bank of Boston's 53rd Annual Economic Conference, Chatham, Massachusetts. Board of Governors of the Federal Reserve System, June 9, 2008.
[9]Krugman, Paul "An Impeccable Disaster." *The New York Times*, September 12, 2011.

University and former chairman of the Council of Economic Advisors under President George W. Bush, has highlighted two major differences that exist between the two measures.[10]

The first difference relates to the goods and services being measured. The GDP deflator calculates the rise in the prices of all goods and services produced domestically. The CPI measures the prices of a basket of goods and services purchased by consumers, irrespective of where they were produced. The former would include the price of an airplane made by Boeing, to use an example of Mankiw, though that item is excluded from the CPI because the average consumer doesn't buy a plane. The latter would include the price of a Mercedes manufactured in Germany and sold in the U.S., while the GDP deflator would exclude that item.

This means that oil prices are largely excluded from the GDP deflator for a country that imports most of its energy products. That effect will cause the CPI to register a higher rate of inflation than the GDP deflator when oil prices are rising. In other words, the GDP deflator may, in some cases, record a rate of inflation closer to the core measure than the headline measure of CPI.

The second major difference relates to the change of the components of the basket of goods. The GDP deflator compares the prices of all goods and services currently produced to the prices of all goods and services produced in a base year. In other words, the actual groups of goods and services automatically change over time. That may limit the use of historical comparisons because the price index is influenced by changes in the composition of GDP. By contrast, the CPI measures a fixed basket of goods and services. It will be changed only periodically by the national statistics agency.

The Federal Reserve's preferred deflator for measuring inflation is that for personal consumption expenditures, a component of GDP. The Federal Open Market Committee explained its reasoning for the switch to the PCE deflator from CPI in its Monetary Policy Report to Congress of February 2000. Members of the FOMC wrote:

> "In past Monetary Policy Reports to the Congress, the FOMC has framed its inflation forecasts in terms of the consumer price index. The chain-type price index for PCE draws extensively on data from the consumer price index but, while not entirely free of measurement problems, has several advantages relative to the CPI. The PCE chain-type index is constructed from a formula that reflects the changing composition of spending and

---

[10]Mankiw, N. Gregory *Principles of Economics*, sixth edition. Mason, OH: South-Western Cengage Learning, 2012.

thereby avoids some of the upward bias associated with the fixed-weight nature of the CPI. In addition, the weights are based on a more comprehensive measure of expenditures. Finally, historical data used in the PCE price index can be revised to account for newly available information and for improvements in measurement techniques, including those that affect source data from the CPI; the result is a more consistent series over time. This switch in presentation notwithstanding, the FOMC will continue to rely on a variety of aggregate price measures, as well as other information on prices and costs, in assessing the path of inflation."[11]

The PCE deflator tends to be about 0.5 of a percentage point below the CPI as a result of measurement differences. As such, the Federal Reserve's implicit target of 2% inflation translates into an implicit target of 1.5% of the PCE deflator.[12]

A GDP deflator has the disadvantage of being less timely than the CPI. The former is released on a quarterly basis and the latter on a monthly basis, though the PCE deflator for the U.S. is available monthly.

The CPI is a lagging indicator. It records price increases that have already materialized. Economists look at other inflation indicators to forecast the future direction of CPI. They include the producer price index, wages, inflation expectations and, in the euro area, money supply.

Producer Price Index

The industrial producer price index measures the selling prices of goods when they leave the factory. Producer prices are also commonly referred to as output prices.

The data are normally published about a month and two or three days after the reference period. This means that the data are released about two weeks after the final release of the CPI for the same month. The PPI – like the CPI – is not seasonally adjusted.

One of the primary differences between the PPI and the CPI relates to intermediate goods. The former is partially made up of them and the latter excludes them. In addition, the difference between the two measures should

---

[11]*Monetary Policy Report to the Congress.* Board of Governors of the Federal Reserve System, February 2000.
[12]Harris, Ethan *Ben Bernanke's Fed: The Federal Reserve After Greenspan.* Boston: Harvard Business Press, 2008.

FIGURE 5.1 Core CPI and core PPI.

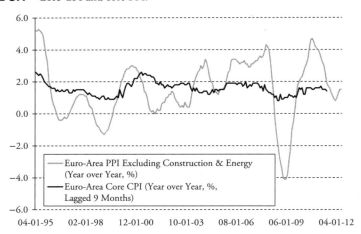

Source: Bloomberg

reflect trade and transport margins and taxes that are added to the prices of the products after they leave the factory.[13]

The index is watched primarily as a gauge of underlying inflationary pressures, which may eventually feed through to consumers. These inflationary pressures are commonly referred to as "in the pipeline." The highest correlation between the year-over-year increase in the PPI excluding construction and energy costs (i.e. core PPI) and the year-over-year increase in the core CPI exists when the latter is lagged by eight to 10 months (Figure 5.1). The monthly correlations between these two time series when the core CPI measure is lagged by seven, eight and nine months all stand at 0.57 using monthly data from January 1995 to November 2010.

The correlation between the headline versions of these two time series is highest when neither is lagged. It stands at 0.81 for the same time period. That is probably due to the influence of energy prices on both of the indices.

Eurostat provides several guidelines related to the compilation of the index. The prices recorded should exclude all taxes. Actual transaction prices should be used as opposed to list prices for accuracy. The prices should refer to the month during which the order was placed as opposed to when the goods actually leave the factory.[14]

---

[13] *Principal European Economic Indicators: A Statistical Guide.* Eurostat, 2009.
[14] *Ibid.*

Labor Costs

The ECB monitors labor costs closely because of their inflationary implications. The best measure of these expenses is unit labor costs because they take into consideration wages and productivity. Unit labor costs are defined as the cost of labor per unit of output and can be calculated by dividing total labor costs by real GDP.

The ECB reports quarterly data on unit labor costs in its monthly bulletin. The figures are found in table 5.1 of the statistical annex. The data can also be found in the statistical data warehouse about 75 days after the end of the reporting period. The breakdown by industry and revisions to previous figures are published about 95 days after the end of the reporting period.[15]

Eurostat reports a labor cost index. It measures the total cost on an hourly basis of employing labor.[16] A breakdown is available of wages and salaries and other labor costs. The data are released on a quarterly basis about 75 days after the end of the reference period.

Labor costs are important because they account for a large share of the overall costs of a business. A rise unaccompanied by an increase in productivity can lead businesses to increase their selling prices, putting upward pressure on CPI. If output per worker – or productivity – rises, employers can afford to increase wages without raising prices.

The ECB often refers to a rise in wages unaccompanied by an increase in productivity as a "second-round effect." For example, throughout 2011, Trichet, in his monthly press statements, frequently made comments such as, "It is of paramount importance that the rise in HICP inflation does not lead to second-round effects in price and wage-setting behaviour and thereby give rise to broad-based inflationary pressures over the medium term."[17]

The phrase expresses the determination to prevent a wage-price spiral. That inflationary dynamic takes hold when workers demand wage increases to keep up with the rise in the price level and employers then have to raise prices in order to afford the higher wage bill. As a result, the aggregate price level rises and workers ask for additional wage increases to compensate for the second rise in prices. Those expectations of rising prices then become embedded in the expectations of wage negotiators and create a vicious cycle.

---

[15] E-mail from ECB to David Powell, July 25, 2012.
[16] *Principal European Economic Indicators: A Statistical Guide*. Eurostat, 2009.
[17] Trichet, Jean-Claude *Introductory Statement to the Press Conference (with Q&A)*. European Central Bank, Frankfurt am Main, April 7, 2011.

One of the most famous historical examples of a wage-price spiral occurred after the oil embargo of 1973 imposed by the Organization of Petroleum Exporting Countries. The rise in the price of oil caused the U.S. CPI to increase by 8.7% year over year by the end of 1973. Inflation rates remained high throughout the decade, hitting 13.3% year over year by the end of 1979.

That price rise contributed to strong wage growth (Figure 5.2). Personal income in the U.S. rose by 11% year over year in December of 1973. That rate of growth remained in double-digit territory for most of the decade, registering 12.5% year over year in December 1979.

Policy makers tolerated elevated levels of inflation because many of them believed in a trade-off between inflation and unemployment. That link was first introduced through the Phillips curve, which is based on the work of Bill Phillips, an economist from New Zealand, who taught at the London School of Economics and Political Science. He discovered an inverse relationship between inflation and unemployment in the British economy and published his findings in 1958 in a paper titled *The Relation between Unemployment and the Rate of Change of Money Wage Rates in the United Kingdom, 1861–1957*.

Milton Friedman later argued the trade-off existed only in the short term and that the curve became vertical in the long term. He believed that inflationary policies would be ineffective in shifting the level of unemployment from its natural rate in the long run. The end result of those pursuits would only be high inflation and high inflation expectations.[18]

FIGURE 5.2 U.S. personal income growth and CPI growth.

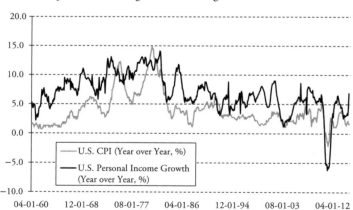

Source: Bloomberg

---

[18]For details, see: Friedman, Milton *Inflation and Unemployment.* Nobel Memorial Lecture, December 13, 1976.

The experience of the 1970s provided support for the views of Friedman. Inflationary policies pursued in the U.S. failed to lower unemployment. By the start of 1975, the inflation rate had risen to 11.8% and the unemployment rate to 8.1%. The period was memorialized by the creation of the "Misery Index," which adds the inflation rate to the unemployment rate. The index peaked at 22 in June 1980 (Figure 5.3).

Central bankers have little ability to control supply shocks such as a spike in oil prices that would cause the headline reading of CPI to rise and could lead to a rise in wage demands. In the face of these cost push inflationary pressures, they can merely threaten employers with rate increases in the event that "second-round effects" or high rates of wage growth are observed.

The monetary authorities can temper aggregate demand by raising interest rates if wages are rising too rapidly. A deceleration of growth should lead to a rise in unemployment and a decrease in the bargaining power of employees to demand wage increases and, by extension, a fall in inflation.

Employment growth tends to lag GDP growth by four quarters (Figure 5.4). The correlation between the year-over-year growth rate of employment with a four-quarter lag and that of GDP from the first quarter of 1998 to the first quarter of 2010 stands at 0.83.

A proxy for suitable wage growth can be determined, though the ECB has refrained from providing a specific target. The Governing Council would probably be satisfied if the increase in wages were to remain in line with its inflation target (close to but below 2%) plus the 10-year average in

FIGURE 5.3 U.S. misery index.

Source: Bloomberg

FIGURE 5.4 Euro-area employment growth and GDP growth.

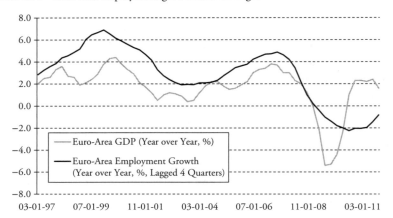

Source: Bloomberg

productivity growth for the euro area. The latter figure is 0.68%. The sum of these two numbers is about 2.5%.

The level of unemployment consistent with price stability is referred to as the non-accelerating inflation rate of unemployment. It is not directly observable, though the OECD publishes its estimates of NAIRU on a biannual basis.

Money Supply

The ECB pays more attention to money supply, when analyzing the inflation outlook, than any other central bank of an advanced economy. The school of thought that assigns a large role to money supply growth for maintaining price stability is called monetarism.

Milton Friedman, who famously said, "Inflation is always and everywhere a monetary phenomenon in the sense that it is and can be produced only by a more rapid increase in the quantity of money than in output," became the high priest of monetarism.[19] His fellow Nobel laureate in economics, Robert Solow, once quipped, "Everything reminds Milton of the money supply. Well, everything reminds me of sex, but I keep it out of the paper."[20]

---

[19]Friedman, Milton *The Counter-Revolution in Monetary Theory*. London: Published for the Wincott Foundation by the Institute of Economic Affairs, 1970.
[20]Krugman, Paul "Who Was Milton Friedman?" *The New York Review of Books*, February 15, 2007.

Monetarists believe in the neutrality of money. The ECB defines it as "a basic economic principle stating that in the long run changes in the money supply only lead to changes in nominal variables but not in real variables."[21] In other words, changes in money supply have no long-term effect on real output, unemployment or real interest rates.

Friedman wanted to abolish the Federal Reserve.[22] He argued that the central bank's attempts to fine tune the economy created instability and proposed replacing the institution with a simple rule to manage the growth of the money supply.

His "k% rule" proposed increasing the money supply by a constant rate each year irrespective of current economic conditions. He proposed an annual increase in the money supply of about 4% to maintain price stability.

That was based on an estimate of long-term output growth of 3% plus 1% to account for the secular decrease in the velocity of money. The velocity of money measures the average frequency with which money is used in a given period of time.[23] Friedman originally favored the use of M2 money supply, though he switched his preference to M1 money supply in the early 1980s.[24]

The major problem with Friedman's rule was that velocity was not constant. The variability of velocity increased throughout the 1980s as technology advanced. One reason for that was that the increased use of credit cards allowed a given level of the money stock to support more transactions and a higher level of nominal spending, raising the velocity of money.[25]

Several major central banks implemented policies of monetary targeting during the 1970s. The Bundesbank pursued that strategy from 1974 until it transferred the responsibility for monetary policy to the ECB in 1999. The

---

[21] *The Monetary Policy of the ECB 2004*. Frankfurt: European Central Bank, 2004.

[22] Roberts, Russell *An Interview With Milton Friedman*. Library of Economics and Liberty, September 4. 2006. {http://www.econlib.org/library/Columns/y2006/Friedmantranscript.html}

[23] Friedman, Milton *A Program for Monetary Stability*. New York: Fordham University Press, 1960 and Orphanides, Athanasios *Taylor Rules*. Finance and Economics Discussion Series: 2007-18. Board of Governors of the Federal Reserve System, January 2007.

[24] Hall, Stephen G., Swamy, P.A.V.B. and Tavlas, George S. "Milton Friedman, the Demand for Money, and the ECB's Monetary Policy Strategy." *Federal Reserve Bank of St. Louis Review*. Federal Reserve Bank of St. Louis, May/June 2012.

[25] Benolkin, Scott and Kahn, George A. "The Role of Money in Monetary Policy: Why Do the Fed and ECB See It So Differently?" *Economic Review, Third Quarter 2007*. Federal Reserve Bank of Kansas City, 2007.

Swiss National Bank also pursued that strategy, though not consistently, for the same time period. The Bank of Canada, the Bank of England and the Federal Reserve implemented monetary targeting regimes during the 1970s and abandoned them in the 1980s.

The Federal Reserve, like most other central banks excluding the ECB, now assigns little weight to the monetary aggregates. In 2006, Chairman Bernanke stated, "It would be fair to say that monetary and credit aggregates have not played a central role in the formulation of U.S. monetary policy since [1982], although policymakers continue to use monetary data as a source of information about the state of the economy."[26]

Bernanke reiterated the Federal Reserve's view of an unstable relationship between the monetary aggregates and inflation. In that same speech, he said, "In practice, the difficulty has been that, in the United States, deregulation, financial innovation, and other factors have led to recurrent instability in the relationships between various monetary aggregates and other nominal variables."

Alan Blinder has been more direct than Bernanke. He wrote, "money demand functions are impossibly unstable and . . . for most periods money is not even cointegrated with income. As Gerry Bouey, a former governor of the Bank of Canada put it. 'We didn't abandon the monetary aggregates, they abandoned us.'" Blinder continued, "In a word, no sturdy long-run statistical relationship exists between nominal GDP and *any* of the Federal Reserve's three official definitions of M for *any* sample that includes the 1990s."[27]

George Kahn and Scott Benolkin, economists at the Federal Reserve Bank of Kansas City, have found that the relationship between money and inflation is more stable in the euro area, even today, than in the U.S. They concluded in a study, "Empirical evidence suggests money is a more useful indicator of future inflation in the Euro area than in the United States. First, over the medium to long run, the correlation between money growth and inflation is greater in the Euro area. Second, the relationship between nominal spending and money growth is more stable in the Euro area than in the United States. And third, unlike in the United States, money growth helps predict inflation in the Euro area in simple regression models."[28] They examined data from the 1980s to 2006.

---

[26]Bernanke, Ben S. "Monetary Aggregates and Monetary Policy at the Federal Reserve: A Historical Perspective." Speech at the Fourth ECB Central Banking Conference, Frankfurt, Germany. Board of Governors of the Federal Reserve System, November 10, 2006.

[27]Blinder, Alan *Central Banking in Theory and Practice*. Cambridge, Mass.: MIT Press, 1998.

[28]Benolkin and Kahn, 2007. Reproduced by permission of the Federal Reserve Bank of Kansas City.

Long after most of the world's central banks had abandoned monetary targeting practices, Otmar Issing, former chief economist of the Bundesbank and architect of the ECB's second pillar, left the ECB as the sole torchbearer of monetarism. He wrote, "The close relationship between the money supply and prices has been proven in countless studies all over the globe and all through history; it is one of the most certain facts in economics – insofar as anything is ever 'certain' in economics."[29]

Paul De Grauwe, John Paulson Chair in European Political Economy at the London School of Economics and Political Science, has directly challenged that assertion. In 2008, he wrote, "After ten years it can now be safely concluded that the attempt at using the growth of M3 as an early indicator of future inflation failed miserably." He concluded, "In a low inflation environment . . . most of the variability of money stock numbers is noise and is unrelated to inflationary dynamics. Most of the noise comes from large portfolio effects and financial innovation."[30]

The Banque de France has expressed disagreement with Issing as well, suggesting that the relationship between money supply and inflation in the euro area may no longer be as strong as it once was. Michele Saint Marc, a former member of the Banque de France's monetary policy committee, said, "It is becoming more and more difficult to justify monetary policy by leaning on a monetary pillar which has had its limitations since the launch of the euro . . . The risk eventually is that it might jeopardise the credibility of a central bank." She added, "The ECB's reference for M3 may seem to be no longer appropriate given the world has changed since Otmar Issing's time at the Bundesbank."[31]

Monetary Aggregates

In general, money supply is divided into four categories: M0 or the monetary base, M1, M2 and M3. The reporting of these figures varies from country to country. For example, the Federal Reserve stopped publishing the M3 monetary aggregate in March 2006. In 2005, the Board of Governors stated, "M3 does not appear to convey any additional information about economic activity that is not already embodied in M2 and has not played a role in the

---

[29]Issing, Otmar *The Birth of the Euro*. Cambridge: Cambridge University Press, 2008.
[30]De Grauwe, Paul "On the Need to Renovate the Eurozone." *International Finance*, 2008.
[31]Pattanaik, Swaha "ECB Must Reconsider M3 Role For Policy – BOF Official." Reuters, May 2, 2007.

TABLE 5.2 Definitions of Euro Area Monetary Aggregates

Liabilities (2)	M1	M2	M3
Currency in circulation	X	X	X
Overnight deposits	X	X	X
Deposits with an agreed maturity of up to 2 years		X	X
Deposits redeemable at notice of up to 3 months		X	X
Repurchase agreements			X
Money market fund shares/units			X
Debt securities issued with a maturity of up to 2 years			X

Source: ECB. Copyright European Central Bank, Frankfurt am Main, Germany. This information may be obtained free of charge from {www.ecb.int}.

monetary policy process for many years."[32] The exact definitions of the monetary aggregates also vary somewhat from country to country, though they are similar around the globe.

The ECB defines the four monetary aggregates as (Table 5.2):[33]

- Base money (M0) includes currency (banknotes and coins) in circulation plus the minimum reserves credit institutions are required to hold with the Eurosystem and any excess reserves they may voluntarily hold in the Eurosystem's deposit facility, all of which are liabilities on the Eurosystem's balance sheet. Base money is sometimes also referred to as the "monetary base".
- Narrow money (M1) includes currency (banknotes and coins) as well as balances which can immediately be converted into currency or used for cashless payments, i.e. overnight deposits.
- "Intermediate" money (M2) comprises narrow money (M1) and, in addition, deposits with a maturity of up to two years and deposits redeemable at a period of notice of up to three months. Depending on their degree of moneyness, such deposits can be converted into components of narrow money, but in some cases there may be restrictions involved, such as the need for advance notification, delays, penalties or fees. The definition of

---

[32]"Discontinuance of M3." *Federal Reserve Statistical Release.* Board of Governors of the Federal Reserve System, November 10, 2005.

[33]*ECB Glossary* {http://www.ecb.int/home/glossary/html/act1a.en.html} and *The ECB's Definition of Euro Area Monetary Aggregates* {http://www.ecb.int/stats/money/aggregates/aggr/html/hist.en.html}. Copyright European Central Bank, Frankfurt am Main, Germany. This information may be obtained free of charge from {www.ecb.int}.

Inflation Measures

M2 reflects the particular interest in analyzing and monitoring a monetary aggregate that, in addition to currency, consists of deposits which are liquid.
- Broad money (M3) comprises M2 and marketable instruments issued by the MFI sector. Certain money market instruments, in particular money market fund (MMF) shares/units and repurchase agreements, are included in this aggregate. A high degree of liquidity and price certainty make these instruments close substitutes for deposits. As a result of their inclusion, M3 is less affected by substitution between various liquid asset categories than narrower definitions of money, and is therefore more stable.

The Governing Council uses M3 money supply growth to assess long-term inflationary pressures through the framework of its second pillar. It has a "reference value", which is less strict than a "target." The central bank states that the "reference value" is "a benchmark for analysing the information content of monetary developments in the euro area" and "monetary policy does not . . . react in a mechanical way to deviations of M3 growth from the reference value."[34] ECB economists Bjorn Fischer, Michele Lenza, Huw Pill and Lucrezia Reichlin confirmed, "deviations were viewed [merely] as triggers for further analysis to identify the cause of the deviation and assess its implications for the outlook for price developments."[35]

The reference value provides considerable leeway for policy makers. Trichet said that rapid money supply growth contributed to the decision to tighten monetary policy in 2005 even though the economic analysis suggested that inflation was not a concern.[36] The four ECB economists named above confirmed, "The progressive increase of official interest rates from December 2005 was – in real time – motivated to an important degree by the monetary analysis."[37]

These words are reminiscent of those of Karl Otto Pohl, former president of the Bundesbank. He quipped that the central bank only took its monetary targets seriously when it was seeking an additional excuse for a decision to raise interest rates.[38]

---

[34] Scheller, Hanspeter K. *The European Central Bank: History, Role and Functions*. Frankfurt: European Central Bank, 2004.

[35] Fischer, Bjorn, Lenza, Michele, Pill, Huw and Reichlin, Lucrezia *Money and Monetary Policy: The ECB Experience 1999–2006*. Preliminary draft, November 6, 2006.

[36] Benolkin and Kahn, 2007.

[37] Fischer, Lenza, Pill and Reichlin, 2006.

[38] Marsh, David *The Most Powerful Bank: Inside Germany's Bundesbank*. New York: Random House, 1992.

The ECB's reference value for M3 money supply is a three-month average of the year-over-year rate of growth of 4.5%.[39] The central bank publishes the data on a monthly basis about 25 days after the end of the reporting period.

The figure was derived from the quantity equation of money.[40] It describes the relationship between monetary growth, inflation, real GDP growth and the velocity of money. Specifically, it states that:

$$\Delta M = \Delta P + \Delta Y - \Delta V$$

where:
ΔM = change in money supply;
ΔP = change in the price level;
ΔY = change in real GDP;
ΔV = change in the velocity of money.

(N.B. This is the same equation from the section on the quantity theory of money on page 53 converted to percentage changes.)

The ECB uses inputs specific to the euro-area economy. It chose its inflation target – less than 2% per year – for the change in the price level. It assumed the medium-term trend in real potential GDP growth – 2–2.5% – for the change in real GDP. It estimated the annual trend decline in the velocity of M3 to be 0.5–1%. From these inputs, the Governing Council decided a reference value of 4.5% was "consistent with maintaining price stability."[41]

Loan Growth

The ECB also appears to watch closely the counterparts of money supply growth as indicators of inflation. They are credit and, more specifically, loan growth (Table 5.3). The monetary aggregates represent the liabilities of the banking system and credit and loan figures represent the assets of the banking system that are funded by those liabilities.

ECB President Mario Draghi, in his monthly press statements, most frequently cites loans to the private sector, adjusted for sales and securitization,

---

[39] *Monetary Policy Glossary*. European Central Bank. {http://www.ecb.int/home/glossary/html/act4r.en.html#265} and *Press Release: The Quantitative Reference Value for Monetary Growth*. Frankfurt: European Central Bank, December 1, 1998.

[40] *The Monetary Policy of the ECB: 2004*. Frankfurt: European Central Bank, 2004.

[41] Issing, 2008.

TABLE 5.3 Breakdown of Loans as Counterpart to M3 by Borrowing Sector, Type and Original Maturity

BREAKDOWN OF LOANS AS COUNTERPART TO M3 BY BORROWING SECTOR, TYPE AND ORIGINAL MATURITY: SEPTEMBER 2012
DATA ADJUSTED FOR SEASONAL EFFECTS
(EUR billions and annual percentage changes)[a]

	End-Of-Month-Level	Monthly Flow[b]			Annual Growth Rate		
	September 2012	July 2012	August 2012	September 2012	July 2012	August 2012	September 2012
BREAKDOWN OF LOANS AS COUNTERPART TO M3[c]							
(1) Loans to households[d]	5240	−8	4	−1	0.3	0.2	0.1
loans adjusted for sales and securitization[e]	*ND*	*−2*	*5*	*1*	*1.0*	*0.9*	*0.9*
(1.1) Credit for consumption	603	−4	−2	−3	−2.1	−2.5	−2.9
(1.2) Lending for house purchase	3812	−5	6	3	0.8	0.8	0.7
(1.3) Other lending	824	0	1	−1	−0.5	−0.6	−0.7
of which: sole proprietors[f]	415	0	−1	−1	1.0	0.8	0.7
(2) Loans to non-financial corporations	4656	8	−7	−21	−0.4	−0.7	−1.4
loans adjusted for sales and securitization[e]	*ND*	*8*	*−6*	*−20*	*−0.2*	*−0.5*	*−1.2*
(2.1) up to 1 year	1142	16	−4	−15	0.1	−0.2	−1.9
(2.2) over 1 year and up to 5 years	828	−3	−5	−6	−2.8	−3.3	−4.1
(2.3) over 5 years	2687	−5	2	0	0.1	−0.1	−0.4
(3) Loans to non-monetary financial intermediaries except insurance corporations and pension funds[g]	963	5	2	4	−2.9	−3.5	−2.0
(4) Loans to insurance corporations and pension funds[g]	87	−1	3	1	−8.6	−11.3	−9.0

a) Figures may not add up due to rounding.
b) Monthly difference in levels adjusted for write-offs/write-downs, reclassification, exchange rate variations and any other changes which do not arise from transactions.
c) Loans granted by monetary financial institutions (MFIs) to non-MFI euro area residents excluding general government.
d) Includes loans to non-profit institutions serving households.
e) Adjusted for the derecognition of loans from the MFI statistical balance sheet due to their sale or securitization.
f) The series is not adjusted for seasonal effects.
g) Excludes reverse repos to central counterparties.
Source: ECB. Copyright European Central Bank, Frankfurt am Main, Germany. This information may be obtained free of charge from [www.ecb.int].

in the section on monetary analysis. For example, in July 2012, the president said, "The annual growth rate of loans to the private sector (adjusted for loan sales and securitisation) declined to 0.4% in May (from 0.8% in April). Annual growth rates for loans to both non-financial corporations and households (adjusted for loan sales and securitisation) also decreased in May, to 0.2% and 1.3% respectively, with negative monthly loan flows to non-financial corporations" (Figure 5.5).[42]

Inflation Expectations

The ECB, like the central banks of most developed economies, monitors inflation expectations closely. They can be measured with inflation-linked bonds – often referred to as "market-based measures" – and surveys.

Market-Based Measures

The inflation-linked government bonds of France provide one of the best market-based measures of inflation expectations for the euro area. They provide a more accurate reading than their German counterparts because the

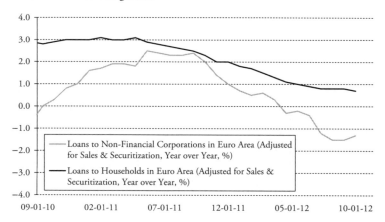

FIGURE 5.5 Euro-area loan growth.

Source: Bloomberg

---

[42]Draghi, Mario *Introductory Statement to the Press Conference (with Q&A)*. Frankfurt: European Central Bank, July 5, 2012. Copyright European Central Bank, Frankfurt am Main, Germany. This information may be obtained free of charge from {www.ecb.int}.

French market is more liquid. France has 147.4 billion euros in outstanding inflation-linked government debt, according to the Bloomberg Professional Service. The equivalent figure for Germany is 55.5 billion euros. The ECB has indicated that it uses the inflation-linked bonds from both countries to measure inflation expectations.[43] These hedges against inflation are also issued by Italy and were issued in the past by Greece.

The ECB watches the five-year forward breakeven inflation rate five years ahead. It is commonly referred to by market participants as the five-year, five-year breakeven rate and measures the expected level of inflation in five years for the following five years. The central bank prefers this measure because it should be less affected by short-term price shocks, such as a sharp rise in oil prices, than the spot breakeven inflation rates.[44]

The difference between inflation-linked bond yields and nominal bond yields contains an expected inflation rate over the life of the bond. In addition, that spread includes risk premia for uncertainty about future inflation outcomes (because compensation is required for the risk inflation may turn out to be higher than expected) and liquidity (because inflation-linked bonds are less actively traded than nominal bonds).[45]

The existence of a premium for inflation risk means that the differences between inflation-linked yields and nominal yields on French and German bonds are not directly comparable. ECB economists Lorenzo Cappiello and Stéphane Guéné have estimated the inflation risk premium on the short- and long-term government bonds of France to be 4 and 21 basis points, respectively, on average. The equivalent figures for those of Germany are 3 and 9 basis points, respectively.[46] Short-term government bonds are defined as those with maturities of between one and three years and long-term instruments are those with durations of more than three years.

All new inflation-linked bonds in the euro area are linked to inflation for the euro area as a whole and not to the rate of inflation for the issuing country. Specifically, they are linked to the euro-area HICP index excluding tobacco.

---

[43]"Assessing the Anchoring of Longer-Term Inflation Expectations." *ECB Monthly Bulletin*. Frankfurt: European Central Bank, July 2012.

[44]*Ibid.*

[45]Garcia, Juan Angel and Van Rixtel, Adrian "Inflation-Linked Bonds From a Central Bank Perspective." ECB Occasional Paper Series, No. 62. Frankfurt: European Central Bank, June 2007.

[46]Cappiello, Lorenzo and Guéné, Stéphane "Measuring Market and Inflation Risk Premia in France and in Germany." ECB Working Paper Series. Frankfurt: European Central Bank, February 2005.

The connection to the measure of price increases that excludes tobacco is the result of French regulations that based the inflation-linked bonds of France, the first country in the euro area to issue these securities, on the domestic CPI excluding tobacco.[47]

France changed the inflation index to that of the euro area as opposed to its domestic figure as the result of an imbalance between supply and demand for inflation-linked government bonds in the euro area.[48] In other words, investors outside of France wanted to buy bonds that provided protection from inflation and they were more concerned with inflation in the euro area as a whole than inflation in France. The first bond linked to the rate of the inflation of the euro area as a whole was issued by the French Treasury in October 2001 with a maturity date of July 2012.

The index that excluded tobacco then became the benchmark for the entire euro area. It has also been used as the index for inflation-linked swaps and HICP futures. The inflation-linked bonds also guarantee redemption at par, providing protection from the risk of deflation.

The ECB has indicated that it watches inflation expectations measured by inflation swaps as well.[49] These derivatives consist of two payments, commonly referred to as legs. One leg is a fixed payment and the second is the actual rate of inflation. For example, party A may agree to pay a pre-determined rate – such as 3% – at the end of the year to party B in exchange for party B paying party A the actual rate of inflation, which may be 2.5%. In theory, the pre-determined rate should represent market expectations for the rate of inflation over the next year and it should include an inflation risk premium similar to that present in inflation-linked government bonds.

The main advantage of inflation-linked swaps over inflation-linked bonds for a user is the ability to customize. In other words, they can be used to hedge the exact duration of an inflation risk, say 2.5 years. Inflation-linked bonds of governments are only issued with standard maturities.

Surveys

Two surveys of inflation expectations are conducted in the euro area. The one most frequently cited by the ECB is its own survey of professional forecasters. The results are published quarterly in the ECB's monthly bulletin

---

[47]Garcia and Van Rixtel, June 2007.

[48]*Ibid.*

[49]"Inflation Expectations in the Euro Area: A Review of Recent Developments." *ECB Monthly Bulletin*. Frankfurt: European Central Bank, February 2011.

and include forecasts for real GDP growth and unemployment in the euro area. This is similar to the survey of professional forecasters published by the Federal Reserve Bank of Philadelphia in the U.S.

The ECB surveys about 75 forecasters from the EU for their short- to longer-term expectations of growth, inflation and unemployment in the euro area. The central bank also asks for the probabilities of different outcomes for the central bank to construct probability distributions (Table 5.4). The horizons of the requested forecasts are one, two and five years ahead.

Erik Nielsen, chief economist of Unicredit and former chief European economist of Goldman Sachs, has refuted the utility of the survey of professional forecasters on inflation expectations. He said to Jürgen Stark at the 2009 The ECB and Its Watchers conference, "I'm part of the professional forecasters. I'm very flattered when you say that that's really what matters to you but I'm going to reveal to you . . . that takes me one second to put in that box because you ask what I think inflation is going to be in 10 years' time . . . I think you're credible so that's 2 percent. Bang. Done. I mean I

TABLE 5.4 Quarterly Survey of Professional Forecasters

	Probabilities of Euro Area Inflation* Year-on-Year Change in the HICP				
	2010	2011	December 2010	December 2011	5 Years Ahead (2014)
less than −1.0%					
−1.0 to −0.6%					
−0.5 to −0.1%					
0.0–0.4%					
0.5–0.9%					
1.0–1.4%					
1.5–1.9%					
2.0–2.4%					
2.5–2.9%					
3.0–3.4%					
3.5–3.9%					
≥ 4.0%					
Total	100	100	100	100	100

*Defined on the basis of the Harmonised Index of Consumer Prices produced by Eurostat. Probabilities should sum to 100%.
Source: ECB. Copied from the ECB's questionnaire for the 2010 Q1 Survey of Professional Forecasters.

can't be bothered with this 1.8, 1.9. Two percent is easier. It's faster. So maybe you pay too much attention to us and should look a little bit more at the consumers."[50]

Research from the ECB appears also to suggest that those forecasts may be based merely on the expectation for the central bank to adhere to its mandate of price stability. The staff economists found that survey participants have tended to forecast rates of inflation for the euro area that have been under the actual outcomes for most of the period since 1999. Specifically, the one-year ahead inflation forecast of 1.7% was below the actual level of inflation by 0.5 of a percentage point, on average, from the first quarter of 1999 to the fourth quarter of 2006. The underestimation for the two-year ahead inflation forecast of 1.8% was 0.4 of a percentage point.[51]

The second survey of inflation expectations is conducted by the EC. The ECB considers this measure to be less important for monetary policy than the survey of professional forecasters because it surveys expectations for "very short periods" and may be more likely to be affected by temporary shocks. The central bank's staff economists calculated the highest correlation between the EC measure of inflation expectations and actual inflation "occurs at the same time or for lags up to seven months, depending on the horizon considered, suggesting that this particular indicator of expectations contains

---

Exhibit 5.1   Question from EC consumer survey

By comparison with the past 12 months, how do you expect that consumer prices will develop in the next 12 months? They will . . .

++ increase more rapidly
+ increase at the same rate
= increase at a slower rate
− stay about the same
— fall
N don't know.

---

[50]Nielsen, Erik Comments made at The ECB and Its Watchers conference, Center for Financial Studies, Frankfurt am Main, Germany, September 4, 2009. Video available at: {https://www.ifk-cfs.de/index.php?id=1608}. Reproduced by permission of Erik Nielsen.

[51]Bowles, Carlos, Friz, Roberta, Genre, Veronique, Kenny, Geoff, Meyler, Aidan and Rautanen, Tuomas *The ECB Survey of Professional Forecasters (SPF): A Review After Eight Years' Experience*. ECB Occasional Paper Series No. 59. Frankfurt: European Central Bank, April 2007.

information about horizons that are much shorter than the 12-month horizon to which the survey question refers."[52]

Jürgen Stark also expressed distrust in the EC's survey of inflation expectations at the aforementioned ECB and Its Watchers conference. He said, "to draw firm conclusions [from the EC survey] about the anchoring of inflation expectations could be misleading . . . what counts is for me the survey of professional forecasters."[53]

---

[52] "Inflation Expectations in the Euro Area: A Review of Recent Developments." *ECB Monthly Bulletin*. Frankfurt: European Central Bank, February 2011.

[53] Stark, Jürgen Comments made at The ECB and Its Watchers conference, Center for Financial Studies, Frankfurt am Main, Germany, September 4, 2009. Video available at: {https://www.ifk-cfs.de/index.php?id=1608}

CHAPTER 6

The European Central Bank

The ECB was born on June 1, 1998. It is the successor to the European Monetary Institute, which was founded in 1994 to prepare for the introduction of the euro, and is headquartered in Frankfurt, Germany.

The ECB is the core of the Eurosystem and the European System of Central Banks. The former is comprised of the ECB and the national central banks that have adopted the euro. The latter is comprised of the ECB and the national central banks of all EU member states regardless of whether they have adopted the euro or not. Denmark and the U.K. negotiated opt-out clauses and are not legally bound to ever join the euro area. All other EU countries have legally committed to eventually joining the euro area.

The main decision-making body of the ECB is the Governing Council. It is made up of the six members of the Executive Board and the 17 governors of the national central banks of the euro area. The Executive Board meets at least once a week.[1] It is charged with implementing the monetary policy of the euro area in accordance with the decisions of the Governing Council, preparing the meetings of the Governing Council and managing the day-to-day business of the ECB.[2] The board's members are appointed by the European Council.

The Governing Council meets twice a month. The meetings are normally in Frankfurt apart from two per year hosted by national central banks. It assesses economic and monetary developments and takes its monetary policy

---

[1] Scheller, 2004.
[2] *The Executive Board*. European Central Bank. {http://www.ecb.int/ecb/orga/decisions/eb/html/index.en.html}

decision at the first meeting of the month. The group attends to other tasks of the ECB at the second meeting of the month.³

Technically, each member of the Governing Council physically present at the meeting has one vote for interest-rate decisions. They are taken by simple majority and the president holds the casting vote.⁴

In reality, members of the Governing Council appear to refrain from voting. "The ECB has never had a formal vote on interest rates. I know this straight from the mouths of horses who between them have attended every single one of the ECB Governing Council's rate-setting meetings since the first one in January 1999," Willem Buiter, chief economist of Citigroup and a former member of the BoE's Monetary Policy Committee, wrote in his blog on the website of the *Financial Times*.⁵ "Instead of voting on the interest rate, the ECB's Governing Council 'reach a consensus' without ever taking a vote. The mystical process through which this consensus is achieved can only be guessed at," he added.

This system of "consensus" has resulted in the will of the majority being squashed by a minority of members of the Governing Council. A majority of the body's members wanted to reduce the main policy rate of the ECB in December 2012 and the move was reportedly blocked by President Mario Draghi and Executive Board members Benoit Coeure and Jörg Asmussen and Bundesbank President Jens Weidmann.⁶

That system may allow the ECB president to impose his will on the Governing Council by only selectively proposing a vote on matters of monetary policy. For example, in August 2012, Draghi appeared to suggest that he would overcome the opposition of Bundesbank President Jens Weidmann to the purchase of government bonds by having the latter outvoted.

At the press conference in August, Draghi said, "It's clear and it's known that Mr. Weidmann and the Bundesbank – although we are here in a personal capacity and we should never forget that – have their reservations about programmes that envisage buying bonds, so the idea is now we have

---

³Scheller, 2004.

⁴*Ibid.*

⁵Buiter, Willem "The ECB Should Vote on Interest Rates, and Then Publish its Minutes." *Financial Times*, July 22, 2008. {http://blogs.ft.com/maverecon/2008/07/the-ecb-should-vote-on-interest-rates-and-then-publish-its-minutes/#}. Reproduced by permission of Willem Buiter.

⁶Black, Jeff and Randow, Jana "Majority of ECB Governing Council Said to Support Rate Cut." Bloomberg News, December 7, 2012.

given guidance, the Monetary Policy Committee, the Risk Management Committee and the Market Operations Committee will work on this guidance and then we'll take a final decision where the votes will be counted."[7]

The president and the vice president host a press conference each month after the first meeting of the Governing Council. The Federal Reserve adopted this practice in April 2011. The ECB releases – and the president reads verbatim – a press statement, which explains the analysis and decision of the Governing Council. A question-and-answer session with journalists follows. The interest-rate decision is announced at 1:45 p.m. in Frankfurt (12:45 p.m. in London and 7:45 a.m. in New York). The press conference starts 45 minutes later at 2:30 p.m. in Frankfurt (1:30 p.m. in London and 8:30 a.m. in New York).

The ECB refrains from publishing minutes, unlike the Bank of England, the Federal Reserve and the Swedish Riksbank. In defense of that decision, Otmar Issing wrote that the word "minutes" suggests:

> "a kind of verbatim account of what went on at the meeting. Reading the minutes is, it would appear, as informative as actually being there, and thus minutes seemingly make for full transparency. Not that any central bank claims that this is so. Minutes are carefully drafted documents that undergo what may be a difficult and protracted internal review process."[8]

He also stated his opinion that little difference exists between the introductory statement from the ECB's monthly press conference and the documents that other central banks refer to as "minutes."

Similarly, the ECB has refused to publish the voting records of its members. This is an attempt to prevent governments from applying pressure to the representatives on the Governing Council from their countries to pursue national interests as opposed to taking a decision based on data for the euro area as a whole.

The statement contains macroeconomic projections for the euro area four times a year. Estimates for GDP and inflation produced jointly by "experts from the ECB and from the euro area national central banks" are released

---

[7]Draghi, Mario *Introductory Statement to the Press Conference (with Q&A)*. Frankfurt: European Central Bank, August 2, 2012. Copyright European Central Bank, Frankfurt am Main, Germany. This information may be obtained free of charge from {www.ecb.int}.

[8]Issing, 2008.

biannually in June and in December. The ECB staff then "complement" those projections with updates in March and in September. The estimates are published in the form of ranges to reflect the degree of uncertainty associated with them.[9] The Governing Council "does not assume responsibility" for those projections.[10]

The ECB publishes a monthly bulletin one week after the monthly press conference. The first article of the publication, the editorial, is close to a verbatim copy of the statement released at the previous press conference. Market economists tend to focus on the special research articles, which appear in the section titled "Boxes" in the table of contents.

The ECB bans its members from discussing monetary policy in the week before each interest-rate decision. This period is referred to as "purdah". The word comes from Urdu and Hindi and means "curtain."[11] It is a reference to the practice of preventing interaction between men and women. The Federal Reserve follows a similar practice.

The practice was reportedly initiated in November 2001 by Wim Duisenberg, the first president of the ECB, to show that the ECB speaks with one voice. His successor, Jean-Claude Trichet, distributed at the monthly meetings a list – assembled by the ECB's press division – of officials who broke the rule.[12]

Traffic Light System

Trichet frequently used verbal signaling as a way to steer the expectations of market participants on future changes in interest rates. Otmar Issing was also an advocate of this policy. He wrote:

> "In the simplest case, certain keywords suffice de facto to signal the intended future decision to market participants. Such 'code words' are easy to identify

---

[9]"ECB Staff Macroeconomic Projections for the Euro Area." *ECB Monthly Bulletin*. Frankfurt: European Central Bank, March 2012. For complete details, see: *A Guide to Eurosystem Staff Macroeconomic Projection Exercises*. Frankfurt: European Central Bank, June 2001.

[10]"The Publication of Eurosystem Staff Economic Projections by the ECB." *ECB Annual Report 2000*. Frankfurt: European Central Bank, 2001.

[11]Ehrmann, Michael and Fratzscher, Marcel "Purdah: On the Rationale for Central Bank Silence Around Policy Meetings." Working Paper Series, No. 868. Frankfurt: European Central Bank, February 2008.

[12]Brockett, Matthew and Thesing, Gabi "Trichet's 'Black List' Fails to Deter Weber as ECB Nears Exit." Bloomberg News, November 4, 2009.

and can be quickly factored into market activity; they can reduce or eliminate uncertainty in the period before meetings of the policy-making body; and they can help to avoid short-run mistakes and hence reduce interest rate volatility."[13]

The most reliable signals from Trichet were the words "vigilance" or "strong vigilance." They indicated that interest rates were to be raised the following month. Only two exceptions to this rule were seen after these code words were originally introduced in 2005. In August 2007, the phrase "strong vigilance" appeared in the monthly press statement and interest rates were held steady the following month. That was probably due to the onset of the global financial crisis. In July 2008, the key policy rate was increased without the word "vigilance" having appeared in the statement the previous month, though the newly introduced phrase "heightened alertness" did appear.

The ECB seems to have started using a traffic light system in 2005. It used the phrase "strong vigilance" in November 2005 for the second consecutive month and the policy rates were increased by 25 basis points in December. During the last month of the year, "monitor closely" appeared in the statement. In January 2006, the phrase "monitor very closely" was included and the following month "vigilance" reappeared. The Governing Council raised interest rates in March, when the same cycle of phrases began again. It appeared to be using the phrase "monitor closely" to signal that an increase was three months away, "monitor very closely" to signal that an increase was two months away, and "vigilance" or "strong vigilance" to indicate that the move would materialize in the following month.

The traffic light theory soon fell apart. The ECB used the phrase "monitor closely" in June 2006 and then jumped to "strong vigilance" the following month without using the intermediate step of "monitor very closely." The Governing Council used the phrase "monitor very closely" in December 2006 and March 2007 when monetary tightening was three months away.

The traffic light system appears to have been used only for tightening cycles. The reduction in interest rates, beginning in late 2008, was free of "code words," though many of those decreases were in response to the snowballing of the financial crisis and the Governing Council lacked the benefit of a multi-month period to warn market participants of its next move. Mario Draghi has avoided the use of code words, though he has yet to preside over a tightening cycle. Interest rates have only been reduced on his watch.

---

[13] Issing, 2008.

Mandate

The ECB's sole mandate is to maintain price stability. That directive was spelled out in the Maastricht Treaty, though the agreement omitted a definition for the term. The Governing Council has defined price stability as "a year-on-year increase in the Harmonised Index of Consumer Prices (HICP) for the euro area of below 2%. Price stability is to be maintained over the medium term."[14] The Governing Council "clarified" in May 2003, "in the pursuit of price stability, it aims to maintain inflation rates below **_but close_** to 2% over the medium term."[15]

The goal differs from that of the Federal Reserve. The American central bank has a dual mandate of pursuing full employment and price stability. Specifically, the Federal Reserve Act charges the Board of Governors and the Federal Open Market Committee "to promote effectively the goals of maximum employment, stable prices, and moderate long-term interest rates."[16]

Otmar Issing and his co-authors defended the sole goal of price stability by claiming an inability to stabilize output and, by extension, influence employment conditions. They wrote, "The uncertainties on the effectiveness of monetary policy as a means to stabilise output fluctuations are mirrored, instead, by the unwillingness to take a specific stance in this respect."[17]

David Blanchflower, a former member of the BoE's Monetary Policy Committee and a professor of economics at Dartmouth College, has strongly disagreed with the ECB's approach. In a commentary piece for Bloomberg News in September 2010, he wrote:

> "The primary objective of the ECB remains to maintain price stability by keeping inflation just below 2 percent. That needs to be changed fast. Inflation targeting didn't prevent the Great Recession of 2009. Plus there is no convincing empirical evidence to suggest that countries targeting inflation have done any better than those that haven't.

---

[14]*Benefits of Price Stability*. European Central Bank. {http://www.ecb.europa.eu/mopo/intro/benefits/html/index.en.html}

[15]Scheller, 2004.

[16]*Federal Reserve Act, Section 2A. Monetary Policy Objectives*. Board of Governors of the Federal Reserve System. {http://www.federalreserve.gov/aboutthefed/section2a.htm}

[17]Angeloni, Ignazio, Gaspar, Vitor, Issing, Otmar and Tristani, Oreste *Monetary Policy in the Euro Area: Strategy and Decision-Making at the European Central Bank*. Cambridge: Cambridge University Press, 2001.

That is pretty telling. All this macro-economic twaddle, suggesting otherwise, is simply wrong. The laughable economic models, with their crazy simplifying assumptions, on which such claims were based, were never confronted with the data.

Trichet's major claim was that surprise inflation would 'destroy the hard-won credibility of central banks worldwide.' This, he argued, would lead to a world with 'higher volatility, higher risk premia and higher nominal and real interest rates.' And ultimately lower growth. That would result in a permanent and substantial loss of credibility once inflation and inflation expectations cease to be anchored.

The ECB president concluded that a 'credible, medium-term orientation on price stability is the best contribution that central banks can make toward sustainable, stable growth.'

There is no empirical basis for such claims; they are nothing more than unsubstantiated assertions. Just because Trichet claims so, doesn't make them so. Prove it."[18]

Paul De Grauwe has accused the ECB of being behind the times with its sole focus on price stability. He likens the mandate to the Maginot Line. During the inter-war period, the French government erected a fortification, named after the minister of war, André Maginot, along its border with Germany. It was designed for a static war like the First World War. The Germans just went around the Maginot Line and invaded France through Belgium and the Netherlands. Essentially, France fell to the Germans because the French were fighting the last war, while the nature of battle had changed.

In July 2008, De Grauwe wrote in the *Financial Times*, "There is a danger that the macroeconomic models now in use in central banks operate like a Maginot Line. They have been constructed in the past as part of the war against inflation. The central banks are prepared to fight the last war. But are they prepared to fight the new one against the financial upheavals and recession? The macroeconomic models they have today certainly do not provide them with the right tools to be successful."[19]

Paul Krugman has expressed a similar thought: "Appropriate macroeconomic policy depends on the situation. Rules designed to prevent irresponsible

---

[18]Blanchflower, David "Trichet's Inflation Ogre is Pure Fiction." Bloomberg News, September 13, 2010. Reproduced by permission of Bloomberg News.

[19]De Grauwe, Paul "Cherished Myths Fall Victim to Economic Reality." *Financial Times*, July 22, 2008. {http://www.ft.com/intl/cms/s/0/b89eb5b2-5804-11dd-b02f-000077b07658.html}. Reproduced by permission of Paul De Grauwe.

inflation and/or deficits may help when inflation is your problem; when you are instead in a depressed economy in a liquidity trap, they become a lead-weighted straitjacket," he wrote.[20]

Two-Pillar Strategy

The goal of price stability is pursued through a two-pillar strategy. The two pillars are economic analysis and monetary analysis (Figure 6.1). The former focuses on real economic activity and financial conditions to assess the short- to medium-term determinants of price developments. The latter focuses on the growth of money supply to assess longer-term risks to price stability. The second pillar serves mainly as a means of "cross-checking, from a medium to long-term perspective, the short to medium-term indications for monetary policy from the economic analysis."[21]

FIGURE 6.1 Monetary policy strategy of the ECB.

```
                The stability-oriented monetary policy strategy of the ECB
                ┌─────────────────────────────────────────────────────┐
                │         PRIMARY OBJECTIVE OF PRICE STABILITY        │
                └─────────────────────────────────────────────────────┘
                                          ↑
                              ┌───────────────────────┐
                              │   Governing Council   │
                              │ takes monetary policy decisions based on an overall assessment
                              │         of the risks to price stability
                              └───────────────────────┘
   ECONOMIC            ↑                                          ↑          MONETARY
   ANALYSIS                                                                  ANALYSIS
              ┌──────────────┐                              ┌──────────────┐
              │   Analysis   │                              │   Analysis   │
              │ of economic  │  ←──── cross-checking ────→  │ of monetary  │
              │ dynamics     │                              │   trends     │
              │ and shocks   │                              │              │
              └──────────────┘                              └──────────────┘
                    ↑                                               ↑
                ┌─────────────────────────────────────────────────────┐
                │              FULL SET OF INFORMATION                │
                └─────────────────────────────────────────────────────┘
```

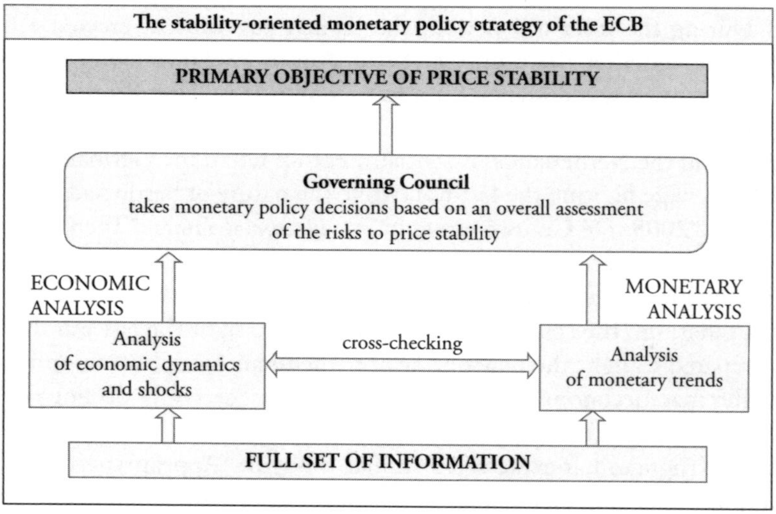

Source: ECB. Copyright European Central Bank, Frankfurt am Main, Germany. This information may be obtained free of charge from {www.ecb.int}.

---

[20]Krugman, Paul "Destructive Responsibility." *The New York Times*, November 30, 2012.
[21]*Monetary Analysis*. European Central Bank. {http://www.ecb.int/mopo/strategy/monan/html/index.en.html}

Monetary Policy Implementation

The ECB conducts open market operations to implement the monetary policy decisions taken by the Governing Council. The implementation is decentralized, with the national central banks executing the operations with counterparties – credit institutions – in their countries. That stands in contrast to the Federal Reserve, which uses a centralized process for its open market operations, with bond dealers as the primary counterparties. All loans from the ECB are made against eligible collateral.

The main policy rate for the euro area is the rate charged on the central bank's main refinancing operations (MRO), which have durations of one week. They had durations of two weeks until the start of 2004.[22] Those procedures can be conducted on a fixed or variable rate basis.[23]

The former offer loans from the central bank at a fixed rate with either full or partial allotment on a pro rata basis. The latter uses an auction for the distribution of credit. The Governing Council sets a minimum acceptable rate and then credit institutions indicate the price they are willing to pay. The ECB decides the size of the overall allotment and then allocates it to the institutions with the highest bids until it is exhausted. Offers at the lowest rate offered and accepted are allotted on a pro rata basis.

The ECB also conducts longer-term refinancing operations (LTRO). The regularly conducted operations are carried out once a month with a maturity of three months. Throughout the financial crisis, irregular operations with maturities of six, 12 and 36 months have also been conducted.

Fine-tuning operations have been used to manage interest rates. They are conducted to smooth changes caused by unexpected liquidity fluctuations.

The ECB calls the fourth type of open market operations "structural operations." They are used to adjust the long-term liquidity position of the banking system of the euro area.

The ECB offers two so-called standing facilities. They are the marginal lending facility and the deposit facility. Eligible counterparties can use the

---

[22] *Implementation Issues Related to the Changes to the Eurosystem's Operational Framework for Monetary Policy, and the Indicative Reserve Maintenance Periods Calendar for 2004.* Frankfurt: European Central Bank, August 1, 2003.

[23] *The Implementation of Monetary Policy in the Euro Area: General Documentation on Eurosystem Monetary Policy Instruments and Procedures.* Frankfurt: European Central Bank, February 2011.

former to receive overnight loans against collateral. The interest rate on that facility is normally 100 basis points above the main refinancing rate. It provides a ceiling for the overnight interest rate in the market. The deposit facility can be used by those institutions to make overnight deposits with the monetary authorities. The interest rate is normally 100 basis points below the main policy rate. It creates a floor for the overnight interest rate in the market.

These penalty rates, which form the so-called corridor, were designed to discourage the use of these facilities. For example, in theory, a bank would only use the overnight deposit facility if more profitable uses for its cash were non-existent.

In practice, it has been used when banks were more worried with the return *of* their cash than the return *on* their cash throughout the financial crisis and with holding an adequate level of cash to meet their liquidity needs. For example, by early March 2012, the level of overnight deposits had risen to a record of 827.5 billion euros (Figure 6.2). The ECB reports these data on a daily basis.

The ECB temporarily changed the width of the corridor during the crisis. The differences of 100 basis points were reduced to 50 basis points in October 2008. That decision was reversed in December 2008 and the change was implemented on January 21, 2009. The corridor was narrowed again in May 2009 to create differences of 75 basis points.

FIGURE 6.2 Balance of overnight deposit facility of the ECB.

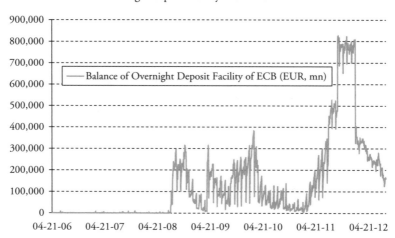

Source: Bloomberg

FIGURE 6.3 One-week Euribor.

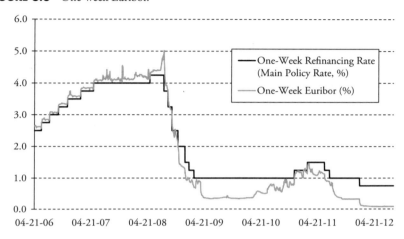

Source: Bloomberg

The corridor system allowed the ECB to ease and tighten monetary policy stealthily throughout the financial crisis without announcing these moves. The monetary authorities were able to push short-term money market rates well below the level of the official policy rate (Figure 6.3). In practice, that was similar to additional interest-rate reductions. The advantage of this procedure for the central bank was the option to tighten monetary policy when the initial signs of economic recovery occurred without having had to incur the wrath of politicians who – along with their voters – were probably still focused on the high levels of unemployment across the euro area.

The financial crisis led the ECB to change – at least temporarily – its liquidity allotment system. The central bank began to offer loans at a fixed interest rate and guaranteed the full amount requested. In addition, it extended the maturities of those loans eventually to a maximum of three years.

Intervention in the Currency Markets

The ECB technically shares responsibility with the Council of the European Union for exchange-rate matters. The responsibility for these issues is spelled out in articles 105 (2) and 109 (2) of the *Treaty on European Union* (The Maastricht Treaty) and article 3.1 of the *Protocol on the Statute of the European System of Central Banks and of the European Central Bank.*

Article 105 (2) of the *Treaty on European Union* states:

"The basic tasks to be carried out through the ESCB shall be:

- to define and implement the monetary policy of the Community,
- to conduct foreign exchange operations consistent with the provisions of Article 109,
- to hold and manage the official foreign reserves of the Member States,
- to promote the smooth operation of the payment systems."

Article 109 (2) of the *Treaty on European Union* states:

"In the absence of an exchange rate system in relation to one or more non-Community currencies as referred to in paragraph 1, the Council, acting by a qualified majority either on a recommendation from the Commission and after consulting the ECB or on a recommendation from the ECB, may formulate general orientations for exchange rate policy in relation to these currencies. These general orientations shall be without prejudice to the primary objective of the ESCB to maintain price stability."

Article 3.1 of the *Protocol on the Statute of the European System of Central Banks and of the European Central Bank* repeats – nearly word for word – Article 105 (2) of the *Treaty on European Union* and the *Treaty Establishing the European Community*.

In reality, the ECB controls intervention in the currency markets because it could always argue that these operations have an effect on price stability. One of the few instances where that argument would fail to hold is sterilized intervention in the currency markets, though experience has shown that sterilized operations are mostly ineffective.

The primacy of the ECB in these decisions has also been asserted by Otmar Issing. He wrote, "While in the USA and Japan the government (finance ministry) has responsibility for such measures, in the case of the euro the task clearly falls to the ECB. At the same time, the Eurogroup is involved in the opinion-forming process."[24]

In the U.S., the decision-making process is the reverse of that for the euro area. The U.S. Treasury is the primary decision taker, while the

---

[24]Issing, 2008.

Federal Reserve holds a secondary role. The Federal Reserve Bank of New York posts on its webpage, "Congress has assigned the U.S. Treasury primary responsibility for international financial policy. In practice, though, the Treasury's FX decisions typically are made in consultation with the Federal Reserve System."[25]

The situation in Japan is similar to that of the U.S. On its website, the Bank of Japan states, "Foreign exchange intervention is, generally speaking, an operation carried out by monetary authorities, such as central banks or finance ministries, buying or selling currencies with the objective of influencing the foreign exchange rate in one way or another. In the case of Japan, the Ministry of Finance is responsible for such operations and the objective is to stabilize the value of the yen. The Bank carries out the actual operations based on instructions from the Finance Minister and acts as the agent."[26]

Taylor Rule

The Taylor Rule can be used as a guide for the required changes to monetary policy. It is named after John Taylor, an economics professor at Stanford University and the former Undersecretary of the Treasury for International Affairs during the first term of President George W. Bush.

The rule suggests that the main policy rate of a central bank should be based on the extent to which inflation may be deviating from a central bank's definition of price stability and employment from the maximum sustainable level.[27] Taylor created his monetary policy rule for a guide to appropriate conditions for the Federal Reserve and the U.S. economy.

The ECB has signaled that the Taylor Rule is used by the Governing Council as a guide to monetary policy, though its suggestions are not pursued in a systematic fashion. Otmar Issing wrote, "The ECB has regularly run Taylor rule estimations with a variety of coefficients, as well as using indicators that also take account of changes in exchange rates or financing conditions. Precisely under conditions of extreme uncertainty, I considered it

---

[25] *U.S. Foreign Exchange Intervention*. Federal Reserve Bank of New York. {http://www.newyorkfed.org/aboutthefed/fedpoint/fed44.html}

[26] *Outline of International Finance*. Bank of Japan. {http://www.boj.or.jp/en/intl_finance/outline/index.htm/}

[27] *The Federal Reserve System: Purposes and Functions*. Board of Governors of the Federal Reserve System, 2011.

very important to monitor such estimations in the background as a kind of benchmark against which to measure our policy."[28]

In his first paper on the Taylor Rule, *Discretion Versus Policy Rules in Practice*, published in 1993, John Taylor proposed the following rule:

$$r = p + .5y + .5(p - 2) + 2$$

where
r = the federal funds rate
p = the rate of inflation over the previous four quarters
y = the percentage deviation of real GDP from a target.

That is,

$$y = 100(Y - Y^*)/Y^*$$

where
Y = real GDP
Y^* = trend real GDP (equals 2.2% per year from 1984.1 through 1992.3).

Countless adjustments have been proposed to the original Taylor Rule since the publication of the first paper.

Fernanda Nechio, an economist at the Federal Reserve Bank of San Francisco, has proposed a version for the euro area.[29] It is:

Target rate = 1 + 1.5 × Inflation − 1 × Unemployment gap

Nechio uses core inflation as a measure for inflation in her study because it enables comparisons with the U.S. This measure of inflation also avoids the problem of a signal to raise interest rates as a result of an oil-price shock.

In his 1993 paper, Taylor seemed to think along similar lines. He examined a case study of the implementation of his rule during the oil-price shock

---

[28]Issing, 2008.
[29]Nechio, Fernanda "Monetary Policy When One Size Does Not Fit All." *Federal Reserve Bank of San Francisco Economic Letter*. Federal Reserve Bank of San Francisco, June 13, 2011.

of 1990 that followed the Iraqi invasion of Kuwait. He concluded, "interest rates should follow the path that would have occurred without the oil price shock."

Nechio uses the unemployment gap as a measure of slack in the economy instead of the deviation of real GDP from a target. The unemployment gap is the difference between the present rate of unemployment and the natural rate of unemployment. The latter is the level that causes inflation to neither accelerate nor decelerate and is often referred to as the non-accelerating inflation rate of unemployment or NAIRU.

An advantage of this measure of economic slack is the frequency of the data. It allows interest rates to be more responsive in the short term to economic developments than the output gap used by Taylor. That is because the employment data are published on a monthly basis and the GDP numbers are released on a quarterly basis. As Taylor points out in his original study, a quarter may be too long to hold the main policy rate steady when the economy falls into recession. It should be lowered rapidly.

The natural rates of unemployment are estimated by the OECD and published twice a year in the *OECD Economic Outlook*. The employment gap plays a role in the monetary policy decisions of the ECB, even though its mandate focuses only on price stability. That's because the output gap – as estimated by NAIRU – influences inflationary pressures.

The Taylor Rule has limitations. They relate mostly to the problems of estimating non-observable variables and the coefficients.

The natural rate of unemployment must be estimated because it is a non-observable variable. For example, the OECD's estimate of the structural unemployment rate for Spain for 2009 was 10.7% in the June 2009 *OECD Economic Outlook* and 14.8% in the May 2012 *OECD Economic Outlook* (Table 6.1).

The coefficients can change over time. The original ones proposed by John Taylor were used because they made the rule fit the actual path of the federal funds rate from 1987 to 1992. He suggested that a period of good economic performance should be identified. A policy rule – including the estimation of the coefficients – should be determined that described the interest-rate-setting behavior of the central bank during that period.[30] That rule could then be used in the future – even when circumstances change – to guide future decisions. He outlined that this may be particularly important if the members of the interest-rate-setting committee change and if their performance should be replicated in the future.

---

[30]Taylor, John B. *Discretion Versus Policy Rules in Practice*. Carnegie–Rochester Conference Series on Public Policy 39, 1993, pp. 195–214.

TABLE 6.1 OECD Estimates of Structural Unemployment for 2009

	Jun-09	May-12
Austria	5.6%	4.4%
Belgium	8.1%	8.0%
Finland	7.5%	8.2%
France	8.3%	8.8%
Germany	8.2%	7.7%
Greece	9.2%	10.5%
Ireland	6.4%	8.8%
Italy	7.1%	7.6%
Netherlands	3.6%	3.7%
Portugal	7.1%	9.1%
Spain	10.7%	14.8%
Euro Area	8.0%	8.8%

Source: OECD

The Taylor Rule is likely to be less useful during a financial crisis or a debt crisis than during a "normal" period. The IMF has warned, "Taylor rules are not likely to be extremely useful in dramatic circumstances, when for example, asset bubbles burst, exchange rate volatility rises, or capital flows get reversed."[31] Taylor originally designed the rule to describe the reaction function of the Federal Reserve during a period when the U.S. economy was free of extreme shocks.

Alan Greenspan shared that opinion. In January 2004, he said, "the prescriptions of formal rules can, in fact, serve as helpful adjuncts to policy, as many of the proponents of these rules have suggested. But at crucial points, like those in our recent policy history – the stock market crash of 1987, the crises of 1997–98, and the events that followed September 2001 – simple rules will be inadequate as either descriptions or prescriptions for policy."[32]

Taylor outlined this issue in his original paper. He used the example of the 1987 crash of the U.S. stock market as an instance of when the Federal Reserve needed more than a simple policy rule to steer the economy and decide on liquidity injections.

---

[31]Carare, Alina and Tchaidze, Robert *The Use and Abuse of Taylor Rules: How Precisely Can We Estimate Them?* IMF Working Paper 05/148. International Monetary Fund, July 2005.
[32]Greenspan, Alan *Risk and Uncertainty in Monetary Policy*. Remarks at the meetings of the American Economic Association, San Diego, California, January 3, 2004.

The Taylor Rule can still be used during such "crucial points" as an indication as to whether monetary policy is accommodative or restrictive. For example, while the utility of the Taylor Rule may have been reduced during the European debt crisis, because the central bank should have taken out insurance against the extraordinary downside risks, the rule can be used to determine if that insurance has been taken out by policy makers.

The first meeting of Mario Draghi provides a good example. According to a Taylor Rule, using the structural unemployment estimates of the OECD from 2012, the main policy rate should have been 2% and the new president reduced the main policy rate to 1.25%.

CHAPTER 7

Other Institutions

The institutions of the EU play important roles in the region's economies and financial markets. Three primary institutions are involved in EU legislation: the Council of the European Union (not to be confused with the European Council), the European Parliament and the EC.

Council of the European Union

The Council of the European Union (formerly known as the Council of Ministers) is one of the two legislative bodies of the bicameral legislature of the EU. It represents the executive branches of the member states and is comprised of one representative from each member state at the ministerial level with responsibility for a given area. For purposes of comparison, the most similar body in the U.S. is the Senate. The frequency of its meetings varies depending on the issue. Economics and finance ministers as well as foreign ministers meet about once a month. The council's main tasks are:[1]

1. Passage of EU laws (it shares with the European Parliament the final say on new EU laws proposed by the European Commission).
2. Coordination of economic policies.
3. Signature of agreements between the EU and other countries.
4. Approval of the annual EU budget.
5. Development of the defense and foreign policies of the EU.
6. Coordination of cooperation between the courts and police forces of member countries.

---

[1] *Council of the European Union*. Official website of the European Union. {http://europa.eu/about-eu/institutions-bodies/council-eu/index_en.htm}

The chair of the council rotates every six months between the 27 member states of the EU. The country that holds the position chairs all of its meetings, proposes guidelines and engineers compromises required for decisions.

European Parliament

The European Parliament is the second of the two legislative bodies of the bicameral legislature. It has 751 directly elected members with five-year terms. The number of seats per country is based on its population. For purposes of comparison, the most similar body in the U.S. is the House of Representatives.

European Commission

The EC is the executive body of the EU. The current president is José Manuel Barroso. The EC is made up of 27 commissioners, one from each EU country. For purposes of comparison with the American system, these positions are similar to those of the U.S. president and his cabinet. The significant differences are that the EC president, like all of the commissioners, is appointed – not elected like the U.S. president – and he has much less power than the American head of state.

The EC claims to represent the interests of Europe as a whole as opposed to the interests of individual countries.[2] The headquarters are in Brussels. The main roles of the EC are:[3]

1. Set objectives and priorities for action.
2. Propose legislation to the European Parliament and Council.
3. Manage and implement EU policies and the budget.
4. Enforce European law.
5. Represent the EU outside of Europe.

The EC has played an important role throughout the financial crisis. It is one of the three members of the so-called Troika, which has negotiated bailout packages for euro-area nations. The other two members are the ECB and the IMF.

---

[2] *About the European Commission.* European Commission. {http://ec.europa.eu/about/index_en.htm}
[3] *Ibid.*

The branch of the EC responsible for economic policy is called the Directorate General for Economic and Financial Affairs (DG ECFIN). It is headed by the Commissioner for Economic and Monetary Affairs, who is presently Olli Rehn. It defines its mission as improving "the economic welfare of the citizens in the European Union and beyond, notably by developing and promoting policies that ensure sustainable economic growth, a high level of employment, stable public finances and financial stability."[4] On its website, the Directorate notes, "Our current priority is to ensure the European economy emerges quickly and strongly from the economic and financial crisis."[5]

The DG ECFIN releases forecasts for key economic variables twice a year – in the spring and the autumn. The forecasts cover the current year and the following year. In between the reports of the spring and autumn, interim forecasts are published for inflation and real GDP for the seven largest member states and for the current year only. For many purposes, the semi-annual forecasts of the IMF may be more useful than the EC forecasts because those of the former include the current year plus five years.

Ecofin

The Economic and Financial Affairs Council also plays an important role in the European economy. It is more commonly known as "Ecofin". It is comprised of the finance ministers of the EU and discusses the region's economic policies. It meets once a month. When the council discusses issues related to the monetary union, the finance ministers from the countries that have not adopted the single currency refrain from voting.

Eurogroup

The Eurogroup is a sub-group of the Ecofin. The former normally meets the day before the Ecofin meeting and focuses on issues related to the monetary union. The group was formalized in the Lisbon Treaty.

---

[4] *Mission Statement*. Directorate General for Economic and Financial Affairs. {http://ec.europa.eu/dgs/economy_finance/organisation/mission_en.pdf}

[5] *Who We Are and What We Do*. Directorate General for Economic and Financial Affairs. {http://ec.europa.eu/dgs/economy_finance/index_en.htm}

The Eurogroup is headed by a president with a term of two and a half years. It is currently Jeroen Dijsselbloem, the finance minister of the Netherlands. The group's meetings are attended by the finance ministers of the countries that have adopted the euro, the commissioner for economic and monetary affairs, currently Olli Rehn, the president of the ECB, presently Mario Draghi, and the Chairman of the Economic and Financial Committee's Eurogroup Working Group, currently Thomas Wieser.

European Council

The European Council became an official institution of the EU with the signing of the Lisbon Treaty. It sets the general political agenda of the EU, though it has no legislative powers. It is headed by its president, currently Herman Van Rompuy, who has a term, which is renewable once, of two and a half years. The council is made up of the heads of governments of the member countries of the EU and the president of the EC. The group meets at least twice every six months.[6]

---

[6] *The European Council – An Official Institution of the EU*. European Council. {http://www.european-council.europa.eu/the-institution?lang=en}

CHAPTER 8

Euro Crisis

The crisis that came to the fore at the end of 2009 in the euro area may be best described as a balance-of-payments crisis created by the region's fixed-exchange-rate regime. The balance of payments is the sum of the current account and the capital and financial account. The current account is the sum of the trade balance and income from foreign investments. The capital and financial account primarily consists of direct and portfolio investment from abroad. This balance-of-payments explanation has been advanced by Paul Krugman of Princeton University, Thomas Mayer of Deutsche Bank and Hans-Werner Sinn of the Ifo Institute, though it is not held universally by economists.

A crisis ensues when the balance of payments is in deficit continuously over a long period of time in the absence of a free-floating exchange rate. If a country runs a current account shortfall, it must be financed by inflows of foreign capital. When capital inflows dry up, a current account deficit must be financed by official sources of capital if the country has a fixed exchange rate.

A country with a free-floating currency, such as the U.S., will, in theory, never experience a balance-of-payments crisis. In this case, the sum of its current and capital and financial accounts should always equal zero. If foreign capital inflows fail to cover the financing gap created by a current account deficit, the currency will weaken until those components completely offset each other.

Origins

The global financial crisis that followed the bankruptcy of Lehman Brothers revealed the problems that had been brewing in the euro area over the previous decade. As Warren Buffett has reportedly quipped, "It's only when the tide goes out that you learn who's been swimming naked."

The adoption of a single monetary policy in 1999 left interest rates too low for some countries of the euro area for most of its first decade. For example, a Taylor Rule, based on coefficients estimated by the Federal Reserve Bank of San Francisco, shows that, in retrospect, the main policy rate was too low for Greece, Ireland, Portugal and Spain throughout most of the 2000s. In April 2006, it should have been about 5.75%, 7.5%, 4.5% and 9% for those countries, respectively (Figure 8.1). The ECB had set the one-week refinancing rate at 2.5%.

The common currency prevented those countries from setting their main policy rates in line with their domestic monetary needs. As Milton Friedman said, "Flexible exchange rates . . . are a means of permitting each country to seek monetary stability according to its own lights, without either imposing its mistakes on its neighbors or having their mistakes imposed on it."[1]

Low interest rates encouraged excessive borrowing from abroad to support domestic consumption and investment. From an accounting point of view, the current account balance equals national savings minus investment. If national savings are too low as a result of high consumption and domestic

FIGURE 8.1 Taylor Rule suggests loose monetary policy in peripheral countries.

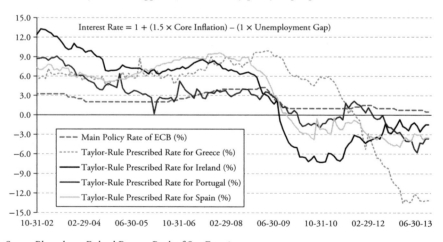

Source: Bloomberg; Federal Reserve Bank of San Francisco

---

[1] Friedman, Milton "The Case for Flexible Exchange Rates" in *Essays in Positive Economics*. Chicago: The University of Chicago Press, 1953.

investment is too high, foreign capital will be required for financing. By the end of 2008, the current account deficits of Greece, Ireland, Portugal and Spain had risen to 14.9% of GDP, 5.7% of GDP, 12.6% of GDP and 9.6% of GDP, respectively (Figure 8.2).

Those credit-fueled booms stoked domestic inflation. The consumer price indices of Greece, Ireland, Portugal and Spain had risen by 39.2%, 40.1%, 33.2% and 37.7%, respectively, from January 1999 to June 2008 (Figure 8.3). The equivalent figure for Germany was 18.9%.

Those price increases led to severe misalignments of real exchange rates within the euro area, even though the nominal exchange rates were fixed. For example, the real effective exchange rate, using CPI as a deflator, of Ireland had appreciated by 30.4% by April 2008 from the first quarter of 1999, according to the data series calculated by the Bank for International Settlements (Figure 8.4). The equivalent figures for Greece, Portugal and Spain were 8.6%, 8% and 15.2%, respectively. The overvalued exchange rates contributed to export growth in the peripheral countries falling short of import growth, exerting additional downward pressure on the current account balances.

The bankruptcy of Lehman Brothers brought an end to the complacency of investors. The collapse of economic growth that ensued caused government budget deficits to balloon. Bondholders became concerned about the ability of some highly indebted countries to service their obligations, which were rapidly rising, and stopped buying sovereign bonds of countries of the euro area with unsound public finances and weak growth prospects.

FIGURE 8.2 Current account deficits balloon.

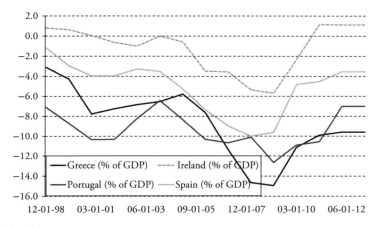

Source: Bloomberg

FIGURE 8.3 Consumer price levels rise in peripheral countries.

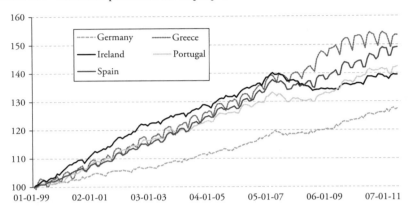

Source: Bloomberg
N.B. Rebased to 100 in January 1999

FIGURE 8.4 Divergences of real exchange rates in euro area.

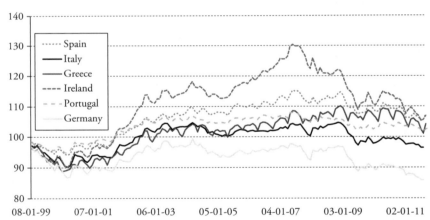

Source: BIS, Bloomberg
N.B. Rebased to 100 at Q1 1999

The first country struck by the crisis was Greece, followed by Ireland, Portugal, Spain and Italy. They began to face large balance-of-payments deficits created by a combination of current account deficits and capital outflows.

Unemployment rates soared in the periphery as those countries began to adjust to the end of the credit boom. By July 2012, the unemployment rates of Greece, Ireland, Portugal and Spain had reached their highest levels since the birth of the monetary union of 25%, 14.8%, 16.3% and 26%,

FIGURE 8.5 Unemployment rates of euro area diverge.

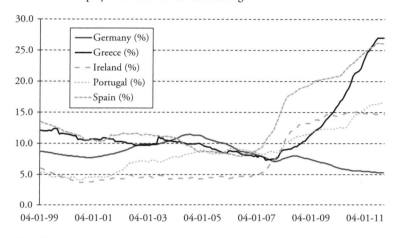

Source: Bloomberg

respectively (Figure 8.5). The figure for Germany had fallen to 5.5%, the lowest level since the country's reunification.

Market participants called into question the sustainability of the euro area as the crisis spread. The single monetary policy appeared ill fitted for a group of nations facing exogenous shocks of varying intensities and at different stages of the business cycle. The debate over the optimality of the euro area as a single currency zone resurfaced.

Optimal Currency Area Theory

Robert Mundell identified factor – capital and labor – mobility as the primary requirement for an optimal currency area. He was awarded the Nobel Prize in Economics in 1999 for "his analysis of monetary and fiscal policy under different exchange rate regimes and his analysis of optimum currency areas."[2]

In a seminal paper, in 1961, Mundell wrote:

> "If the world can be divided into regions within each of which there is factor mobility and between which there is factor immobility, then each of

---

[2] *Press release.* The Royal Swedish Academy of Sciences, October 13, 1999. {http://www.nobelprize.org/nobel_prizes/economics/laureates/1999/press.html}

these regions should have a separate currency which fluctuates relative to all other currencies . . . If labor and capital are insufficiently mobile within a country then flexibility of the external price of the national currency cannot be expected to perform the stabilization function attributed to it, and one could expect varying rates of unemployment or inflation in the different regions. Similarly, if factors are mobile across national boundaries then a flexible exchange system becomes unnecessary."[3]

The euro area fails to meet the requirement for factor mobility completely. Many workers within the monetary union face constraints in seeking employment in other countries from cultural and linguistic barriers, even though they face no legal impediments.

Research conducted by the EU has highlighted this problem. Lewis Dijkstra and Zuzana Gakova, economists at the EC, found, "a very low rate of cross-border labour mobility accounting for only 0.14 percent of the EU's working age population" in 2006. The authors compared that figure with data for the U.S., where "the share of the working age population who moved to another state amounted to 2 percent."[4]

Paul Krugman and Thomas Mayer credit Peter Kenen with having identified the second requirement for an optimal currency area.[5] In 1969, in a paper titled *The Theory of Optimum Currency Areas: An Eclectic View*, Kenen pointed out that fiscal transfers can cushion the economic hardship that labor mobility – or lack thereof – fails to alleviate. He concluded, "fixed-rate countries must be armed with a wide array of budgetary policies to deal with the stubborn 'pockets of unemployment' that are certain to arise from export fluctuations combined with an imperfect mobility of labor."[6]

---

[3] Mundell, Robert A. "A Theory of Optimum Currency Areas." *The American Economic Review*. Volume 51, No. 4, September 1961. Reproduced by permission of the American Economic Association.

[4] Dijkstra, Lewis and Gakova, Zuzana *Labour Mobility Between the Regions of the EU-27 and a Comparison With the USA*. European Union Directorate-General for Regional Policy, 02/2008.

[5] Krugman, Paul "Revenge of Optimum Currency Area." *The New York Times*, June 24, 2012 and Mayer, Thomas *Europe's Unfinished Currency: The Political Economics of the Euro*. London: Anthem Press, 2012.

[6] Kenen, Peter B. "The Theory of Optimum Currency Areas: An Eclectic View" in *Monetary Problems of the International Economy*. Edited by Robert A. Mundell and Alexander K. Swoboda. Chicago: The University of Chicago Press, 1969.

The euro area has also failed to meet this second requirement of the optimal currency area. "In 2008, transfers among EMU member states amounted to only 0.1 percent of GDP, compared to interregional transfers equivalent of 2.3 percent of GDP in the U.S.," Thomas Mayer pointed out in his book, *Europe's Unfinished Currency*, citing data from a McKinsey Study.[7]

The differences in economic performance that characterized the euro area after the start of its crisis would likely have been less important if the residents of the various euro-area nations had been ready to complete a "transfer union" to mitigate differences in national income, as suggested by Kenen. The political will required for those policies was absent in Europe.

As Jim O'Neill, former chairman of Goldman Sachs Asset Management, said, "If I relate it to virtually all the crises I've gone through in my now nearly 31 years, most of them usually involved big balance-of-payments problems and if you look at the euro area, there isn't a balance-of-payments problem [for the euro area as a whole] so on one level it's the most unnecessary crisis I've ever seen . . . if they're going to behave as genuine united states of Europe, the crisis is finished."[8]

Holger Schmieding disagrees with those skeptical about the sustainability of the euro area. He has argued, "In real life, no country or region can fully conform to the textbook ideal of an 'optimum currency area.' The relevant question then is whether the Eurozone offers its members adequate opportunities to adjust within the strictures of monetary union. The German example shows that it does. After 2003, Germany turned itself from the 'sick man of Europe' into the most dynamic of the major European economies. It did so without the ability to set its own interest rates or steer its own exchange rate. This German experience is shaping the German and ECB response to the euro crisis."[9]

Fiscal Consolidation

The ECB, under President Jean-Claude Trichet, initially asserted that fiscal consolidation would increase confidence and boost growth. Wolfgang Münchau, a commentator for the *Financial Times*, retorted that he could

---

[7]Mayer, 2012.
[8]O'Neill, Jim Interview by Thomas Keene at FX12: The Bloomberg Summit, October 16, 2012. Reproduced by permission of Jim O'Neill.
[9]Schmieding, Holger *Tough Love: The True Nature of the Euro Crisis*. Berenberg Bank, August 20, 2012. Reproduced by permission of Berenberg Bank.

not "see how somebody with a solid training in macroeconomics, and with minimal sense of honesty and decency, could come up with the fairy tale of an expansionary fiscal contraction."[10] Paul Krugman has frequently attacked the notion of what he refers to as the "confidence fairy" as well.

The fiscal consolidation programs implemented by the peripheral countries of the euro area ended up having devastating effects on output and the IMF eventually concluded that fiscal multipliers were larger than they had previously thought. The fund defines the fiscal multiplier as "the ratio of change in output to an exogenous change in the fiscal deficit."[11] In other words, it is the effect on the level of GDP induced by a change in the fiscal deficit caused by a budget cut or an increase in taxes.

The staff economists had originally used figures of about 0.5. They later found the fiscal multipliers were probably between 0.9 and 1.7. That means a reduction in government spending of $1 reduces GDP by about $0.9 to $1.7 in "an environment of substantial economic slack, monetary policy constrained by the zero lower bound, and synchronized fiscal adjustments across numerous economies."[12]

Quantitative and Qualitative Easing

The ECB injected tremendous sums of liquidity into the economy in an effort to quell the crisis. The largest flows came from the two three-year longer-term refinancing operations in December 2011 and February 2012. The Governing Council also decided to purchase government bonds in the secondary markets.

The three-year longer-term refinancing operations were a mix of qualitative and quantitative easing. Willem Buiter has proposed the following definitions of those two terms, though no universally-agreed-upon definitions exist.[13]

---

[10]Münchau, Wolfgang "Why Europe's Officials Lose Sight of the Big Picture." *Financial Times*, October 17, 2011.

[11]Schindler, Martin, Spilimbergo, Antonio and Symansky, Steve *Fiscal Multipliers*. IMF Staff Position Note, International Monetary Fund, May 20, 2009.

[12]"Are We Underestimating Short-Term Fiscal Multipliers?" *World Economic Outlook: Coping with High Debt and Sluggish Growth*. International Monetary Fund, October 2012.

[13]Buiter, Willem "Quantitative Easing and Qualitative Easing: A Terminological and Taxonomic Proposal." *Financial Times*, December 9, 2008. {http://blogs.ft.com/maverecon/2008/12/quantitative-easing-and-qualitative-easing-a-terminological-and-taxonomic-proposal/#axzz2MalsPVfo}. Reproduced by permission of Willem Buiter.

Qualitative easing

A shift in the composition of the assets of the central bank towards less liquid and riskier assets, holding constant the size of the balance sheet (and the official policy rate and the rest of the list of usual suspects). The less liquid and more risky assets can be private securities as well as sovereign or sovereign-guaranteed instruments. All forms of risk, including credit risk (default risk) are included.[14]

Quantitative easing

An increase in the size of the balance sheet of the central bank through an increase in its monetary liabilities (base money), holding constant the composition of its assets. Asset composition can be defined as the proportional shares of the different financial instruments held by the central bank in the total value of its assets. An almost equivalent definition would be that quantitative easing is an increase in the size of the balance sheet of the central bank through an increase in its monetary liabilities that holds constant the (average) liquidity and riskiness of its asset portfolio.

The ECB increased the size of the monetary base of the euro area by 577.8 billion euros from the end of the third quarter of 2011 to the end of the second quarter of 2012, a period that included the two three-year longer-term refinancing operations. By June 2012, the ratio of the monetary base to GDP for the euro area was 18.6% (Figure 8.6). The equivalent figure for the U.S. was 16.8%. It also shifted the composition of the assets on its balance sheet by accepting a wide variety of collateral in exchange for those loans.

The sharp increase in the size of the monetary base had a limited effect on inflation because the money multiplier had collapsed in the euro area as it had in the U.S. The money multiplier is the ratio of the money supply to the monetary base. For example, the ratio of M3 to the monetary base for the euro area declined to 5.5 by the end of the second quarter of 2012 from 10.2 at the end of the third quarter of 2008 (Figure 8.7).

The major difference between the ECB's "Longer-Term Refinancing Operations" and the Federal Reserve's "Long-Term Asset Purchases" was the immediate objective – not the increases in the respective monetary bases. The former tried to secure funding for a liquidity-strapped banking sector – and, one

---

[14]In an e-mail on March 2, 2013 to David Powell, Willem Buiter noted that qualitative easing, as he defined it, is now generally referred to as credit easing by the Federal Reserve and as enhanced credit easing by the ECB.

FIGURE 8.6 Euro-area monetary base soars.

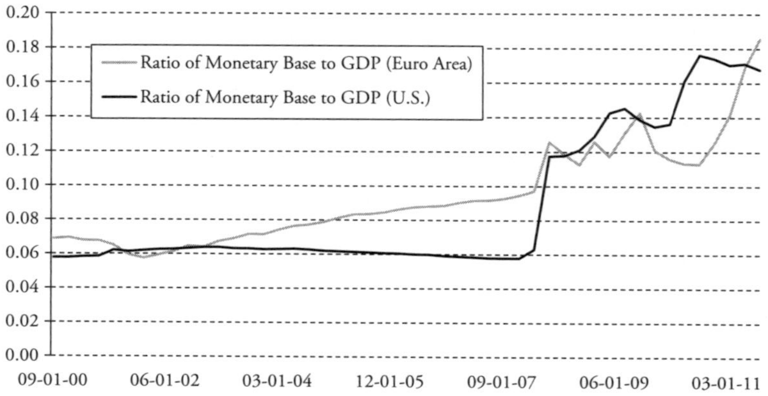

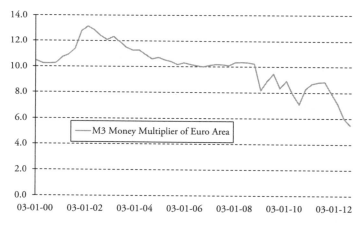

Source: Bloomberg

FIGURE 8.7 M3 money multiplier falls.

Source: Bloomberg

could argue, sovereigns – and the latter aimed to ease the stance of its monetary policy by lowering the level of long-term interest rates in the U.S.

The major operational difference between the two programs was that the ECB's refinancing operations had pre-determined reversal dates and the Federal Reserve had refrained from indicating when it will sell its assets or when it will stop reinvesting the proceeds of maturing bonds. In theory, if the ECB decides not to roll over its loans, the three-year LTROs will be unwound automatically three years after their start dates. In other words, the Federal Reserve has conducted outright purchases of privately-held assets and the ECB has made collateralized loans, which are commonly referred to in finance as repo – or repurchase – operations.

Government Bond Purchases

The ECB also bought bonds of the peripheral countries in the secondary markets through its Securities Markets Programme, which was terminated when the Outright Monetary Transactions program was announced in September 2012. The total of securities held under that effort was 219.5 billion euros at its height. The sterilization of those purchases was mostly cosmetic because the balance of the program was small relative to the size of the central bank's liquidity operations.

The program proved controversial because the ECB is prohibited by its founding treaty from financing governments of the euro area. Article 104 of the Maastricht Treaty states, "Overdraft facilities or any other type of credit facility with the ECB or with the central banks of the Member States (hereinafter referred to as 'national central banks') in favour of Community institutions or bodies, central governments, regional, local or public authorities, other bodies governed by public law, or public undertakings of Member States shall be prohibited, as shall the purchase directly from them by the ECB or national central banks of debt instruments."[15] Axel Weber, president of the Bundesbank, and Jürgen Stark resigned in protest.

The proposal in the summer of 2012 to renew sovereign bond purchases by the central bank proved to be equally controversial at the Bundesbank. Mario Draghi appeared to suggest that the representative of the German central bank would just be outvoted. As already stated, at the press conference in August, he said, "It's clear and it's known that Mr Weidmann and the Bundesbank – although we are here in a personal capacity and we should never forget that – have their reservations about programmes that envisage buying bonds, so the idea is now we have given guidance, the Monetary Policy Committee, the Risk Management Committee and the Market Operations Committee will work on this guidance and then we'll take a final decision where the votes will be counted."

---

[15] *Treaty on European Union.* {http://eur-lex.europa.eu/en/treaties/dat/11992M/htm/11992M.html}

Jens Weidmann increased his resistance to the program. He discussed his resignation with the board of the Bundesbank in the run up to the September meeting of the ECB's Governing Council and decided to stay to fight against the bond-purchasing program, according to *Bild*, a German newspaper.[16] As Wim Duisenberg reportedly said, "The Bundesbank is like cream – the more you whip it the harder it gets."[17]

The Bundesbank appeared to have been side-lined by the German government after Mario Draghi announced the start of the Outright Monetary Transactions program. In the aftermath of the announcement, Angela Merkel said that Germany was "in line" with the ECB's approach to defending the euro.[18] Jim O'Neill described the actions of the German chancellor as having reduced the Bundesbank to a "protest group."[19] Jürgen Stark, after having resigned from the ECB, began to refer to the OMTs as "Out-of-Mandate Transactions."[20]

The German government had previously trumped the will of the country's central bank to meet its political objectives. The most prominent example related to the exchange rate between the currencies of East and West Germany at the time of reunification. The Bundesbank was in favor of an exchange rate of two to one for the East German mark to the Deutsche mark.

The German government prevailed with an exchange rate of one to one for wages, salaries, rents, leases, pensions and savings accounts up to 4000 East German marks for savers between 15 and 59 years old with a limit of 6000 East German marks for those who were older and 2000 East German marks for those who were younger. An exchange rate of two to one applied to all other financial assets of GDR residents. Assets held by people outside East Germany were converted at an exchange rate of three to one.[21]

The combination of an overvalued exchange rate and subsequent wage increases pushed many companies into bankruptcy and crippled the East

---

[16] Webb, Alex "Bundesbank's Weidmann Has Considered Resignation, Bild Reports." Bloomberg News, August 31, 2012.

[17] Brost, Marc and Von Heusinger, Robert "Interview with Jean-Claude Trichet, President of the European Central Bank and Die Zeit." Frankfurt: European Central Bank, July 23, 2007.

[18] Czuczka, Tony and Donahue, Patrick "Merkel Says Germany Backs Draghi's Conditions for ECB Aid." Bloomberg News, August 16, 2012.

[19] O'Neill, Jim Interview by Thomas Keene at FX12: The Bloomberg Summit, October 16, 2012.

[20] Black, Jeff "Draghi's Go-to ECB Seen Risking Credibility Through Overload." Bloomberg News, December 7, 2012.

[21] For full details, see: Bofinger, Peter "The German Monetary Unification (Gmu): Converting Marks to D-Marks." *Federal Reserve Bank of St. Louis Review*, July/August 1990, Volume 72.

German economy.[22] Former Bundesbank President Karl Otto Pohl remarked, "We introduced the DM with practically no preparation or possibility of adjustment, and, I would add, at the wrong exchange rate . . . So the result is a disaster, as you can see. I am not surprised, I predicted it."[23]

With the opposition of the Bundesbank overcome, the ECB's Governing Council stated the objectives of the program to buy government bonds were related to monetary policy. They claimed, "The objective of this programme is to address the malfunctioning of securities markets and restore an appropriate monetary policy transmission mechanism."[24] Willem Buiter retorted, "I'm sure that's part of the reason, reason number 75 out of 76. But the real reason is to keep the sovereigns funded."[25]

These liquidity operations failed to stem the panic in the euro area, though the promise from the ECB to buy unlimited quantities of government bonds calmed financial markets in the summer of 2012. The liquidity operations – along with the European Financial Stability Mechanism and the European Stability Mechanism – were largely designed to solve liquidity crises not solvency crises. Several euro-area countries may be facing the latter.

Measures of National Solvency

No precise definition exists for solvency when the word is applied to a country. A private corporation is considered insolvent when its liabilities are greater than its assets. The largest asset of any sovereign nation – the present value of future tax receipts – is difficult to value because the valuation depends on the unknown future levels of several variables, with the most important probably being economic growth. That makes a precise classification of a nation as solvent or insolvent difficult.

The IMF tends to base the sustainability of a nation's debt on the debt-to-GDP ratio over a forecast horizon. If it fails to decline at some future point, the nation's fiscal policy may be unsustainable and eventually its debt may be

---

[22]For a full account of the economic problems created by high wages in the former East Germany after reunification, see: Sinn, Hans-Werner *Can Germany Be Saved?: The Malaise of the World's First Welfare State*. Cambridge, Mass.: The MIT Press, 2007.
[23]Jeffries, Ian *Socialist Economies and the Transition to the Market*. London: Routledge, 1993.
[24]*Press Release: ECB Decides on Measures to Address Severe Tensions in Financial Markets*. Frankfurt: European Central Bank, May 10, 2010.
[25]Buiter, Willem Speech at The ECB and Its Watchers XI conference. Center for Financial Studies, Frankfurt am Main, June 15, 2012.

as well. The organization tends to avoid using the words "solvent" and "insolvent" when talking about a country. Economists from the IMF say:

> "The fiscal policy stance can be regarded as unsustainable if, in the absence of adjustment, sooner or later the government would not be able to service its debt. If no realistic fiscal adjustment can prevent this situation from arising, not only fiscal policy, but also public debt would be unsustainable."[26]

A proxy for national solvency can be derived from the research of Carmen Reinhart and Kenneth Rogoff. It is a debt-to-GDP ratio of 90%. A country with a level of indebtedness above that figure may be on the road to insolvency.

The preferred remedy of the two economists is debt restructuring. They have advocated writing down bank and sovereign debt to "unlock growth" when a nation becomes overly indebted.[27] In the case of the euro-area crisis, they have said, "In our view, the only way to break this feedback loop [*between debt and growth*] is to have dramatic write-downs of debt."[28]

In a seminal paper, *Growth in a Time of Debt*, the two economists concluded, "The relationship between government debt and real GDP growth is weak for debt/GDP ratios below a threshold of 90 percent of GDP. Above 90 percent, median growth rates fall by 1 percent . . . the threshold for public debt is similar in advanced and emerging economies."[29]

---

[26]Fiscal Affairs Department and the Strategy, Policy, and Review Department. *Modernizing the Framework for Fiscal Policy and Public Debt Sustainability Analysis*. International Monetary Fund, August 5, 2011. Reproduced by permission of the International Monetary Fund.

[27]Reinhart, Carmen M. and Rogoff, Kenneth S. "Debt, Growth and the Austerity Debate." *The New York Times*, April 25, 2013.

[28]Reinhart, Carmen M. and Rogoff, Kenneth S. "Reinhart and Rogoff: Responding to Our Critics." *The New York Times*, April 25, 2013. Italicized words inserted by David Powell.

[29]Reinhart, Carmen M. and Rogoff, Kenneth S. "Growth in a Time of Debt" *American Economic Review Papers and Proceedings*, January 7, 2010. The results of this paper were criticized in April 2013 by a group of researchers from the University of Massachusetts Amherst. Reinhart and Rogoff largely stood by their findings, though they admitted that some mistakes had been made. In addition, they cited work from the IMF with similar conclusions. They pointed out that, in the *World Economic Outlook* published in April 2013, the IMF stated, "Much of the empirical work on debt overhangs seeks to identify the 'overhang threshold' beyond which the correlation between debt and growth becomes negative. The results are broadly similar: above a threshold of about 95 percent of G.D.P., a 10 percent

In an article published by Bloomberg News, the authors later stressed that the 90% number is an approximate guideline. It is not a threshold for complete catastrophe.[30] A country may not be on the verge of meltdown at 91% or completely safe at 89%.

In a later paper, *Debt Overhangs: Past and Present*, Reinhart and Rogoff, with a third author, Vincent Reinhart, wrote that when the debt-to-GDP ratio passes the 90% threshold, growth averages 1.2% less than in other periods. "That is, debt levels above 90 percent are associated with an average growth rate of 2.3 percent (median 2.1 percent) versus 3.5 percent in lower debt periods. Notably, the average duration of debt overhang episodes was 23 years, implying a massive cumulative output loss." They cited high taxes and low government investment that may be associated with those high levels of debt as forces weighing on economic growth.[31]

Manmohan Kumar and Jaejoon Woo, economists at the IMF, came to a similar conclusion. They found a debt-to-GDP ratio of more than 90% has a significant negative effect on growth.[32] They attributed the adverse effect to "a slowdown in labor productivity growth, mainly due to reduced investment and slower growth of the capital stock per worker."

The indebtedness appears to have been particularly detrimental for the countries of the euro area. The debt-to-GDP ratios of Japan, the U.K. and the U.S. were at least as high as those of several peripheral countries of the euro area. The sensitivity of investors may have been linked to the fact that borrowing in the euro for a euro-area nation is similar to borrowing in a foreign currency, because the country lacks the ability to "print its way" out of its problems.

---

increase in the ratio of debt to G.D.P. is identified with a decline in annual growth of about 0.15 to 0.20 percent per year." For the full response of Reinhart and Rogoff, see: Reinhart, Carmen M. and Rogoff, Kenneth S. "Reinhart and Rogoff: Responding to Our Critics." *The New York Times*, April 25, 2013. For further details of the *World Economic Outlook* issue referred to in their response and quoted above, see: International Monetary Fund "Public Debt Overhang and Private Sector Performance." *World Economic Outlook: Hopes, Realities and Risks*. April 2013.

[30]Reinhart, Carmen M. and Rogoff, Kenneth S. "Too Much Debt Means the Economy Can't Grow." Bloomberg News, July 14, 2011.

[31]Reinhart, Carmen M., Reinhart, Vincent R. and Rogoff, Kenneth S. "Debt Overhangs: Past and Present." Working Paper 18015, NBER Working Paper Series. National Bureau of Economic Research, April 2012.

[32]Kumar, Manmohan S. and Woo, Jaejoon "Public Debt and Growth." IMF Working Paper 10/174. International Monetary Fund, July 2010.

Membership of the monetary union effectively cut off the ability of the peripheral nations to use inflation and – some euro-skeptic economists would argue – growth to pay off their debts. These were the forces that enabled many of the developed nations to reduce their debt loads after the Second World War.

The sustainability of government debt is also likely to be linked to the investor base. Countries that are heavily dependent on foreign investors to finance their deficits are unlikely to be able to sustain levels of debt as high as those with domestically financed deficits. For example, in Japan, the gross government debt-to-GDP ratio stood at 229.6% at the end of 2011. Of that debt, 92.5% was held by domestic investors.

The euro area lacks the luxury of Japan. Of euro-area government bonds, 51.1% are held by non-euro-area residents.[33] The numbers for non-resident holdings of government debt are broadly similar throughout the monetary union, with a few exceptions (Table 8.1).[34]

TABLE 8.1 Percentage of Debt Held by Foreigners

	Nonresident Holding of Marketable Central Government Debt, 2012 (percent of total)	Nonresident Holding of General Government Debt, 2012 (percent of total)
Austria	71.2	83
Belgium		57.9
Finland	95.3	90.6
France	62.9	64.1
Germany	57.3	61.7
Greece		55.9
Ireland	76.5	60.5
Italy	43.1	35.2
Netherlands		56
Portugal		54.2
Slovak Republic	35.2	41.1
Slovenia	60.9	50.3
Spain	43.8	28
Euro Area		51.1

Source: ECB, IMF

---

[33]The ECB reported general government debt held by non-residents of the euro area stood at 44.6% of GDP and gross outstanding general government debt stood at 87.3% of GDP, as of February 18, 2013. (44.6/87.3 = 51.1). For the latest data, see: {http://www.ecb.europa.eu/stats/keyind/html/sdds.en.html}

[34]For the country breakdown, see: *Fiscal Monitor. Taking Stock: A Progress Report on Fiscal Adjustment*. International Monetary Fund, October 2012.

Target2 Balances

The ECB became the largest source of external funding for debtor countries through its so-called Target2 system, which is a cross-border payment system for the national central banks in the euro area. Target is an acronym for Trans-European Automated Real-Time Gross Settlement Express Transfer. Target2 replaced its predecessor Target. This source of "back-door" funding was brought to the public's attention by a series of articles written by Hans-Werner Sinn.

Sinn and his co-author, Timo Wollmershäuser, summarized Target2 balances as measures of intra-euro-area balance-of-payments deficits and surpluses and provided the following definition:

> "Target balances are claims and liabilities of the individual central banks of the Eurozone vis-à-vis the Eurosystem that are booked as such in the balance sheets of the NCBs [National Central Banks]. Target balances measure accumulated deficits and surpluses in each euro country's balance of payments with other euro countries."[35]

Those intra-euro-area claims and liabilities mostly netted to zero before the onset of the financial crisis because private capital inflows to the peripheral countries were large enough to meet private and public demand for foreign funding and capital flight was not a problem. The net claims of the Bundesbank were close to zero in mid-2007. The same was also true for Greece, Portugal and Spain. They had ballooned to 751 billion euros by August 2012 for the Bundesbank (Figure 8.8). The liabilities of the central banks of those peripheral economies totaled 107.9 billion euros, 72 billion euros, and 428.6 billion euros, respectively, by that month.

Those claims and liabilities had become huge relative to the size of national economies. The net claims of the Bundesbank were about 29% of German GDP by that date. The liabilities amounted to about 52% of GDP for Greece, 43% of GDP for Portugal and 40% of GDP for Spain.

Sinn and Wollmershäuser contend that the payments system allowed "a secret bail-out activity that the parliaments of the Eurozone were unaware of when they decided on the open rescue programmes." They calculated the credit advanced to Greece, Ireland, Italy, Portugal and Spain through

---

[35] Sinn, Hans-Werner and Wollmershäuser, Timo "Target Loans, Current Account Balances and Capital Flows: The ECB's Rescue Facility." *International Tax and Public Finance*, July 2012.

FIGURE 8.8 Target2 balances explode.

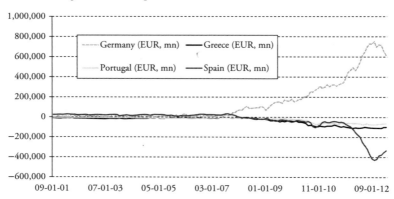

Source: Bloomberg

the Target2 system totaled 650 billion euros by the end of 2011. That compared with official aid – extended and committed – by all euro-area countries of 172 billion euros at the time of their study.[36]

The Target2 system made the Bundesbank the most exposed central bank to a complete break-up of the euro area. In the event of disintegration, the German central bank and its continental peers with positive balances "would have claims against a system that no longer exists." Sinn and Wollmershäuser calculated that "German, Dutch and Finnish savers had to accept a swap of marketable foreign assets for mere Target claims to the tune of 16,000 to 18,000 euros per working person, respectively."

The losses sustained by the Bundesbank would, in theory, be much smaller than its net claims in the event of a peripheral nation leaving the monetary union as long as the currency zone didn't completely disintegrate.

---

[36]In an e-mail on March 8, 2013 to David Powell, Hans-Werner Sinn noted that he would add "the net payment orders measured by Target by themselves reduced the stock of M0 in the deficit countries and increased it in the surplus countries. However, as this would have meant a quick drying up of local liquidity provision in the former and excess liquidity in the latter, the outflows were sterilized by creating and lending out more money in the deficit countries and destroying money and redeeming the stock of refinancing credit in the surplus countries. You could also say that the Target balances indirectly measure the shift in the (electronic) printing press from the surplus to the deficit countries. This would be a good metaphor. Basically, countries like Greece and Portugal have been financed with the (electronic) printing press since the beginning of the crisis."

TABLE 8.2 Euro-Area NCBs' Contributions to the ECB's Capital

NCB	Capital Key %	Paid-up Capital (€)	Adjusted for P&L
Nationale Bank van België/ Banque Nationale de Belgique	2.4	220,583,718.02	3.5
Deutsche Bundesbank	18.9	1,722,155,360.77	27.1
Eesti Pank	0.2	16,278,234.47	0.3
Central Bank of Ireland	1.1	101,006,899.58	1.6
Bank of Greece	2.0	178,687,725.72	2.8
Banco de España	8.3	755,164,575.51	11.9
Banque de France	14.2	1,293,273,899.48	20.3
Banca d'Italia	12.5	1,136,439,021.48	17.9
Central Bank of Cyprus	0.1	12,449,666.48	0.2
Banque centrale du Luxembourg	0.2	15,887,193.09	0.2
Central Bank of Malta	0.1	5,747,398.98	0.1
De Nederlandsche Bank	4.0	362,686,339.12	5.7
Oesterreichische Nationalbank	1.9	176,577,921.04	2.8
Banco de Portugal	1.8	159,181,126.31	2.5
Banka Slovenije	0.3	29,901,025.10	0.5
Národná banka Slovenska	0.7	63,057,697.10	1.0
Suomen Pankki – Finlands Bank	1.3	114,029,487.14	1.8
Total	**70.0**	**6,363,107,289.36**	100.0

Source: ECB

That is because those losses would legally have to be distributed across the central banks of the euro area based on their shares of the paid-in capital of the ECB (Table 8.2). In other words, because Germany's contribution to the paid-in capital of the ECB is 27%, the Bundesbank would only have to bear 27% of the losses linked to its Target2 balances.

That figure would have to be adjusted in the event of a country's departure to account for the new percentages of paid-in capital of the remaining nations. The formula was originally based on the country's share of euro-area GDP. The remaining members would redistribute the losses that should have been borne by the departing country.

Resolution

The resolution of the crisis will likely be multi-faceted. It may involve the departure of one or more countries from the euro area, haircuts to the government debt of some countries and to some private debt, relative price changes within the euro area as well as inflation.

Euro-area policy makers have thus far largely based their plans for a solution on relative price changes within the euro area apart from the restructuring of Greek government debt. They have also pushed for the peripheral countries to do most of the adjusting. In the June 2012 edition of the central bank's monthly bulletin, the staff of the ECB wrote:

> "Rebalancing competitiveness across euro area countries implies that price and cost growth in countries that have previously seen excesses in this respect need to be significantly lower than the euro area average during a transition phase. At the same time, several of the euro area economies that increased their competitiveness in the past are likely to temporarily experience price and cost growth above the euro area average. However, the more competitive countries need to avoid – also in this transition phase – excessive wage increases that would lead to higher unemployment."[37]

This suggests that the central bank desires an asymmetric adjustment. "Significantly lower than the euro-area average" sounds more below the mean than "above the euro-area average" is greater than it. The average should be their definition of price stability – "below but close to 2%." Above average may therefore mean about 3% and significantly lower than average probably means at least a decline to 0%.

The process of "internal devaluation" will only be able to be achieved through rises in unemployment in those countries. As John Maynard Keynes stated, "Deflation does not reduce wages 'automatically.' It reduces them by causing unemployment."[38] That is because workers rarely accept wage cuts, preventing downward adjustment. Firing tends to be the path of least resistance. Wage cuts are necessary because wages are normally the largest cost of a firm and therefore strongly influence the prices of the company's products.

That outcome may prove difficult to implement because of the pain associated with a rise in unemployment rates in the peripheral countries. The two greatest price adjustments are required in Greece and Portugal, according to a Goldman Sachs study quoted by Hans-Werner Sinn. Those

---

[37]"Rebalancing of Competitiveness Within the Euro Area and its Implications for Inflation." *ECB Monthly Bulletin*. Frankfurt: European Central Bank, June 2012. Copyright European Central Bank, Frankfurt am Main, Germany. This information may be obtained free of charge from {www.ecb.int}.

[38]Keynes, John Maynard *Essays in Persuasion*. London: Macmillan and Co., Limited, 1931.

two countries need their price levels to drop by about 30% and 35%, respectively.[39] History suggests that the social consequences of such an adjustment may be disastrous. Sinn wrote, "Germany had a wage cut of 30% from 1929 to 1933 and a price cut of 23%. This drove the country to the brink of a civil war."[40]

The adjustment required – and the potential backlash from voters – to remain in the EMU is reminiscent of the problems that led to the breakdown of the gold standard after the First World War. One of the major lessons from that experience was the pursuit of external balance – the elimination of trade deficits – over internal balance – a low level of unemployment – was incompatible with the development of modern democracies and the increased spread of suffrage.

Barry Eichengreen has summed up the argument as it related to the gold standard:

> "What was critical for the maintenance of pegged exchange rates . . . was protection for governments from pressure to trade exchange rate stability for other goals. Under the nineteenth-century gold standard the source of such protection was insulation from domestic politics . . . Because the right to vote was limited, the common laborers who suffered most from hard times were poorly positioned to object to increases in central bank interest rates [*or unemployment rates*] adopted to defend the currency peg . . . Governments were therefore free to take whatever steps were needed to defend their currency pegs . . . Come the twentieth century, these circumstances were transformed. It was no longer certain that, when currency stability and full employment clashed, the authorities would opt for the former. Universal male suffrage and the rise of trade unionism and parliamentary labor parties politicized monetary and fiscal policymaking."[41]

By contrast, Thomas Mayer has argued that the price adjustment will eventually most likely be made in the creditor countries, especially Germany,

---

[39]Sinn, Hans-Werner "A Crisis in Full Flight." *Project Syndicate: A World of Ideas*, April 25, 2012. {http://www.project-syndicate.org/commentary/a-crisis-in-full-flight}

[40]Sinn, Hans-Werner "Greece Probably Will, and Should, Leave the Euro Zone." *The Economist*, July 20, 2011. {http://www.economist.com/economics/by-invitation/contributors/Hans-Werner%20Sinn}

[41]Eichengreen, Barry *Globalizing Capital: A History of the International Monetary System.* Princeton: Princeton University Press, 1996. Italicized words in the quote inserted by David Powell.

rather than the debtor countries. He wrote, "With outright budgetary transfers from the creditor to the debtor countries unlikely and the latter also probably unable to achieve internal real depreciation through deflation of goods, services and asset prices, the path of least resistance seems to be an appreciation in creditor countries through the inflation of goods, services and asset prices. With representatives of debtor countries holding a majority of votes in the ECB's Governing Council, a policy of easy money and exchange rate depreciation that leads to overheating in the creditor countries seems most likely."[42]

Milton Friedman argued that a price adjustment could be most easily achieved by just adopting a free-floating currency. The abandonment of the fixed-exchange-rate regime would largely eliminate the need for sharp price increases in the creditor countries or decreases in the debtor countries.

The Nobel laureate compared the situation to daylight savings time. In 1953, he wrote, "The argument for flexible exchange rates is, strange to say, very nearly identical with the argument for daylight savings time. Isn't it absurd to change the clock in the summer when exactly the same result could be achieved by having each individual change his habits? All that is required is that everyone decide to come to his office an hour earlier, have lunch an hour earlier, etc. But obviously it is much simpler to change the clock that guides all than to have each individual separately change his pattern of reaction to the clock, even though all want to do so. The situation is exactly the same in the exchange market. It is far simpler to allow one price to change, namely, the price of foreign exchange, than to rely upon changes in the multitude of prices that together constitute the internal price structure."[43]

A freely floating – and significantly weaker – exchange rate could potentially provide the stimulus needed in the peripheral countries to break their economic downturns. An extremely weak currency would probably drastically reduce imports and promote export growth, especially in the tourism industry. In addition, the sharp increase in the prices of foreign goods would likely reorient demand toward the domestic economy, lowering the level of unemployment.

A country's problems would fail to be solved completely by the abandonment of the euro. That move could be debilitating for the balance sheets of

---

[42]Mayer, Thomas "Euroland's Hidden Balance-of-Payments Crisis." Deutsche Bank, October 26, 2011. Reproduced by permission of Deutsche Bank.
[43]Friedman, 1953.

its banks, corporations and households as well as the sovereign. They could end up with assets denominated in a weak currency and liabilities in a strong currency, potentially leading to a wave of bankruptcies.

Departure from the Euro Area

No formal departure procedure exists because membership was meant to be irrevocable. Article 50 of the Lisbon Treaty provided guidelines for a state's departure from the EU, though not from EMU. Phoebus Athanassiou of the ECB has argued that a state cannot leave the monetary union without leaving the entire EU from a legal point of view.[44] Regardless of the present legal framework, a sovereign state can try to negotiate anything such as leaving the monetary union while remaining in the free-trade area of the EU through a change to the legal framework.

In the words of Nouriel Roubini, "Only time will tell whether betting the house to save the garage was the right move."[45]

Tools for Analyzing Debt Sustainability

A debt sustainability analysis can be conducted to model the debt-to-GDP ratio of a country to determine its solvency according to the aforementioned definitions. As a starting point, the IMF states that a detailed analysis of the sustainability of a country's debt is needed when the debt-to-GDP ratio exceeds 60% or is projected to do so over the forecast horizon.[46]

The key ratio to focus on is gross government debt to GDP. The IMF uses that ratio as opposed to net government debt to GDP because the former allows for cross-country comparisons with the "greatest degree of reliability and coverage."[47] Reinhart and Rogoff use gross government debt to GDP as the debt-to-GDP ratio for their analysis.

---

[44]Athanassiou, Phoebus "Withdrawal and Expulsion from the EU and EMU: Some Reflections." Legal Working Paper Series, No. 10. Frankfurt: European Central Bank, December 2009.

[45]Roubini, Nouriel "Early Retirement for the Eurozone?" *Project Syndicate: A World of Ideas*, August 15, 2012. {http://www.project-syndicate.org/commentary/early-retirement-for-the-eurozone-by-nouriel-roubini}

[46]Fiscal Affairs Department and the Strategy, Policy, and Review Department *Modernizing the Framework for Fiscal Policy and Public Debt Sustainability Analysis*. International Monetary Fund, August 5, 2011.

[47]*Ibid.*

A model of the debt-to-GDP ratio produces those forecasts. It requires assumptions of a country's primary budget balance, which excludes the interest payments on government debt, real GDP growth, inflation and the average cost of debt. The latest historical measure of the debt-to-GDP ratio is also required.

Forecasts for the first three variables can be found on the IMF's website in the database of the latest version of its *World Economic Outlook*. The publication (and the associated online database) is released twice a year, normally in April and September/October, according to the website. Updates are published in January and July with a sub-set of revised estimates for some indicators. The latest historical measure of the debt-to-GDP ratio can also be found in the database.

An analyst should assume that these forecasts represent a best-case scenario for a country in crisis. In August 2011, IMF economists warned, "Timmermann (2006) found that *World Economic Outlook* real GDP forecasts showed a tendency to systematically exceed outcomes. This phenomenon was particularly prevalent in countries with an IMF-supported program. Such bias was found to be most statistically significant in the next-year forecast."[48]

The resignation letter of Peter Doyle, an economist at IMF, appears to confirm the political pressure brought to bear on the teams focused on forecasting. He protested loudly against the "European bias" of the organization.[49]

European Department
Washington DC
June 18, 2012

To Mr. Shaalan, Dean of the IMF Executive Board

> Today, I addressed the Executive Board for the last time – because I am leaving the Fund.
> Accordingly, I wanted first to formally express my deep appreciation to the Swedish, Israeli, and Danish authorities with whom I have worked recently, as well as all others with whom I have worked earlier, for their extraordinary generosity towards me personally.
> But I also wanted to take this opportunity to explain my departure.
> After twenty years of service, I am ashamed to have had any association with the Fund at all.
> This is not solely because of the incompetence that was partly chronicled by the OIA report into the global crisis and the TSR report on surveillance ahead of the Euro Area crisis. Moreso, it is because the substantive difficulties in these

---

[48] *Ibid.* Reproduced by permission of the International Monetary Fund.
[49] {http://cnnibusiness.files.wordpress.com/2012/07/doyle.pdf}

crises, as with others, were identified well in advance but were suppressed here. Given long gestation periods and protracted international decision-making processes to head off both these global challenges, timely sustained warnings were of the essence. So the failure of the Fund to issue them is a failing of the first order, even if such warnings may not have been heeded. The consequences include suffering (and risk of worse to come) for many including Greece, that the second global reserve currency is on the brink, and that the Fund for the past two years has been playing catch-up and reactive roles in the last-ditch efforts to save it.

Further, the proximate factors which produced these failings of IMF surveillance – analytical risk aversion, bilateral priority, and European bias – are, if anything, becoming more deeply entrenched, notwithstanding initiatives which purport to address them. This fact is most clear in regard to appointments for Managing Director which, over the past decade, have all-too-evidently been disastrous. Even the current incumbent is tainted, as neither her gender, integrity or élan can make up for the fundamental illegitimacy of the selection process. In a hierarchical place like this, the implications of those choices filter directly to others in senior management, and via appointments, fixed term contracts, and succession planning of senior staff, they go on to infuse the organization as a whole, overwhelming everything else. A handicapped Fund, subject to those proximate roots of surveillance failure, is what the Executive Board prefers. Would that I had understood twenty years ago that this would be the choice.

There are good salty people here. But this one is moving on. You might want to take care not to lose the others.

Yours Sincerely,
Peter Doyle

cc. Ms Nemat Shafik   Mr Stanley Fischer
    Mr Stephan Ingves   Mr Benny Anderson
    Mr Alex Gibbs   Mr Eric Meyer
    Mr Amit Friedman   Mr Martin Holmberg
    Mr Reza Moghadam   Mr Mark Plant
    Mr Brad McDonald

A proxy for the average cost of debt can be taken from the bond market. If the average maturity of a country's bonds is six years, the six-year government bond yield can be used as an estimate for the level with which the average cost of debt will eventually converge, as long as the current maturity profile is maintained. That bond yield and the average maturity of a country's government debt can be found on the Bloomberg Professional Service. The latter is obtained by using the {DDIS <GO>} function.

The real growth rate and the rate of inflation must be used to calculate the nominal rate of growth. This can be done with the following formula:

Nominal Growth = ((1 + Real Growth Rate) × (1 + Inflation Rate)) − 1

TABLE 8.3 Debt-to-GDP Ratio Calculator

	Real GDP Growth	Inflation	Nominal Growth	Primary Budget Balance (% of GDP)	Average Cost of Debt	Interest Payments (% of GDP)	Total Budget Balance	Debt (% of GDP)
2011	0.4%	3.1%	3.8%	−7.0%	4.3%	−2.5%	−9.1%	68.5%
2012	−1.5%	2.4%	0.9%	−4.5%	4.8%	−3.3%	−7.8%	75.7%
2013	−1.3%	2.4%	1.1%	−2.2%	4.8%	−3.6%	−5.8%	80.7%
2014	1.0%	1.5%	2.5%	−0.8%	4.8%	−3.8%	−4.6%	83.2%
2015	1.6%	1.5%	3.1%	0.1%	4.8%	−3.9%	−3.8%	84.5%
2016	1.7%	1.4%	3.1%	1.1%	4.8%	−3.9%	−2.8%	84.8%
2017	1.7%	1.4%	3.1%	1.7%	4.8%	−3.9%	−2.2%	84.4%

Source: Bloomberg, IMF

The burden from interest payments must also be calculated. This can be done using the following formula:

Interest Payments as Percentage of GDP_2
$$= ((\text{Debt-to-GDP Ratio}_1/(1 + \text{Nominal Growth}_2)) \times \text{Average Cost of Debt}_2) \times -1)$$

The total budget balance as a percentage of GDP can be calculated with the formula:

Total Budget Balance as Percentage of GDP
$$= \text{Primary Budget Balance as Percentage of GDP} + \text{Interest Payments as Percentage of GDP}$$

The debt-to-GDP ratio can be modeled using the following formula:

$$\text{Debt-to-GDP Ratio}_2 = (\text{Debt-to-GDP Ratio}_1/(1 + \text{Nominal Growth}_2)) + ((\text{Interest Payments as Percentage of GDP}_2 \times -1) + (\text{Primary Budget Balance as Percentage of GDP}_2 \times -1))$$

These formulas can then be input into an Excel spreadsheet to produce Table 8.3.

An analyst can then enter a different average cost of debt (Figure 8.9) or rate of real growth to determine the effects of those changes.

FIGURE 8.9 Debt-to-GDP ratio with different average-cost-of-debt assumptions.

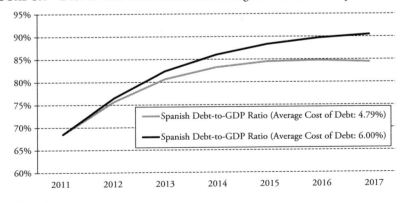

Source: Bloomberg

Box 8.1   Government budget balances

Economists use a variety of terms to describe a country's current fiscal position. The cleanest read on a country's fiscal situation is the structural primary budget balance.

The most often cited terms are:

Budget balance: The government's budgetary surplus or deficit.
Primary budget balance: The budget balance excluding interest payments on government debt.
Cyclically-adjusted budget balance: The budget balance adjusted for all the effects of the business cycle. Economists at the ECB estimate that for every percentage-point gap between GDP and the estimated potential level of GDP for the euro area as a whole, a 0.5 percentage-point deterioration of the budget balance occurs as a result of the business cycle.[50]
Cyclically-adjusted primary budget balance: The budget balance adjusted for all the effects of the business cycle excluding interest payments on government debt.
Structural budget balance: The cyclically-adjusted budget balance excluding the effects of one-off events such as bank recapitalizations.
Structural primary budget balance: The cyclically-adjusted budget balance excluding the effects of one-off events such as bank recapitalizations and interest payments on government debt.

---

[50]"Cyclical Adjustment of the Government Budget Balance." *ECB Monthly Bulletin*. Frankfurt: European Central Bank, March 2012.

CHAPTER 9

Germany

Germany has become the most important country in the euro area because of its large economy. The strength of the domestic economy has been made most visible over the past few years by the resilience of the labor market at a time when most other countries in the euro area and the U.S. faced the highest rates of unemployment in decades. The resilience of the labor market was due mainly to the stabilization policies engineered by the government of Angela Merkel during the financial crisis and structural reforms introduced by her predecessor, Gerhard Schröder.

Labor Market

The Merkel government introduced a temporary work program called *Kurzarbeit* – meaning "short-term work" in German – during the financial crisis. Employers were able to reduce the hours of their workers by the percentage required by the needs of the business up to 100% in order to avoid mass lay-offs. The employee had to go through training and skill development in the extreme of working hours being reduced to nothing.[1]

The maximum period for an employee to participate in the scheme eventually became 24 months after several extensions. The government wanted to subsidize the costs of retaining workers who would be needed again when the economic downturn ended and avoid paying for obsolete workers.

---

[1] "Short-Time Work of 'Kurzarbeit': Frequently Asked Questions." German Missions in the United States. {http://www.germany.info/Vertretung/usa/en/07__Climate__Business__Science/02__Bus__w__Germany/FAQ/FAQ__ShortTimeWork.html}

The companies continued to pay 60% of the foregone net salary and were reimbursed that sum by the local government employment agency. The figure could have risen to 67% if the household contained at least one child. The social contributions of the employee for pensions, health care, long-term care and unemployment benefits continued to be paid. That bill was split during the first six months by the employer and the employment agency. After that period, 100% of the bill was paid by the state. The government also partially financed training for works using the scheme.

The labor scheme cost the state about $16 billion in 2009, according to the German government.[2] From October 2008 to June 2009, over 2.6 million employees at over 80,000 companies participated in the scheme, according to Dr Stephen J. Silvia, a professor of International Economic Relations at American University.[3]

Silvia concluded that the stimulus provided by the government was most effective for a "V-shaped" recovery because it "preserved the export-oriented manufacturing base." The subsidies would have proved more costly in the event of an "L-shape" recovery characterized by anemic demand for German exports and it would have prevented necessary adjustments.

Much of the adjustment required to return the German labor market to health took place under the previous government. Germany faced an economic crisis by the late 1990s. The country suffered from mass unemployment and began to be known as the "sick man of Europe," a term which had previously been used to describe the U.K. before Margaret Thatcher rose to power.[4]

The primary reasons for the economic malaise were exorbitant rises in wages and a welfare state that provided greater financial incentives to stay at home, collecting financial assistance from the state, than to return to the workplace. The unemployment rate trended upward throughout the 1990s (Figure 9.1), creating a sense of crisis for the German government. It plateaued at 9.7% in 1997–1998.

The Hartz reforms bear the name of the man who led the commission that designed them. In 2002, Schröder appointed the personnel director of Volkswagen, Dr Peter Hartz, to head the "Commission on Modern Services

---

[2] *Ibid.*

[3] Silvia, Stephen J. "Keynes in Lederhosen: Assessing the German Response to the Financial Crisis." *AICGS Transatlantic Perspectives.* American Institute for Contemporary German Studies at Johns Hopkins University, June 2009.

[4] For example, see: Schmieding, Holger "Germany: The Sick Man of Europe?" *European Monitor.* Merrill Lynch, 1998.

FIGURE 9.1 German unemployment soars after reunification.

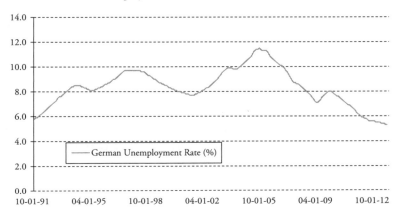

Source: Bloomberg

for the Labour Market" charged with proposing reforms of the Federal Labor Office called *Bundesagentur für Arbeit*, or BA, in German, and delivering a final report six weeks before the federal elections of 2002. The agency had been rocked by a scandal in early 2002 related to data falsification that overstated its job placement record.

In 2002, Schröder ran on a platform to tackle mass unemployment in Germany and the report of the Hartz Commission became a focus of the campaign. "Released just six weeks before the election, the 340-page document bore little resemblance to the prototype of a government report, in style, layout or structure: the summary read more like a manifesto, ending as it did with an appeal to the 'professionals of the nation' to bring forward proposals to reduce unemployment, and it appeared to be aimed at the media and the public rather than at policy elites," according to a report from the OECD by William Tompson.[5]

The chancellor began a push to implement the Hartz recommendations when he started his second term in 2002. The four Hartz laws were adopted within two years of the publication of the report. The first two bills were passed in the autumn of 2002. The third and fourth bills emerged in March 2003 as part of the government's plans for economic reform termed "Agenda 2010."

---

[5]Tompson, W. *The Political Economy of Reform: Lessons from Pensions, Product Markets and Labour Markets in Ten OECD Countries*, OECD Publishing, 2009. {http://dx.doi.org/10.1787/9789264073111-en}

The reforms focused mainly on the reintegration of the unemployed into the labor market. They steered clear of rigidities such as employment protection and collective bargaining.

Hartz I focused on the creation of Personnel-Service Agencies. These organizations were meant to act as temporary employment agencies. They were to treat "the unemployed as placement clients rather than passive benefit recipients." Hartz II concentrated on the rules governing "mini jobs," decreasing the burden of social security contributions linked to that form of employment. Hartz III dealt with putting the unemployed back to work and reducing unemployment benefits. Hartz IV also related to changes to the financial assistance given to the unemployed.[6]

Box 9.1   Summary of Hartz reforms from the OECD

Four new federal laws were adopted in 2002–03 pursuant to the Hartz Commission report:

1. Hartz I (December 2002) encompassed: the establishment of so-called "Personnel-Service Agencies" all over Germany; reform of the Law on Temporary Employment and Labour Leasing; the requirement of early registration even for impending unemployment; stricter rules for taking up "reasonable" employment; transfer of the burden of proof concerning rejected job offers onto the job-seeker; and the introduction of training vouchers.
2. Hartz II (December 2002) included: the provision of new benefits for business start-ups (*Ich-AG*); reform of the minor employment relationships ("mini-job") legislation;[1] promotion of household services; preparations for the organisation of Job Centres combining employment and social welfare services; and reorganisation of the BA with a view to making it a more effective service provider.
3. Hartz III (October 2003) continued the reform of the BA[2] to focus its activities more clearly on reintegration of the unemployed and introduced some changes in the rules governing partial retirement. The most controversial element of this bill was the provision allowing the BA to cut benefits by up to 30 percent if recipients of unemployment benefit refused a job offer without adequate grounds for doing so.

---

[6]For an in-depth discussion of reforms, see: Tompson, 2009.

> 4. Hartz IV (July 2004) restructured unemployment benefits. Entitlement to the old income-related UI benefit (henceforth to be known as unemployment benefit I or UB I) was limited to a maximum of 12 months for those under 55 and to 18 months for older workers. Thereafter, the unemployed were eligible for the new flat-rate unemployment benefit II (UB II). Hartz IV also further tightened the definition of a "reasonable" job.[3] (The Hartz IV law itself did not curtail the duration of UB I, and, as noted above, the Hartz Commission had shied away from making such a recommendation. However, this measure was adopted at the same time as Hartz IV, in a separate Labour Market Reform Act, and it thus came to be identified with Hartz IV in public debates on the issue.)
>
> [1]The legislation raised the limit for low-paid work exempt from social security contributions and introduced a rising scale of contributions for incomes of EUR 400 to EUR 800 a month.
> [2]Henceforth re-named the *Bundesagentur für Arbeit* or Federal Labour Agency.
> [3]This included the requirement that "standard regional wages" must be accepted even if they are below union wages.
> *Source:* OECD. Reproduced by permission of the OECD.

Tompson attributed the passages of these laws to the proverbial "perfect storm." He concluded, "sharply rising unemployment increased the pressure on the government to be seen to be taking action to combat joblessness, the scandal at the BA put those responsible for the labour-market *status quo* on the defensive, and the approach of elections made it harder for the trade unions or SPD traditionalists to challenge government policy in public."

The economic reforms eventually cost Schröder his job. He deliberately lost a parliamentary vote of confidence in 2005 in order to trigger a general election after facing electoral losses in North Rhine-Westphalia, Germany's most populous state.[7] After his party suffered losses in the general election, he was succeeded as German chancellor by Angela Merkel in November 2005.

Political Institutions

Germany is a parliamentary democracy. The country's parliament is called the Bundestag. Its members elect the chancellor after a general election.

---

[7]*Profile: Gerhard Schroeder*. BBC News, September 9, 2005. {http://news.bbc.co.uk/2/hi/europe/2242899.stm}

Each German voter has two votes. The first is for a candidate of the constituency and the second is for their preferred party.

In terms of the first vote, the candidate with the most votes wins regardless of their political affiliation. This is a first-past-the-post system. These votes produce 299 members of the Bundestag – one for each constituency in Germany. These seats are about half of those in the Bundestag.

The second vote is for a party list. This is a system of proportional representation. For example, if a party wins 50% of the votes cast as part of the "second vote," that party will be granted 50% of all the seats in the Bundestag. If 150 candidates from that party were to win seats as part of the "first vote," 149 individuals from a list of candidates of each party would be chosen, starting with the top of the list, as part of the "second vote."

"Overhang mandates" – known in German as *Überhangmandaten* – can create extra seats for a party. For example, if a party wins 50% of the vote under the "second vote," it is entitled to 299 seats in the Bundestag. That same party may have actually won 308 seats under the system of the "first vote." In this case, it is allotted its 299, according to the outcome of the "second vote" and is given nine "overhang mandates." In this case, the Bundestag would have 607 members until the next election.

The "second vote" contains a cut-off clause of 5%. A political party must gain at least that percentage of the vote in order to be allotted seats. This is to prevent splinter parties, which weakened the Weimar Republic, from being represented in parliament. The exception to this rule is if a party wins three seats under the "first vote" without winning at least 5% under the "second vote."

The German Constitutional Court has ruled that the system must be altered before the federal election of 2013.[8] Under the new system, the role of *Überhangmandaten* will change.

To re-use the previous example, in the current system, if a party wins 50% of the vote under the "second vote," it is entitled to 299 seats in the Bundestag. That same party may have actually won 308 seats under the system of the "first vote." In this case, it is allotted its 299, according to the outcome of the "second vote" and is given nine "overhang mandates." Under the new law, the opposition (assuming, for purposes of simplification, that only one opposition party exists) would be given an extra nine seats as well to preserve the ratio of 1:1 that resulted from the "second vote." In this case, the Bundestag would have 616 members until the next election.

A general election takes place every four years. It must take place between 46 and 48 months after the legislative term begins, according to the German

---

[8]"Politicians in Proportion: How Germany, Seeking the Best of All Worlds, Fiddles With its Voting Rules." *The Economist*, December 1, 2012.

TABLE 9.1 German Chancellors Since 1945

Chancellor	Years	Political Party
Angela Merkel	2005–Present	CDU
Gerhard Schröder	1998–2005	SPD
Helmut Kohl	1982–1998	CDU
Helmut Schmidt	1974–1982	SPD
Willy Brandt	1969–1974	SPD
Kurt Georg Kiesinger	1966–1969	CDU
Ludwig Erhard	1963–1966	CDU
Konrad Adenauer	1949–1963	CDU

Source: The Press and Information Office of the Federal Government of Germany

Basic Law.[9] The exact date of the election is decided by the president and must be on a Sunday or a public holiday, according to the Federal Electoral Law.[10]

Political Parties

Germany has six major political parties. They are the Christian Democratic Union, the Christian Social Union, the Free Democratic Party, the Green Party, the Left Party and the Social Democratic Party.

The CDU is the main conservative party. Its website states its policies are "based on Christian values." The party was formed in the aftermath of the Second World War and united Catholics and Protestants. It espouses the "economic and social model of the 'Social Market Economy.'"[11] The party's traditional strongholds are in southwest and western Germany, according to Spiegel Online.[12] The first post-war chancellor, Konrad Adenauer, and the architect of the post-war economic miracle, the *Wirtschaftswunder*, Ludwig Erhard, were members of the CDU. In total, five of the eight post-war chancellors were members of the party (Table 9.1).

---

[9] *Basic Law for the Federal Republic of Germany (Grundgesetz)*. Translated into English by Inter Nationes. {http://www.iuscomp.org/gla/statutes/GG.htm#39}

[10] *Federal Electoral Law (Bundeswahlgesetz)*. Translated into English by Inter Nationes. {http://www.iuscomp.org/gla/statutes/BWG.htm#ToC19}

[11] "Successful Policies for Over 50 Years." *CDU Deutschlands.* {http://www.cdu.de/english/history.htm}

[12] "Where Do They Stand?: A Quick Guide to Germany's Political Parties." Spiegel Online. {http://www.spiegel.de/international/germany/where-do-they-stand-a-quick-guide-to-germany-s-political-parties-a-651388.html}

The CSU is the sister party of the CDU in the state of Bavaria. It was also founded after the Second World War and has never had a member of its party rise to the position of chancellor of the Federal Republic. The party, which is limited operationally to Bavaria, has been part of a joint political party with the CDU in the national parliament since 1949.[13]

The FDP is a pro-business party. It supports the free market economy and individual liberty. The group is referred to as the party of the privileged few by its critics, according to Spiegel Online. It has been in government, as part of coalitions with either the CDU or the SPD, for 41 years, which is longer than any other party.[14]

The Green Party is an environmentalist party. More specifically, it works for "environmental protection and sustainable development, democracy and human rights, social justice, peace and multilateral international policies," according to its website. A member of the party first won a seat in parliament in 1983. The group was part of a coalition government with the SPD from 1998 to 2005.

The Left Party is a socialist party. It was formed in 2007 when the Party of Democratic Socialism, which is the successor to the communist party of the former East Germany, and Electoral Alternative for Labour and Social Justice (WASG) from the western part of Germany combined.

The SPD is a center-left movement.[15] It has historically represented the working class. It is Germany's second largest political party and, founded in 1875, is the country's oldest. Three of the eight post-war chancellors were members of the party.

Germany has a second parliamentary body called the Bundesrat. Its members represent the 16 *länder* of the country. In this sense, it is similar to the U.S. Senate, with members that represent the individual states of the country. The Bundesrat refers to itself as "one of the five constitutional bodies in Germany."[16] The other four are the Bundestag, the Federal President, the Federal Government (the chancellor and the federal ministers) and the Federal Constitutional Court.

---

[13] *CSU*. {http://www.csu.de/partei/international/english.htm}

[14] "Where Do They Stand?: A Quick Guide to Germany's Political Parties." Spiegel Online. {http://www.spiegel.de/international/germany/where-do-they-stand-a-quick-guide-to-germany-s-political-parties-a-651388.html}

[15] *Ibid.*

[16] *Bundesrat*. {http://www.bundesrat.de/cln_227/EN/Home/homepage__node.html?__nnn=true}

The Bundesrat is the third major body for the passage of a law in Germany. The Federal Government initiates most bills. The Bundestag votes on all of those bills. The Bundesrat's approval is required for certain bills called "consent bills." They fall into three categories:

1. Amendments to the constitution.
2. Those that "impinge in a particular manner on the finances of the federal states."
3. Those that "impinge on the organizational and administrative jurisdiction of the federal states."[17]

The Bundesrat can also vote on the other types of bills called objection bills, though these bills may, ultimately, be passed without the approval of the Bundesrat.

Members of the Bundesrat are appointed by governments of the German states. The body has 69 members and they are assigned according to the size of the population of each state. All members from a state must vote en bloc.

Germany has a federal president as well, though the role is mostly ceremonial. The president is elected by a Federal Convention, which consists of all members of the Bundestag and a number of people from the parliaments of the German states. The term is for five years and is renewable once.

---

[17]"Consent and Objection Bills." *Bundesrat*. {http://www.bundesrat.de/cln_227/nn_11592/EN/funktionen-en/gesetzgebung-en/zust-einspr-en/zust-einspr-en-node.html?__nnn=true}

CHAPTER 10

France

The French and German governments – as a duo – have been the driving force behind many of the episodes of European integration since the end of the Second World War. Similarly, the EU's response to the debt crisis was initially driven by Angela Merkel and Nicolas Sarkozy. The team became known as "Merkozy."

The German chancellor appears likely to be less close to the newly-elected French president, François Hollande, who comes from the other side of the political spectrum. Some commentators have referred to the new team as "Merde," which means "shit" in French.

The president of France is the main representative of the country on the international stage. Institutional practice leaves the matters of diplomacy and defense to the president – as opposed to the prime minister – except in the case of "cohabitation." That occurs when the prime minister and the president come from different political parties.

This situation can change the national hierarchy. The webpage of the National Assembly states, "The actual powers of the President of the Republic can change in certain circumstances: when the presidential and the parliamentary majority coincide, the office of the President has primacy; on the contrary, a period of 'cohabitation' provides actual political supremacy to the Prime Minister."[1]

The role of the president was elevated to a level commensurate with that in the U.S. when the Fifth Republic was founded by Charles de Gaulle in 1958. The general wanted more than a ceremonial position for the president, as in Germany. He declared his actions could not be limited "to the

---

[1] *The President of the Republic*. Assemblée Nationale. {http://www.assemblee-nationale.fr/english/synthetic_files/file-02.asp}

inauguration of chrysanthemums."[2] The new constitution made the president elected directly by the people.

The president has a five-year term. The presidential election normally consists of two rounds of voting. If a candidate fails to gain 50% of all votes, a second round is held with only the two candidates who received the most votes during the first round.

The president appoints the prime minister. The only constraint he faces is the political composition of the National Assembly. In other words, a president must appoint someone who can command the support of the majority of deputies either because that majority comes from his own political party or can be formed through coalition-like voting patterns. The prime minister proposes the other government ministers to the president.

The parliament is comprised of the National Assembly and the Senate. The former is elected directly by the people and the latter by an electoral college made up of about 150,000 grand electors. Deputies of the National Assembly are meant to represent the nation as a whole and not the geographic *département* from which he or she comes. By contrast, the Senators are meant to represent their geographic regions – not the nation as a whole.

Members of the National Assembly have five-year terms. They are all up for election at the same time. These terms can be interrupted by dissolution of the chamber by the president of the republic. The National Assembly was dissolved by the president in 1962, 1968, 1981, 1988 and 1997. It has 577 members. Its primary functions are passing laws and supervising the government.

The National Assembly is the stronger of the two houses. A bill normally has to be passed by both chambers of the government to become law. The National Assembly – with a few exceptions – may make the final decision in the event of dispute.

Members of the Senate have six-year terms. Half of them are up for election every three years. The Senate cannot be dissolved. It has 348 members. The Senate can propose legislation. It also supervises the government along with the National Assembly.

---

[2] *Ibid.*

CHAPTER 11

United Kingdom

The U.K. declined to join the economic and monetary union that gave birth to the continent's common currency. As such, the country has maintained its own monetary policy and currency. In retrospect, that decision appears to have been beneficial to the country.

The Bank of England

The Bank of England has an explicit inflation target. The target currently stands at 2% and is set by the government. Each year in the budget, the Chancellor of the Exchequer announces the inflation target of the government. It has never been changed from 2% since this framework was born in 1997.

Operational independence was granted to the central bank in May 1997. If the national interest demands it, the government is able to direct the central bank's interest rate policy for a limited period, according to the 1998 Bank of England Act.

The targeted measure of inflation is the increase of the CPI. It is a symmetrical target. An undershoot is judged to be as bad as an overshoot. If the target is missed by more than 1% – on the upside or the downside – the governor is obligated to write a letter to the Chancellor of the Exchequer explaining the reasons behind the miss of the target and the proposals of the Bank to return inflation to the target. The letters have been published an hour after the release of the inflation report.

Box 11.1   Letter to the Chancellor of the Exchequer

BANK OF ENGLAND
LONDON EC2R 8AH

13 February 2012

The Rt Hon George Osborne
Chancellor of the Exchequer
HM Treasury
1 Horse Guards Road
London
SW1A 2HQ

Dear Chancellor,

The Office for National Statistics (ONS) will publish data tomorrow showing that CPI inflation was 3.6% in January. In November I wrote an open letter to you because CPI inflation had remained more than one percentage point above the 2% target. As it is three months since I last wrote to you, and the rate of inflation is more than one percentage point above the target, I am writing a further open letter on behalf of the Monetary Policy Committee.

In accordance with our remit, this letter explains why inflation has moved away from the target, the period within which we expect inflation to return to the target, the policy action that the Committee is taking to deal with it, and how this approach meets the Government's monetary policy objectives. Following our usual procedure, the Bank of England will publish this open letter at 10.30 am tomorrow. The Committee's latest judgements on the outlook for output and inflation will be published in the February *Inflation Report* on Wednesday 15 February.

Why has inflation moved away from the target?

CPI inflation has been above the 2% target since the end of 2009, prompting a series of open letters. As described in those previous letters, and in the Bank's quarterly *Inflation Reports*, inflation was pushed up over that period by increases in VAT, import prices and energy prices that were largely unexpected. In contrast domestically generated inflation has been subdued.

The effect of the factors that temporarily pushed up inflation is now waning. CPI inflation peaked in September 2011 at 5.2% and has fallen back in each month since then, to 3.6% in January. As expected, the sharp decline in the latest CPI figure largely reflected the impact of the increase in VAT in January 2011 dropping out of the twelve-month comparison. Since September, the contributions of petrol and food prices have also fallen back. Nevertheless CPI inflation remains well above the 2% target.

Over what period does the MPC expect inflation to return to target?

The Committee's best collective judgement is that CPI inflation will continue to fall back to around the target by the end of 2012. In coming months, that further moderation is likely to reflect the declining contributions from petrol prices and any remaining VAT impact, together with recently announced cuts to domestic energy prices. The upward pressure from past rises in energy and import prices should dissipate further over 2012, and the margin of spare capacity that has built up in the economy is likely to continue to bear down on wages and prices beyond that.

But the pace and extent of the fall in inflation remain highly uncertain. Key factors include the degree to which slack in the labour market restrains wages, and the rate at which firms rebuild their profit margins. Any further external price shocks, precipitated for example by heightened tensions in oil exporting countries, could also have a material impact on the inflation outlook.

The MPC's February *Inflation Report* will set out the Committee's latest projections in more detail.

What policy action are we taking?

Monetary policy affects inflation only with a lag. The key consideration when setting monetary policy is, therefore, the medium-term outlook for inflation, and the balance of risks around it, rather than its current rate. With external price pressures diminishing, and the underlying weakness in domestically generated inflation likely to persist, the Committee's assessment of the inflation outlook at its February meeting was that, in the absence of further policy action, the balance of risks around the inflation target in the medium term lay to the downside. That is why we judged that it was appropriate to increase the size of the asset purchase programme, financed by the issuance of central bank reserves, by £50 billion to a total of £325 billion, while maintaining Bank Rate at 0.5%.

Although the Committee expects that programme of asset purchases to take three months to complete, we will re-evaluate the outlook for inflation and our policy stance every month. In the coming months, we will pay particular attention to prospects for the euro area and their implications for the banking system and credit conditions; the degree of spare capacity in the economy and its impact on domestically generated inflation; and measures of inflation expectations and their effect on pay and prices. The MPC stands ready to react as necessary to changes in the balance of risks to the inflation outlook.

(Continued)

> **How does this approach meet the Government's monetary policy objectives?**
>
> The unwelcome combination of sluggish growth and high inflation over the past two years is a reflection of the need for the economy to rebalance following the financial crisis and associated deep recession, together with rises in the costs of energy and imports. Although inflation is now falling broadly as expected, the process of rebalancing still has a long way to go. Growth remains weak and unemployment is high. While the MPC can use Bank Rate or asset purchases to help ease the transition, there is a limit to what monetary policy can achieve when real adjustments are required. The best contribution that monetary policy can make to high and stable levels of growth and employment is to respond flexibly and transparently to bring inflation back to target. The Committee remains determined to set policy to ensure that inflation is on track to meet the target in the medium term.
>
> I am copying this letter to the Chairman of the Treasury Committee, through which we are accountable to Parliament, and will place this letter on the Bank of England's website for public dissemination.
>
> *Source:* Bank of England. {http://www.bankofengland.co.uk/monetarypolicy/Documents/pdf/cpiletter120214.pdf}

Inflation has historically been higher in the U.K. than in the U.S. or Germany. The average rate of price increases from the end of 1960 to August 2012 was 5.6%. The figures for the latter countries were 4% and 2.8%, respectively.

Inflation was particularly high during the years that preceded the governments of Margaret Thatcher, especially during those of her predecessors from the Labour Party, James Callaghan and Harold Wilson. Inflation peaked at 26.9% in 1975. As part of her economic plan, she attempted to slay the inflationary dragon. During her first campaign as leader of the Conservative Party, Margaret Thatcher famously held two bags of groceries containing the amount one pound could buy in 1974 and the amount one pound could buy in 1979 to illustrate the erosion of purchasing power caused by inflation over the five-year period (Figure 11.1).

Interest-rate decisions are taken by the Monetary Policy Committee. The group's interest rate announcement is normally made on the first Thursday after the first Monday of the month. The meeting is followed by an announcement at noon. A statement is released if monetary policy has

FIGURE 11.1   Margaret Thatcher illustrates the effects of inflation.

Source: Mirrorpix. Reproduced by permission of Mirrorpix.

been changed. Otherwise, no explanation of the decision is disseminated. A press conference is held by the governor once a quarter when the Inflation Report is released.

The MPC consists of nine members. They are the governor, two deputy governors, the chief economist of the BoE, the executive director for markets and four external members. The latter are selected by the Chancellor of the Exchequer to enable the MPC to benefit from outside opinion.

A representative from the Treasury also joins the monthly meetings, though he or she is not permitted to vote. That person is present to brief the committee on fiscal policy developments and those related to the broad economic strategy of the government. He or she also keeps the Chancellor updated on monetary policy matters.

Each member of the MPC has one vote. The decisions are not based on a consensus of opinion. The governor's vote has the same weight as that of any other member of the MPC. Mervyn King has even been outvoted on several occasions.

This contrasts with the voting behavior at the Federal Reserve. Ben Bernanke and Alan Greenspan were never outvoted. Paul Volcker threatened to resign when he was outvoted once.[1]

---

[1] For a full description of Volcker's threat to resign, see: Greider, William *Secrets of the Temple*. New York, Simon & Schuster, 1987.

In his book, *A Term at the Fed*, Laurence Meyer, a former member of the Board of Governors of the Federal Reserve System, wrote:

> "Once the majority view (which, as I've already mentioned, is that of the Chairman) is apparent at FOMC meetings, the Committee is expected to rally around it. This means that most votes are unanimous – and when there are dissents, they are typically limited to one or two opposing votes. This is sometimes referred to as a system of 'collective responsibility' for decisions, in which the majority view is adopted and supported by the entire body.
>
> There are, nevertheless, occasional dissents. Indeed, while most votes are unanimous, one or two dissents are not unusual. A third, however, would be viewed as a sign that the FOMC is in open revolt with the Chairman's leadership . . .
>
> . . . I came to think of the voting process as a game of musical chairs. There were two imaginary red chairs around the table – the 'dissent chairs.' The first two FOMC members who sat in those chairs were able to dissent. After that, no one else could follow the same course."[2]

The personality of Mervyn King appears to have been as dominant as that of Alan Greenspan, even though public dissent has been more prevalent at the BoE than the Federal Reserve. David Blanchflower, a former member of the MPC, wrote a damning review of King's management style in the *New Statesman*:

> "It's never easy replacing a tyrant but there are huge benefits from doing so. The pain is usually worth it. A tyrant looks to his own advantage rather than that of his subjects and uses extreme and cruel tactics – which pretty much sums up how I feel Mervyn King has run the Bank of England in his role as governor since 2003. His second five-year term is up at the end of June 2013 and, at long last, a replacement is being sought. The Labour government reappointed him for a second term in 2008 and subsequently regretted it. Then there were no obvious candidates to replace him but there are now.
>
> The terms of both Charlie Bean, deputy governor for monetary policy, and Spencer Dale, chief economist, are coming to an end as well. They have been in charge of forecasting, which has been pretty hopeless these many years. It's time to start again on the forecasting front, so this is a great

---

[2]Meyer, Laurence H. *A Term at the Fed*. New York: Harper Collins, 2006.

opportunity to put them both out to pasture. A great opportunity, then, to clean the house and bring in new blood.

King has controlled the Bank with an iron fist, slaying any dissenters in his path. He follows in the tradition established by Montagu Norman, who was governor from 1920 to 1944: it's his way or the highway. I recall a meeting in which King told the Treasury representative to tell the then prime minister to shut up. I have never worked at a place that had such low morale. I clashed with King many times when I was a member of the Monetary Policy Committee (MPC) but I had an endowed professorship to go back to at Dartmouth College. Fortunately, my career didn't depend on him."[3]

The MPC meeting lasts for two days. The first day consists of an update on the latest economic data and items for discussion are determined. The second day consists of a summary of the first day and each member explains his or her view on how monetary policy should be set. The governor then puts to a vote a position he believes the majority will support and a vote is taken. The members who opposed the decision taken are asked the level at which they believe interest rates should be set, or, recently, the level of quantitative easing. That information is reported in the minutes of the meeting.[4]

The MPC normally also meets the Friday before the two-day session. The gathering is referred to as the pre-MPC meeting. The most recent economic data are presented to the committee along with an analysis of economic trends. The business agents of the BoE report on business conditions around the country after having met with managers of businesses to discuss economic developments and prospects.

The minutes are published on the Wednesday two weeks after the meeting. They summarize the views of each member rather than provide a verbatim account of the meeting.

The quarterly inflation report provides an in-depth analysis of the British economy. The report provides growth and inflation forecasts over a two-year horizon for two scenarios. That horizon has been chosen presumably because the BoE has stated that changes to its main policy rate can take up to two

---

[3]Blanchflower, David "Mervyn King is a Tyrant, But Who Will Succeed Him at the Bank?" *New Statesman*, April 18, 2012. Reproduced by permission of *New Statesman*. For a second assessment of Mervyn King by David Blanchflower, see: Blanchflower, David "King's Men Fiddle With U.K. Forecasts." Bloomberg News, July 13, 2010.

[4]*Monetary Policy Committee*. Bank of England. {http://www.bankofengland.co.uk/monetary policy/Pages/overview.aspx}

years to have their full impact on inflation.[5] The first is unchanged monetary policy and the second is based on the policy changes priced in the financial markets. The issuance of the report is followed by a press conference with the governor of the central bank and journalists. This is the BoE's equivalent of the ECB's monthly gathering.

King chose a different delivery style than Trichet. The former eschewed the code words used by the latter. In a May 2007 speech, the governor of the BoE said, "Explaining our analysis at some length is a richer source of information for markets than code words or statements about the future path of interest rates. Less weight should be placed on the short statements that are published with the announcements of our decisions because such statements, as we have seen elsewhere, run the risk of becoming monetary policy by code word."[6]

The forecasts are published as probability distributions as opposed to single point forecasts. The range of potential outcomes – also known as fan charts – is used to emphasize "the inevitable uncertainty around the outlook for the economy."[7] The fan charts are characterized by a central projection, which is the most likely path in the opinion of the BoE and is the mode of potential outcomes, a degree of uncertainty, which is expressed through the width of the probability distributions, and the skew, which represents the mean of the potential outcomes. The BoE releases the data used to compile the charts one week later.

The BoE, like the ECB, has standing facilities. Eligible financial institutions can borrow from the BoE using the "Operational Standing Lending Facility" and can deposit funds at the central bank using the "Operational Standing Deposit Facility." The interest rates on these facilities are normally 100 basis points above and below the official Bank Rate, respectively, throughout the month except on the last day of the monthly reserves maintenance period when the corridor is lowered to 25 basis points.

---

[5] *"Quantitative Easing Explained: Putting More Money Into Our Economy to Boost Spending."* Bank of England.

[6] King, Mervyn "The MPC Ten Years On." Speech to the Society of Business Economists, May 2, 2007. {http://www.bankofengland.co.uk/publications/Documents/speeches/2007/speech309.pdf}

[7] Elder, Rob, Kapetanios, George, Taylor, Tim and Yates, Tony "Assessing the MPC's Fan Charts." *Bank of England Quarterly Bulletin*, Autumn 2005.

The corridor changes when the official Bank Rate falls below 0.50%. The interest rate on the lending facility is set 25 basis points above the Bank Rate and that on the deposit facility has a lower bound of 0%.[8]

Quantitative Easing

The BoE announced the onset of quantitative easing in the U.K. in March 2009 with a size of 75 billion pounds. The size of the program was increased by 50 billion pounds in May 2009, by 50 billion pounds in August 2009, by 25 billion pounds in November 2009, by 75 billion pounds in October 2011, by 50 billion pounds in February 2012 and by 50 billion pounds in July 2012 (Table 11.1). That last addition increased the size of the QE program to 375 billion pounds, or about 24% of GDP.

The program lowered yields on U.K. government bonds and boosted real GDP and inflation. Long-term gilt yields fell by about 100 basis points in response to the first 200 billion pounds in QE from March 2009 to January 2010.[9] More specifically, the staff economists have calculated, using a simple regression model, that each additional 1 billion pounds in unanticipated QE purchases leads to a 0.62 basis point fall in gilt yields when announced.

QE has also had an effect on other asset prices. The asset purchase announcements in 2009 caused yields of investment-grade corporate bonds to fall by 70 basis points and those of sub-investment-grade bonds to decline

TABLE 11.1 U.K. Quantitative Easing Announcements

Date	Size	Cumulative
March-09	£75 Billion	£75 Billion
May-09	£50 Billion	£125 Billion
August-09	£50 Billion	£175 Billion
November-09	£25 Billion	£200 Billion
October-11	£75 Billion	£275 Billion
February-12	£50 Billion	£325 Billion
July-12	£50 Billion	£375 Billion

Source: Bloomberg

---

[8]*Bank of England Market Notice: Sterling Monetary Framework.* Bank of England, August 6, 2009.
[9]Joyce, Michael, Tong, Matthew and Woods, Robert "The United Kingdom's Quantitative Easing Policy: Design, Operation and Impact." *Quarterly Bulletin.* Bank of England, Third Quarter, 2011.

FIGURE 11.2 QE transmission channels.

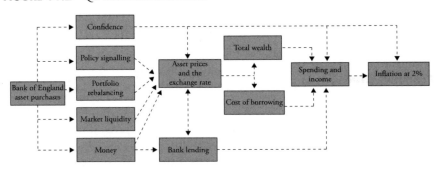

Source: Bank of England. {http://www.bankofengland.co.uk/publications/Documents/quarterlybulletin/qb1103.pdf}

by 150 basis points.[10] They also estimated a 20% rise of equity prices in response to the monetary stimulus. They calculated the combined effect of the boost to the prices of corporate and government bonds and equities to have been a 16% increase to households' net financial wealth in the U.K.

The goal of QE was to boost nominal spending in order to meet the central bank's inflation target. The monetary easing contributed to that goal by boosting asset prices, lowering the exchange rate and increasing bank lending, in theory (Figure 11.2).

Using "conservative average estimates" from three models, George Kapetanios, Haroon Mumtaz, Ibrahim Stevens and Konstantinos Theodoridis, economists from the central bank, concluded that the 200 billion pounds in QE undertaken in 2009 boosted the level of real GDP by around 1.5% and annual CPI inflation by about 1.25 percentage points.[11]

The first 200 billion pounds was equivalent to reducing the BoE's main policy rate by 150 to 300 basis points, according to the study by Joyce, Tong and Woods. They stated that the internal forecasting model suggests that a 100-basis-point rate reduction increases CPI inflation by about 0.5 of a percentage point after 18 to 24 months. They then calculated the rate reduction required to spur the change of inflation created by QE – an estimated 0.75 to 1.50 percentage points.

---

[10]*Ibid.*

[11]Kapetanios, George, Mumtaz, Haroon, Stevens, Ibrahim and Theodoridis, Konstantinos *Assessing the Economy-Wide Effects of Quantitative Easing.* Working Paper No. 443. Bank of England, January 2012.

FIGURE 11.3 Broad money and nominal GDP.

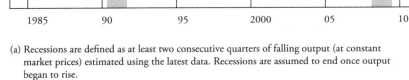

(a) Recessions are defined as at least two consecutive quarters of falling output (at constant market prices) estimated using the latest data. Recessions are assumed to end once output began to rise.
(b) The series is constructed using M4 growth prior to 1998 Q4, and growth in M4 excluding intermediate OFCs thereafter. For the definition of intermediate OFCs, see footnote (a) in Table 1.C.
(c) At current market prices. The latest observation is 2009 Q4.

Source: Bank of England. {http://www.bankofengland.co.uk/publications/Documents/inflationreport/ir10may.pdf}

The MPC monitors M4 money supply growth, excluding intermediate other financial corporations, to judge the efficacy of its QE policy. The policy makers view this measure of money supply as most closely related to nominal spending (Figure 11.3).[12]

GDP

The U.K. publishes three estimates of GDP. The first estimate is released three and a half weeks after the end of the quarter, making it the fastest produced

---

[12]Janssen, Norbert "Measures of M4 and M4 Lending Excluding Intermediate Other Financial Corporations." *Monetary & Financial Statistics*, Bank of England, May 2009.

GDP estimate of any major industrialized country.[13] The report consists only of a GDP measure based on output data because no expenditure or income data are available at the time.

The first estimate is based on data from about 40,000 businesses. The Office for National Statistics normally has returned forms from that number of respondents for each of the first two months of the quarter. Only about half of the 40,000 forms for the third month of the quarter have been published by the time the first quarter estimate is published. That encompasses about 44% of the data on economic output.[14] The remainder of the first estimate is based on output from forecasting models.

The second estimate is published about a month after the first estimate or seven and a half weeks after the end of the reporting period. It includes additional output data and expenditure and income data. The revisions reported with the second estimate only relate to the first estimate during the first three quarters of the year. Data for the four previous quarters may be revised when the report for the last quarter of the year is released. The second estimate is based on 83% of the data on economic output.

The third estimate is reported about three months after the end of the reporting period. It updates the output, expenditure and income data. Revisions reported with this release may relate to periods as far back as the first quarter of the previous calendar year. The third estimate is based on 92% of the data on economic output.

The ONS has found evidence that the first estimates understate growth, though the downward bias has diminished in recent years. The statisticians found that:

1. Revisions have most often been upward.
2. The sizes of revisions have decreased since the mid-1990s.
3. Since that period, revisions that materialized during the 24 months after the end of the reporting period, when most of the non-methodological changes will have been accounted for, have averaged only 0.05 of a percentage point.

---

[13] Brown, Gary, Buccellato, Tullio, Chamberlin, Graeme, Dey-Chowdhury, Sumit and Youll, Robin *Understanding the Quality of Early Estimates of Gross Domestic Product*. Office for National Statistics.

[14] *Information Paper: Quality and Methodology Information*. Office for National Statistics, August 17, 2012.

The study concluded: "Although there is some evidence of historical upward bias in revisions, its extent and direction have not been stable or predictable. Further, any such bias appears to have been smaller since the mid-1990s, and insignificantly different from zero. Overall, revisions are not sufficiently large, regular or predictable to be able to support any procedure of incorporating bias adjustments into early estimates."[15]

Inflation Measures

The CPI is the most important measure of inflation in the U.K. It is the index used for the Bank of England's inflation target. It has also been used since April 2011 for the indexation of benefits, tax credits and public service pensions.[16] Its calculation is harmonized, according to Eurostat rules, with the CPI measures across the EU in order to compare apples with apples. The only time CPI data have been revised was when the index was rebased at the start of 2006.

The retail price index is also a widely watched measure of inflation in the U.K. It is the most long-standing measure of inflation in the country and is still used for other purposes such as the inflation index for inflation-protected government bonds. RPI data are never revised. The two most significant differences between CPI and RPI relate to the population base and the items selected to have their prices measured.

The population base for the two prices indices is different. CPI covers private and institutional households and foreign visitors to the country. The RPI excludes institutional households, foreign visitors, the highest income households and pensioner households that are mainly dependent on state benefits.[17]

The items in the price basket of goods and services also differ. The most significant difference is the exclusion from CPI of mortgage interest payments, house depreciation (a measure of maintenance costs for a home) and council tax.

The RPI has core measures as well. The ONS publishes RPIX, which is the RPI excluding mortgage interest payments, and RPIY, which is the RPI excluding mortgage interest payments and indirect taxes.

---

[15]Brown, Buccellato, Chamberlin, Dey-Chowdhury and Youll. Source: Office for National Statistics licensed under the Open Government Licence v.1.0.
[16]"Consumer Price Indices, July 2012." *Statistical Bulletin*. Office for National Statistics, August 14, 2012.
[17]*Ibid.*

The Bank of England used RPIX as the reference for its inflation target from 1992 to 2003. The policy makers chose a measure that excluded mortgage interest payments because those costs normally rise if interest rates go up. If the central bank had targeted the headline figure, an interest rate increase to curb inflation would actually cause inflation, as measured by the RPI, to increase.

Wage growth is another important measure of domestically-generated inflation for the BoE. The MPC has historically viewed earnings growth of 4.5% year over year as consistent with its inflation target, though Mervyn King has stated, "but this does not imply that there is some magical threshold defining 'acceptable' and 'unacceptable' rates of earnings growth."[18]

The rationale for the figure is related to the inflation target and productivity growth. In a 1998 speech, King explained that 2% is linked to the historical levels of annual productivity growth and 2.5% is linked to the annual inflation target, which was 2.5% for the RPIX at that time. The rate of wage growth compatible with the BoE's new inflation target – 2% for the CPI – was presumably the same because the reduction to 2% from 2.5% was only due to differences in the way the two indices measured inflation and not an attempt to lower the rate of annual price increases.

The ONS publishes data on wage growth about six weeks after the end of the reporting period. The statistical agency reports the headline figures as the year-over-year rate of growth of a three-month average of total pay (including bonuses) and the same reading on regular pay (excluding bonuses). The reading that excludes bonuses may provide the clearest reading of inflationary pressures by excluding one-off payments.

House Prices

Measures of house prices tend to be watched in the U.K. more than in continental Europe. That may be because policy makers at the central bank have watched them closely when setting monetary policy throughout the boom and bust cycles that have characterized the British housing market.

The four longest-established house price indices are published by the Land Registry, the Office for National Statistics (when its predecessor from the Office of the Deputy Prime Minister is included), Halifax and Nationwide, according to a study by Gregory Thwaites and Rob Wood of the Bank of

---

[18]King, 1998.

England.[19] The former two indices are figures compiled by the government and the latter two by private lenders.

The measurement of house prices is more difficult than that of consumer goods. The study by Thwaites and Wood signaled three of the features of houses that make their prices difficult to measure on a nationwide basis. They are:

1. Houses are all different. They have different locations, sizes, neighborhoods, etc.
2. Sale prices may be different from asking prices. By contrast, consumer goods usually sell at advertised prices.
3. Houses are normally sold infrequently. Only 7% of the nation's housing stock was sold per year during the 1990s, according to the study's authors.

The major indices each have their own strengths and weaknesses. The measure published by the Land Registry is based on 100% of sales registered in England and Wales and is therefore free of sampling errors, though it is published around two months after the month of the reporting period. The ONS measure covers a large sample as well, though it has a long publishing lag.

The measures compiled by private lenders are published with lags less than those of the official measures, though the sample sizes are smaller. The market share of Halifax/Lloyds Banking Group is 19.9% of gross mortgage lending in the U.K., according to the Council of Mortgage Lenders (Table 11.2).[20] The equivalent figure for Nationwide is 12.1%.

The Rightmove index is comprehensive and timely. According to Rightmove, 90% of all homes sold in the U.K. are posted on the website, and it is released around two to three weeks into the reporting period. The downside of the measure is that it is based on asking prices, which may be significantly different from selling prices (Figure 11.4). Buyers frequently negotiate a lower price than the seller's demand.

The earlier in the sales process the price is recorded, the less accurate the house price index may be. Rightmove records the asking prices. Halifax, Nationwide and Hometrack record the prices at the stage of mortgage approval. The ONS records the price when the transaction is completed and the Land Registry when the transaction is registered.

---

[19] Thwaites, Gregory and Wood, Rob "The Measurement of House Prices." *Quarterly Bulletin.* Bank of England, Spring 2003.

[20] For the full report, see: {www.cml.org.uk/cml/publications/newsandviews/118/441}

TABLE 11.2 Largest Mortgage Lending by Gross Lending

Gross mortgage lending in year

			2011		2010	
Rank 2011	Rank (2010)	Name of group	£bn	Estimated market share	£bn	Estimated market share
1	(1)	Lloyds Banking Group	28.0	19.9%	30.0	22.2%
2	(2)	Santander	23.7	16.8%	24.2	17.9%
3	(3)	Barclays	17.1	12.1%	16.9	12.5%
3	(5)	Nationwide BS	17.1	12.1%	12.2	9.0%
5	(4)	The Royal Bank of Scotland	14.6	10.4%	16.2	12.0%
6	(6)	HSBC Bank	13.3	9.4%	11.3	8.3%
7	(7)	Northern Rock plc	4.9	3.5%	4.2	3.1%
8	(10)	Yorkshire BS	4.1	2.9%	2.8	2.1%
9	(8)	Coventry BS	4.0	2.8%	3.5	2.6%
10	(13)	ING Direct	3.0	2.1%	1.1	0.8%
11	(11)	Clydesdale Bank	2.7	1.9%	1.7	1.3%
12	(9)	Co-operative Financial Services	1.6	1.1%	3.3	2.4%
13	(16)	Skipton BS	1.5	1.1%	0.4	0.3%
14	(14)	Leeds BS	1.2	0.9%	1.0	0.7%
15	(15)	Principality BS	0.8	0.6%	0.8	0.6%
15	(12)	Bank of Ireland	0.8	0.6%	1.2	0.9%
17	(24)	UBS	0.4	0.3%	0.1	0.1%
17	(16)	Nottingham BS	0.4	0.3%	0.4	0.3%
17	(24)	Aldermore Mortgages	0.4	0.3%	0.1	0.1%
20	(16)	Aviva Equity Release	0.3	0.2%	0.4	0.3%

Notes:

1. Most figures are shown on a calendar year basis. Where we are not able to obtain calendar year figures we have used published results for the organization's financial year which ended in the same year.
2. All figures relate to calendar year except: Clydesdale Bank & Paragon Sep 11.
3. Where possible, gross lending figures are shown net of portfolios purchased.
4. Figures are rounded to the nearest £100 million and ranked on the same basis.
5. Wherever possible, figures are shown on a financial services group basis.
   Figures for previous years have been adjusted to account for any mergers and acquisitions occurring in the latest year.
6. Figures for lenders outside CML membership are taken from published accounts, and may not be on a basis that is fully comparable with those from CML members.
7. The table is truncated at the point below which, due to significant clustering, rankings are not robust or meaningful. In 2011 over 20 lenders not shown in this table had gross lending of £100 million or £200 million on a rounded basis.

Source: CML Research. Reproduced by permission of the Council for Mortgage Lenders.

FIGURE 11.4 House purchase timeline and house price indices.

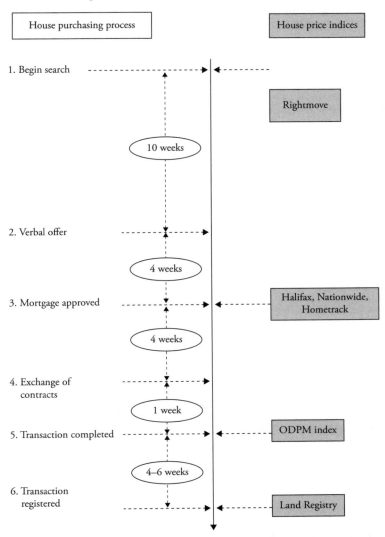

Source: Bank of England. {http://www.bankofengland.co.uk/publications/Documents/quarterlybulletin/qb0301.pdf}

Several of the indices lack seasonal adjustments. That makes month-over-month comparisons difficult because prices typically rise in the spring and fall in the winter along with seasonal demand for housing. The indices published by Hometrack, the Land Registry, the Office for National Statistics and Rightmove are not seasonally adjusted.

> **Box 11.2 U.K. house price indices**
>
> **Halifax**
>
> Sample: Loans approved for house purchase
> Seasonally adjusted: Yes
> Weights used: 1983 Halifax loan approvals
> Publication date: Around the fifth day of the month following the reporting period
>
> **Hometrack**
>
> Sample: Survey of approximately 4000 estate agents' estimates of local average prices
> Seasonally adjusted: No
> Weights used: England and Wales housing stock
> Publication date: Around the first day of the month following the reporting period
>
> **Land Registry**
>
> Sample: 100% of sales registered in England and Wales
> Seasonally adjusted: No
> Weights used: None
> Publication date: Around two months after the month of the reporting period
>
> **Nationwide**
>
> Sample: Loans approved for house purchase
> Seasonally adjusted: Yes
> Weights used: Rolling average of Survey of Mortgage Lenders, Land Registry and Nationwide transactions
> Publication date: Around the first day of the month following the reporting period
>
> **Office for National Statistics**
>
> Sample: Council of Mortgage Lenders' eligible completions; the sample included 65–70% of all U.K. mortgage completions in 2011
> Seasonally adjusted: No
> Weights used: Rolling average of U.K. transactions
> Publication date: Around six weeks after the month of the reporting period

> **Rightmove**
>
> Sample: Sellers' asking prices posted on website
> Seasonally adjusted: No
> Weights used: England and Wales housing stock
> Publication date: Around two to three weeks into the reporting period
>
> *Source:* Bank of England, Bloomberg, Hometrack, the Land Registry, Office for National Statistics

The Royal Institution of Chartered Surveyors also provides a monthly report on the U.K. housing market, though it is a sentiment survey as opposed to an index of house prices. The headline reading relates to the change in house prices in England and Wales over the previous months. The 11 questions of the survey are:[21]

1. How have house prices changed over the last three months? (up/same/down)
2. Over the last month how have the number of new enquiries regarding property purchases changed? (up/same/down)
3. Over the last month how has the number of new instructions changed? (up/same/down)
4. Over the last month how did the number of agreed sales change? (up/same/down)
5. Over the next three months how do you expect house price levels to change? (up/same/down)
6. Over the next twelve months how do you expect house price levels to change? (up/same/down)
7. Over the next three months how do you expect the number of agreed sales to change? (up/same/down)
8. Over the next twelve months how do you expect the number of agreed sales to change? (up/same/down)
9. How many dwellings have been sold during the last three months, i.e. where contracts have been exchanged? (Number)
10. How many dwellings are there currently for sale, i.e. where contracts have not been exchanged? (Number)
11. How many branches do these relate to? (Number)

---

[21] *RICS UK Housing Market Survey, August 2012.* Royal Institution of Chartered Surveyors, September 11, 2012. Reproduced by permission of the RICS.

Political Institutions

The U.K. is a parliamentary democracy. The parliament has a lower house – the House of Commons – and an upper house – the House of Lords. The role of the monarchy is largely ceremonial.

The House of Commons is the elected chamber. Members of parliament consider and propose new laws. The political party with the greatest number of seats in the House of Commons forms a government. The head of that party becomes the prime minister.

The House of Lords is unelected. It has about 700 members who are appointed for life, 26 members who are archbishops or bishops from the Church of England and 92 hereditary members. Its members "share the task of making and shaping laws and checking and challenging the work of the government."[22]

The U.K. has two main political parties and one additional mainstream party. The former two are the Conservative Party and the Labour Party. The third party is the Liberal Democratic Party.

The Conservative Party stands on the right wing of the political spectrum, though its policies are probably more closely aligned with those of the Democratic Party than the Republican Party in the U.S. It is the oldest political party in the world.[23] The party, under the leadership of Margaret Thatcher, drove the country's period of deregulation and privatization.

The Labour Party stands on the left wing of the political spectrum. The group presided over much of the economic chaos of the 1970s. The party's website states, "Callaghan presided over one of the most difficult periods of Government for Labour, with rampant inflation, crippling industrial action led by increasingly militant trade unions, and culminating in the disastrous 'winter of discontent' of 1978–9, when rubbish went uncollected and dead bodies unburied."[24] Tony Blair reinvented the party under the label of "New Labour" in the 1990s and the 2000s.

The Liberal Democratic Party is a centrist party. Its head, Nick Clegg, has said, "We are not on the left and we are not on the right. We have our

---

[22] *What the Lords Does.* UK Parliament. {http://www.parliament.uk/business/lords/work-of-the-house-of-lords/what-the-lords-does/}

[23] *The History of the Conservative Party.* The Conservative Party. {http://www.conservatives.com/People/The_History_of_the_Conservatives.aspx}

[24] *History of the Labour Party.* The Labour Party. {http://www.labour.org.uk/history_of_the_labour_party2}

own label: Liberal."[25] The group was born from a merger of the Liberal Party and the Social Democratic Party in 1988. The newly formed party entered into government for the first time in 2010 as part of a coalition led by the Conservative Party.

A general election in the U.K. will be held every five years since the passing of the Fixed-Term Parliament Act in 2011. It will take place on the first Thursday of May.

A general election can be called under two circumstances at a different time. The first is if a motion of no confidence is passed by simple majority and 14 days elapse without a new government having been formed. The second is if two-thirds of the total number of seats in the House of Commons (including those that are vacant) agree to a general election. Previously, a Parliament was able to sit for a maximum of five years with the prime minister choosing the date of the general election within that period.

---

[25]Clegg, Nick Speech to the Liberal Democrat Spring Conference, March 13, 2011.

CHAPTER 12

Switzerland

The Swiss National Bank

The Swiss National Bank is the central bank of Switzerland. It was established in 1907 and has a head office in Berne and one in Zurich. Its primary task, like many of its international counterparts, is price stability. The SNB defines that concept as "a rise in the national consumer prices index of less than 2 percent per year."[1]

The SNB announces its interest rate decisions four times a year – in March, June, September and December. This quarterly schedule differs from the monthly schedule of the BoE and the ECB.

The SNB has several key elements to its monetary policy strategy. They are:

1. A definition of price stability.
2. Inflation forecasts for a three-year horizon.
3. A target range for its main policy rate.
4. A minimum exchange rate for the euro versus the Swiss franc since September 2011.

The inflation forecasts assume that the main policy rate will be unchanged over a three-year horizon. The SNB considers this horizon to correspond roughly with the period of time needed for monetary policy changes to affect output and prices. This differs from the two-year horizon normally referenced by the BoE and the ECB. The inflation forecasts are published each quarter in the press statement released after the quarterly meetings. The SNB also holds

---

[1] *The Swiss National Bank in Brief*, seventh edition. Swiss National Bank, June 2012.

a press conference in June and December. The central bank reserves the right to change monetary policy in between meetings if necessary.

The SNB's main policy rate is the three-month Swiss franc Libor published by the British Bankers Association. The announced target normally has a range of 100 basis points and the central bank attempts to keep that interest rate in the middle of the range. The range of the target has been reduced to 25 basis points – from 0% to 0.25% – since August 2011. The SNB influences the level of that rate by absorbing money or providing money to the market through its open market operations.

The Governing Board of the SNB is responsible for monetary policy decisions. It consists of three members who are appointed for six-year terms by the Federal Council – a body of the country's federal government – based on the recommendations of the Bank Council – a body that oversees the central bank.

The SNB also has three alternate board members. The central bank reports that the "Board of Deputies is responsible for planning and implementing the strategic guidelines on the SNB's conduct of business. It is also responsible for the SNB's ongoing operations and ensures coordination in all operational matters that are of inter-departmental significance."[2]

The SNB is partially privately owned, unlike the other major central banks of Europe. Forty-five percent of the shares are held by private persons. Fifty-five percent are held by public shareholders such as cantons and cantonal banks. The Confederation of Switzerland has no shares.[3]

KOF Leading Indicator

One of the most widely watched economic indicators for Switzerland is the KOF Economic Barometer. It is published by the KOF Swiss Economic Institute on a monthly basis during the last week of the reporting period. KOF, or *Konjunkturforschungsstelle*, means economic research institute in German. The indicator has the highest correlation with a lead over GDP of one to two quarters (Figure 12.1).[4]

---

[2] *Ibid.*
[3] *The National Bank as a Joint-Stock Company*. Swiss National Bank. {http://www.snb.ch/en/system/print/en/iabout/snb/org/id/snb_org_stock}
[4] "*KOF Economic Barometer*" KOF Swiss Economic Institute. {http://www.kof.ethz.ch/en/indicators/economic-barometer/}

FIGURE 12.1 KOF leading economic indicator and Swiss GDP.

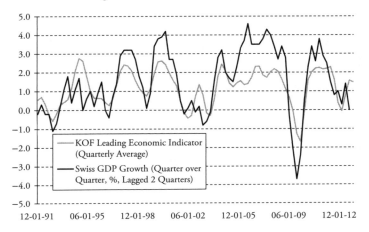

Source: Bloomberg

The index is derived from the aggregation of data from three "module indicators." They are a banking module, a construction module and a core GDP module. The banking and construction industries are separated from the rest of the economy because of their cyclical nature. The core GDP figure is based on the output of three models, which focus on Swiss industry, Swiss consumption and exports to the EU. The three "module indicators" are weighed using the value added ratios from the national accounting procedures to create a headline number. It is seasonally adjusted.

Twenty-five indicators are used to calculate the headline figure. Ten are published monthly and 15 appear on a quarterly basis. With the figures in parentheses indicating the number of indicators taken from the source and their frequencies, they are:[5]

Banking Module
- KOF banking surveys (6 Q)
- Banking statistics, SNB (3 M)
- Employment statistics, Federal Statistical Office (1 Q)

---

[5] *"The KOF Economic Barometer: Design and Structure of the KOF Economic Barometer"* KOF Swiss Economic Institute. {http://www.kof.ethz.ch/static_media/filer_public/2012/09/16/konjunkturbarometer_methodik_en_1.pdf}

Construction Module
- KOF construction survey (3 Q)
- KOF planning sector survey (1 Q)
- Building permits for subscribers to the *Baublatt* journal, computation KOF (1 M)

Core GDP Module: Measurement Model Swiss Industry
- KOF industry survey (3 M)

Core GDP Module: Measurement Model Swiss Consumption
- KOF retail trade survey (1 M)
- KOF hotel and restaurant trade survey (1 Q)
- Consumer survey, Federal Department of Economic Affairs (1 Q)
- Advertising statistics, media focus (1 M)

Core GDP Model: Measurement Model Export Destination EU
- Industry survey, European Commission (1 M, 2 Q)

CHAPTER 13

Sweden

The Riksbank is the world's oldest central bank. It is independent with an explicit inflation target. The target currently stands at 2%. The central bank lacks an explicit time horizon for a return of inflation to its target when deviations occur, though it normally aims for a return in two years.[1] The headline CPI reading is the inflation measure for the official target.

The Riksbank paid special attention to CPIX prior to 2008, though that measure's special status has been revoked. CPIX excludes households' mortgage interest expenditure and the direct effects of changes in indirect taxes and subsidies.

In June 2008, Riksbank Deputy Governor Barbro Wickman-Parak announced: "Our target variable is the CPI. We want to be clear about this. Our strategy and inflation target stand firm. Over the years, another measure of inflation, the CPIX, has played a prominent role alongside the CPI. The Riksbank has previously assumed that the CPI and the CPIX will converge in the long term. We no longer believe that this will be the case. The CPIX will be phased out, but this will not have a tangible effect on future interest rate decisions."[2]

Statistics Sweden publishes another reading of underlying inflation – CPIF – on behalf of the Riksbank. The CPIF is the CPI with a fixed interest rate. That measure – like the RPIX in the U.K. – has avoided reporting a rise in inflation as the central bank raises its policy rate to combat a rise in inflation.

---

[1] "*Forecasts and Interest Rate Decisions.*" {http://www.riksbank.se/en/Monetary-policy/Forecasts-and-interest-rate-decisions/}

[2] *Press Release: The Riksbank to Phase Out the CPIX Inflation Measure.* Sveriges Riksbank, June 9, 2008.

The central bank uses its repo rate – the rate for banks that borrow money from the Riksbank for a period of seven days – as its main policy rate. The Riksbank also has standing facilities. The deposit rate is the yield on overnight deposits with the central bank. It is normally 75 basis points below the repo rate. The lending rate is the price for overnight borrowing from the central bank. It is normally 75 basis points above the repo rate. Borrowing from the central bank does not convey a negative signal about the financial condition of a bank, in contrast to borrowing from the Federal Reserve in the U.S.[3]

Monetary policy is decided by an executive board. It consists of six members. One of them is the governor of the Riksbank, who has the casting vote. The Executive Board is appointed by the General Council of the Riksbank, which is appointed by the Riksdag, the Swedish parliament.

The Executive Board meets six times a year. It votes on the level of the repo rate and on forecasts for the repo rate for the following three years at each meeting. It releases a press statement the day after each meeting. The press statement contains the central bank's forecasts for inflation, GDP growth, unemployment and the repo rate (Table 13.1). A press conference with the

TABLE 13.1 Forecasts from the Riksbank

Forecasts for inflation in Sweden, GDP and the repo rate

Annual percentage change, annual average

	2011	2012	2013	2014
CPI	3.0 (3.0)	1.2 (1.1)	1.3 (1.7)	2.6 (2.8)
CPIF	1.4 (1.4)	1.1 (1.0)	1.6 (1.7)	2.0 (2.1)
GDP	3.9 (3.9)	1.5 (0.6)	1.9 (1.7)	2.8 (2.8)
Unemployment, 15–74 years, per cent	7.5 (7.5)	7.6 (7.6)	7.6 (7.7)	6.9 (7.0)
Repo rate, per cent	1.8 (1.8)	1.5 (1.5)	1.4 (1.6)	2.0 (2.3)

Note: The assessment in the July 2012 Monetary Policy Report is shown in brackets.
Sources: Statistics Sweden and the Riksbank.

Forecast for the repo rate

per cent, quarterly averages

	2012 Q2	2012 Q3	2012 Q4	2013 Q3	2014 Q3	2015 Q3
Repo rate	1.5	1.5 (1.5)	1.3 (1.4)	1.4 (1.6)	2.2 (2.4)	2.9 (3.1)

Note: The assessment in the July 2012 Monetary Policy Report is shown in brackets.
Source: The Riksbank.

---

[3]Mitlid, Kerstin and Vesterlund, Magnus "Steering Interest Rates in Monetary Policy – How Does it Work?" *Economic Review.* Sveriges Riksbank, 2001.

governor, at which journalists can ask questions, is held after the publication of the press statement.

A monetary policy report is published in conjunction with the monetary policy decisions three times a year. The report contains the central bank's economic forecasts. An update to the monetary policy report is published the other three times a year with some economic forecasts as well.

The Riksbank also publishes the minutes of its meetings with a delay of about two weeks. These minutes tend to read more like a verbatim account of the discussions than those of the BoE.

The Riksbank attracted attention during the financial crisis when it reduced its overnight deposit rate to −0.25%, though the move was nearly meaningless in reality. According to the central bank's minutes, at the September 2009 meeting, First Deputy Governor Svante Öberg stated: "Although the Riksbank formally has a deposit rate of minus 0.25 per cent, this is of marginal significance. Approximately SEK 100 billion of the bank's total deposits of around SEK 300 billion are deposited overnight at 0.15 per cent interest, and approximately SEK 200 billion are deposited in a one week Riksbank Certificate at an interest rate of 0.25 per cent. Only a very small percentage is deposited at the advertised deposit rate."[4]

---

[4]*Minutes of the Executive Board's Monetary Policy Meeting, No. 4*. Sveriges Riksbank, September 16, 2009.

CHAPTER 14

Norway

The Norges Bank has an explicit inflation target. It stands at 2.5% and refers to headline consumer price inflation. The central bank also lacks an explicit time horizon for a return of inflation to its target when deviations occur. It will "depend on disturbances to which the economy is exposed and the effects on prospects for the path for inflation and the real economy."[1]

The central bank tends to focus on core readings of inflation in practice. It states, "the direct effects on consumer prices resulting from changes in interest rates, taxes, excise duties and extraordinary temporary disturbances are not taken into account."[2]

Statistics Norway publishes measures of underlying inflation, which assist with the implementation of monetary policy. CPI-ATE is a measure of CPI adjusted for tax changes and excluding energy products. The central bank has stated that this measure underestimates the overall inflation rate because it excludes the trend change in energy prices.[3] As a result, the Norges Bank has created an index called CPIXE, which is CPI adjusted for tax changes and excluding temporary fluctuations in energy prices. It is released on the same day as Statistics Norway publishes its monthly inflation report.

The Norges Bank has less independence than many other modern central banks. It must submit matters of "special importance" to the Ministry of Finance before taking a decision, according to the Norges Bank Act of 1985,

---

[1] *Monetary Policy Report*. Norges Bank, October 2012.
[2] *Ibid.*
[3] Nordbo, Einar W. *Staff Memo: CPIXE and Projections for Energy Prices*. No. 7. Norges Bank, 2008.

though that term was left undefined.[4] The central bank has, in recent years, refrained from considering small interest rate changes as matters of "special importance," though significant changes in monetary policy, such as those seen during the financial crisis, must be submitted to the Ministry of Finance.

Monetary policy is decided by an executive board. It is headed by the governor and the deputy governor and consists of seven members who are all appointed by the government. The governor and the deputy governor are appointed for six-year terms, which can be renewed once. The other members are appointed for four-year terms, which can be renewed until a period of service reaches 12 years.

The Executive Board meets every six weeks to take a decision on monetary policy. The decision is announced at 2:00 p.m. (1:00 p.m. London time) on the day of the meeting and a press statement is released simultaneously. A press conference with the governor or deputy governor is held at the same time.

The Norges Bank's key policy rate is the sight deposit rate. It is part of a standing facility and is the interest rate paid to banks on their deposits up to a quota with the central bank. The level of deposits that exceeds the quota is remunerated at 100 basis points below the sight deposit rate. The central bank also operates a lending deposit facility with a rate 100 basis points above the main policy rate. The central bank refrains from conducting regular market operations.

A monetary policy report is published three times a year. Normally it is released in March, June and October/November. It contains an in-depth assessment of the Norwegian economy. The Norges Bank refrains from publishing minutes of its meetings.

The Norges Bank tends to focus on the mainland economy when assessing economic conditions. This excludes the exploration of crude oil and natural gas, services activities incidental to oil and gas, transport via pipelines and ocean transport.[5]

The central bank and the government focus on the mainland economy because it represents the long-term income-generating capacity of the nation. The OECD has underlined that overall GDP overstates the sustainable income potential of the country, though mainland GDP slightly understates

---

[4]Gjedrem, Svein "Making Use of the Central Bank." Speech at the Norges Bank Symposium "What is a Useful Central Bank?", November 17, 2010.

[5]*Concepts and Definitions in National Accounts.* Statistics Norway, 2012. {http://www.ssb.no/english/subjects/09/01/terms/}

FIGURE 14.1 Market value of the government pension fund.

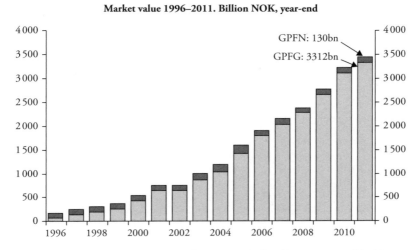

Source: Norges Bank and Norwegian Ministry of Finance. Reproduced by permission of the Norwegian Ministry of Finance.

it because returns on financial assets from the nation's sovereign wealth fund are not included in that measure.[6]

The Norges Bank also manages the Government Pension Fund. It is among the world's largest sovereign wealth funds. The fund's value was 3.4 trillion Norwegian kroner at the end of 2011 (Figure 14.1).[7] That was about $569 billion.

The fund holds mostly foreign assets to avoid putting upward pressure on the Norwegian currency and the advent of "Dutch disease." This term refers to a situation in which the manufacturing sector of a country suffers from a lack of competitiveness as a result of currency appreciation brought on by the sale of natural resources to trading partners.

---

[6] *Economic Policy Reforms 2011: Going For Growth.* Organization for Economic Cooperation and Development, 2011.
[7] *Market Value of the Government Pension Fund.* Norwegian Ministry of Finance. {http://www.regjeringen.no/en/dep/fin/Selected-topics/the-government-pension-fund/market-value-of-the-government-pension-f.html?id=699635}

Bibliography

Abberger, Klaus and Nierhaus, Wolfgang *The Ifo Business Cycle Clock: Circular Correlation with the Real GDP*. CESIfo Working Paper No. 3179, Ifo Institute, 2010.

Allard, Céline, Catalan, Mario, Everaert, Luc and Sgherri, Silvia *Explaining Differences in External Sector Performance Among Large Euro Area Countries*. International Monetary Fund, October 12, 2005.

Angeloni, Ignazio, Gaspar, Vitor, Issing, Otmar and Tristani, Oreste *Monetary Policy in the Euro Area: Strategy and Decision-Making at the European Central Bank*. Cambridge: Cambridge University Press, 2001.

Antonucci, Daniele, Baker, Melanie, Bartsch, Elga and Sleeman, Cath *European Economics: A Practitioner's Guide to European Macro Indicators*. Morgan Stanley, June 4, 2010.

Apel, Emmanuel *Central Banking Systems Compared: The ECB, the Pre-Euro Bundesbank, and the Federal Reserve System*. London: Routledge, 2003.

Ardagna, Silvia *Debt Sustainability: A Tool for Our Clients*. Bank of America–Merrill Lynch, December 8, 2010.

Ashley, James and Hayes, Simon "Clearing the Fog: How Useful Are Short-Term Economic Indicators?" *World Economics,* Volume 11, No. 2, April–June 2010.

Assemblée Nationale *General Framework*. {http://www.assemblee-nationale.fr/english/framework.asp}

Assemblée Nationale *The National Assembly and the Senate – General Characteristics of the Parliament*. {http://www.assemblee-nationale.fr/english/synthetic_files/file-04.asp}

Assemblée Nationale *The President of the Republic*. {http://www.assemblee-nationale.fr/english/synthetic_files/file-02.asp}

Athanassiou, Phoebus *Withdrawal and Expulsion from the EU and EMU: Some Reflections*. Legal Working Paper Series, No. 10. Frankfurt: European Central Bank, December 2009.

Atkins, Ralph "Hawkish ECB Treads Fine Line on Growth." *Financial Times*, January 27, 2011.

Auerbach, Alan J. and Kotlikoff, Laurence J. *Macroeconomics: An Integrated Approach*, second edition. Cambridge, Mass.: The MIT Press, 1998.

Bank of America–Merrill Lynch *Global Economic Weekly: Europe Sneezes, The US Catches a Cold,* August 6, 2010.

Bank of America–Merrill Lynch *Morning Market Tidbits: PMIs Not Good Predictors of GDP*. May 8, 2012.
Bank of England {http://www.bankofengland.co.uk}
Bank of England *Monetary Policy Committee*. {http://www.bankofengland.co.uk/monetarypolicy/Pages/overview.aspx}
Bank of England "*Quantitative Easing Explained: Putting More Money into Our Economy to Boost Spending.*"
Bank of England, *The Framework for the Bank of England's Operations in the Sterling Money Markets*. November 2006.
Bank of England *Bank of England Market Notice: Sterling Monetary Framework*. August 6, 2009.
Bank of England *Inflation Report*, May 2010. {http://www.bankofengland.co.uk/publications/Documents/inflationreport/ir10may.pdf}
Bank of England *Bank of England and The Times Interest Rate Challenge: Target Two Point Zero*. 2012.
Bank of Japan *Outline of International Finance*. {http://www.boj.or.jp/en/intl_finance/outline/index.htm/}
Basic Law for the Federal Republic of Germany (Grundgesetz). Translated into English by Inter Nationes. {http://www.iuscomp.org/gla/statutes/GG.htm#39}
The Basics. Bbalibor. {http://www.bbalibor.com/bbalibor-explained/the-basics}
Bayoumi, Tamim, Harmsen, Richard and Turunen, Jarkko *Euro Area Export Performance and Competitiveness*. International Monetary Fund, June 2011.
BBC *Profile: Gerhard Schroeder*. BBC News, September 9, 2005. {http://news.bbc.co.uk/2/hi/europe/2242899.stm}
BBC *Q&A: Quantitative Easing*. BBC News, July 5, 2012.
Belke, Ansgar and Polleit, Thorsten *Monetary Economics in Globalised Financial Markets*. Heidelberg: Springer, 2009.
Benolkin, Scott and Kahn, George A. "The Role of Money in Monetary Policy: Why Do the Fed and ECB See It So Differently?" *Economic Review,* Third Quarter 2007. Federal Reserve Bank of Kansas City, 2007.
Bernanke, Ben S. "Monetary Aggregates and Monetary Policy at the Federal Reserve: A Historical Perspective." Speech at the Fourth ECB Central Banking Conference, Frankfurt, Germany. Board of Governors of the Federal Reserve System, November 10, 2006.
Bernanke, Ben S. "Globalization and Monetary Policy." Speech to the Stanford Institute for Economic Policy Research. Board of Governors of the Federal Reserve System, March 2, 2007.
Bernanke, Ben S. "Outstanding Issues in the Analysis of Inflation." Speech at the Federal Reserve Bank of Boston's 53rd Annual Economic Conference, Chatham, Massachusetts. Board of Governors of the Federal Reserve System, June 9, 2008.
Black, Jeff "Draghi's Go-to ECB Seen Risking Credibility Through Overload." Bloomberg News, December 7, 2012.

Black, Jeff and Randow, Jana "Majority of ECB Governing Council Said to Support Rate Cut." Bloomberg News, December 7, 2012.
Blanchflower, David "King's Men Fiddle with U.K. Forecasts." Bloomberg News, July 13, 2010.
Blanchflower, David "Trichet's Inflation Ogre is Pure Fiction." Bloomberg News, September 13, 2010.
Blanchflower, David "Mervyn King is a Tyrant, But Who Will Succeed Him at the Bank?" *New Statesman,* April 18, 2012.
Blinder, Alan *Central Banking in Theory and Practice.* Cambridge, Mass.: MIT Press, 1998.
Board of Governors of the Federal Reserve System {http://www.federalreserve.gov}
Board of Governors of the Federal Reserve System *Federal Reserve Act, Section 2A. Monetary Policy Objectives.* {http://www.federalreserve.gov/aboutthefed/section2a.htm}
Board of Governors of the Federal Reserve System *Monetary Policy Report to the Congress.* February 2000.
Board of Governors of the Federal Reserve System "Discontinuance of M3." *Federal Reserve Statistical Release,* November 10, 2005.
Board of Governors of the Federal Reserve System *The Federal Reserve System: Purposes and Functions.* 2011.
Board of Governors of the Federal Reserve System "*Economic Projections of Federal Reserve Board Members and Federal Reserve Bank Presidents, September 2012.*" September 13, 2012.
Bofinger, Peter "The German Monetary Unification (Gmu): Converting Marks to D-Marks." *Federal Reserve Bank of St. Louis Review,* Volume 72, July/August 1990.
Boone, Laurence and Worthington, Huw *European Government Monitor: Is Further Tightening Desirable?* Barclays Capital, September 1, 2010.
Boone, Peter and Johnson, Simon *Policy Brief: The European Crisis Deepens.* Peterson Institute for International Economics, January 2012.
Bowles, Carlos, Friz, Roberta, Genre, Veronique, Kenny, Geoff, Meyler, Aidan and Rautanen, Tuomas *The ECB Survey of Professional Forecasters (SPF): A Review After Eight Years' Experience.* ECB Occasional Paper Series No. 59. Frankfurt: European Central Bank, April 2007.
Brockett, Matthew and Thesing, Gabi "Trichet's 'Black List' Fails to Deter Weber as ECB Nears Exit." Bloomberg News, November 4, 2009.
Brost, Marc and Von Heusinger, Robert "Interview with Jean-Claude Trichet, President of the European Central Bank and Die Zeit." Frankfurt: European Central Bank, July 23, 2007.
Brown, Gary, Buccellato, Tullio, Chamberlin, Graeme, Dey-Chowdhury, Sumit and Youll, Robin *Understanding the Quality of Early Estimates of Gross Domestic Product.* Office for National Statistics.
Brown, Gordon *Remit for the Monetary Policy Committee of the Bank of England and the New Inflation Target.* HM Treasury, December 10, 2003.

Buiter, Willem "The ECB Should Vote on Interest Rates, and Then Publish its Minutes." *Financial Times*, July 22, 2008. {http://blogs.ft.com/maverecon/2008/07/the-ecb-should-vote-on-interest-rates-and-then-publish-its-minutes/#}

Buiter, Willem "Quantitative Easing and Qualitative Easing: A Terminological and Taxonomic Proposal." *Financial Times*, December 9, 2008. {http://blogs.ft.com/maverecon/2008/12/quantitative-easing-and-qualitative-easing-a-terminological-and-taxonomic-proposal/#axzz2MalsPVfo}

Buiter, Willem Speech at the conference "The ECB and Its Watchers XI," Center for Financial Studies, Frankfurt am Main, June 15, 2012.

Buiter, Willem, Michels, Jürgen and Rahbari, Ebrahim "The Implications of Intra-Euro Area Imbalances in Credit Flows." *Policy Insight*, No. 57. Centre for Economic Policy Research, August 2011.

Bundesrat {http://www.bundesrat.de/cln_227/EN/Home/homepage__node.html?__nnn=true}

Bundesrat "Consent and Objection Bills." {http://www.bundesrat.de/cln_227/nn_11592/EN/funktionen-en/gesetzgebung-en/zust-einspr-en/zust-einspr-en-node.html?__nnn=true}

Bündnis 90/Die Grünen *Welcome to the Website of the Green Parliamentary Group in the German Bundestag*. {http://www.gruene-bundestag.de/service-navigation/english_ID_2000025.html}

Bureau of Economic Analysis *Gross Domestic Product: Fourth Quarter and Annual 2011 (Third Estimate); Corporate Profits: Fourth Quarter and Annual 2011*. March 29, 2012.

Bureau of Economic Analysis *National Income and Product Accounts: Gross Domestic Product, 2nd Quarter 2012 (Advance Estimate)*. July 27, 2012.

Burns, Arthur F. and Mitchell, Wesley C. *Measuring Business Cycles*. Cambridge, Mass.: NBER, 1946.

Calculating the Ifo Business Climate. {http://www.cesifo-group.de/ifoHome/facts/Survey-Results/Business-Climate/Calculating-the-Ifo-Business-Climate.html}

Cappiello, Lorenzo and Guéné, Stéphane *Measuring Market and Inflation Risk Premia in France and in Germany*. ECB Working Paper Series. Frankfurt: European Central Bank, February 2005.

Carare, Alina and Tchaidze, Robert *The Use and Abuse of Taylor Rules: How Precisely Can We Estimate Them?* IMF Working Paper 05/148. International Monetary Fund, July 2005.

CDU "Successful Policies for Over 50 Years." *CDU Deutschlands*. {http://www.cdu.de/english/history.htm}

Central Statistics Office Ireland {http://www.cso.ie/en/}

Centre for Economic Policy Research *Euro Area Business Cycle Dating Committee*. {http://www.cepr.org/data/dating/default.asp}

Chinn, Menzie D. *A Primer on Real Effective Exchange Rates: Determinants, Overvaluation, Trade Flows and Competitive Devaluation*. Working Paper 11521. National Bureau of Economic Research, July 2005.

Chinn, Menzie D. "Effective Exchange Rates" in *The Princeton Encyclopaedia of the World Economy*. Editors in chief, Kenneth A. Reinert and Ramkishen S. Rajan; Associate editors, Amy Jocelyn Glass and Lewis S. Davis. Princeton: Princeton University Press, 2009.

Clegg, Nick Speech to the Liberal Democrat Spring Conference, March 13, 2011.

Conservative Party *The History of the Conservative Party*. {http://www.conservatives.com/People/The_History_of_the_Conservatives.aspx}

Council of the European Union. Official website of the European Union. {http://europa.eu/about-eu/institutions-bodies/council-eu/index_en.htm}

Council of Mortgage Lenders *CML News & Views*, Issue no. 14, July 25, 2012. {www.cml.org.uk/cml/publications/newsandviews/118/441}

CSU. {http://www.csu.de/partei/international/english.htm}

Czuczka, Tony and Donahue, Patrick "Merkel Says Germany Backs Draghi's Conditions for ECB Aid." Bloomberg News, August 16, 2012.

De Grauwe, Paul "Cherished Myths Fall Victim to Economic Reality." *Financial Times*, July 22, 2008. {http://www.ft.com/intl/cms/s/0/b89eb5b2-5804-11dd-b02f-000077b07658.html}

De Grauwe, Paul "On the Need to Renovate the Eurozone." *International Finance*, 2008.

De Lucia, Clemente and Lucas, Jean-Marc "How Different Are the Fed and ECB?" *Conjoncture*. BNP Paribas, April–May 2007.

Deo, Stephane, Donovan, Paul and Hatheway, Larry "Euro Break-Up – The Consequences." *Global Economic Perspectives*, September 6, 2011.

Destatis {https://www.destatis.de/EN/Homepage.html}

Destatis *Detailed Results on the Gross Domestic Product in the 4th Quarter of 2011*. February 24, 2012.

Deutsche Bundesbank "Macroeconomic Effects of Changes in Real Exchange Rates." *Deutsche Bundesbank Monthly Report*, March 2008.

Die Linke *Die Linke: History and Structure*. {http://en.die-linke.de/index.php?id=9694}

Dijkstra, Lewis and Gakova, Zuzana *Labour Mobility Between the Regions of the EU-27 and a Comparison with the USA*. European Union Directorate-General for Regional Policy, 02/2008.

Directorate General for Economic and Financial Affairs *Who We Are and What We Do*. {http://ec.europa.eu/dgs/economy_finance/index_en.htm}

Draghi, Mario *Introductory Statement to the Press Conference (with Q&A)*. Frankfurt: European Central Bank, July 5, 2012.

Draghi, Mario *Introductory Statement to the Press Conference (with Q&A)*. Frankfurt: European Central Bank, August 2, 2012.

Dutta, Neil and Harris, Ethan S. *Europe Sneezes, the US Catches a Cold*. Bank of America–Merrill Lynch, August 06, 2010.

Economic and Financial Affairs Directorate General *Mission Statement* {http://ec.europa.eu/dgs/economy_finance/organisation/mission_en.pdf}

The Economist Guide to Economic Indicators: Making Sense of Economics, seventh edition. Hoboken, NJ: John Wiley & Sons, Inc., 2011.

Ehrmann, Michael and Fratzscher, Marcel *Purdah: On the Rationale for Central Bank Silence Around Policy Meetings*. Working Paper Series, No. 868. Frankfurt: European Central Bank, February 2008.

Eichengreen, Barry *Globalizing Capital: A History of the International Monetary System*. Princeton: Princeton University Press, 1996.

Elder, Rob, Kapetanios, George, Taylor, Tim and Yates, Tony "Assessing the MPC's Fan Charts." *Bank of England Quarterly Bulletin*, Autumn 2005.

Ellis, Luci *Measuring the Real Exchange Rate: Pitfalls and Practicalities*. Reserve Bank of Australia, August 2001.

Euro Area Economic and Financial Data. {http://www.ecb.europa.eu/stats/keyind/html/sdds.en.html}

Euro Panel. Bbalibor. {http://www.bbalibor.com/panels/eur}

European Banking Federation *Euribor Panel Banks* {http://www.euribor-ebf.eu/euribor-org/panel-banks.html}

European Banking Federation *Euribor Rates* {http://www.euribor-ebf.eu/euribor-org/euribor-rates.html}

European Central Bank {http://www.ecb.int}

European Central Bank *The ECB's Definition of Euro Area Monetary Aggregates*. {http://www.ecb.int/stats/money/aggregates/aggr/html/hist.en.html}

European Central Bank *ECB Glossary*. {http://www.ecb.int/home/glossary/html/act1a.en.html}

European Central Bank *Benefits of Price Stability* {http://www.ecb.europa.eu/mopo/intro/benefits/html/index.en.html}

European Central Bank *The Executive Board* {http://www.ecb.int/ecb/orga/decisions/eb/html/index.en.html}

European Central Bank *Monetary Analysis*. {http://www.ecb.int/mopo/strategy/monan/html/index.en.html}

European Central Bank *Monetary Policy Glossary*. {http://www.ecb.int/home/glossary/html/act4r.en.html#265}

European Central Bank *Protocol on the Statute of the European System of Central Banks and of the European Central Bank*. {http://www.ecb.int/ecb/legal/pdf/en_statute_2.pdf}

European Central Bank *Strategy*. {http://www.ecb.int/mopo/strategy/html/index.en.html}

European Central Bank *Press Release: The Quantitative Reference Value for Monetary Growth*. December 1, 1998.

European Central Bank "The Publication of Eurosystem Staff Economic Projections by the ECB." *ECB Annual Report 2000*. 2001.

European Central Bank *A Guide to Eurosystem Staff Macroeconomic Projection Exercises*. June 2001.

European Central Bank "Recent Findings on Monetary Policy Transmission in the Euro Area." *ECB Monthly Bulletin*, October 2002.

European Central Bank *Press Release: Implementation Issues Related to the Changes to the Eurosystem's Operational Framework for Monetary Policy, and the Indicative Reserve Maintenance Periods Calendar for 2004.* August 1, 2003.

European Central Bank *The Monetary Policy of the ECB 2004.* 2004.

European Central Bank "Output, Demand and the Labour Market." *ECB Monthly Bulletin*, July 2009.

European Central Bank "Loans to the Non-Financial Private Sector Over the Business Cycle in the Euro Area." *ECB Monthly Bulletin*, October 2009.

European Central Bank *Quarterly Survey of Professional Forecasters (SPF).* (Questionnaire for the 2010 Q1 Survey of Professional Forecasters). January 15, 2010.

European Central Bank *Press Release: ECB Decides on Measures to Address Severe Tensions in Financial Markets.* May 10, 2010.

European Central Bank *The Implementation of Monetary Policy in the Euro Area: General Documentation on Eurosystem Monetary Policy Instruments and Procedures.* February 2011.

European Central Bank "Inflation Expectations in the Euro Area: A Review of Recent Developments." *ECB Monthly Bulletin*, February 2011.

European Central Bank "Patterns of Euro Area and U.S. Macroeconomic Cycles – What Has Been Different This Time?" *ECB Monthly Bulletin*, May 2011.

European Central Bank "Cyclical Adjustment of the Government Budget Balance." *ECB Monthly Bulletin*, March 2012.

European Central Bank "ECB Staff Macroeconomic Projections for the Euro Area." *ECB Monthly Bulletin*, March 2012.

European Central Bank "Rebalancing of Competitiveness Within the Euro Area and its Implications for Inflation." *ECB Monthly Bulletin*, June 2012.

European Central Bank "Assessing the Anchoring of Longer-Term Inflation Expectations." *ECB Monthly Bulletin*, July 2012.

European Central Bank *Press Release: Monetary Developments in the Euro Area September 2012.* October 25, 2012.

European Commission *About the European Commission.* {http://ec.europa.eu/about/index_en.htm}

European Commission Directorate-General for Economic and Financial Affairs *The Joint Harmonised EU Programme of Business and Consumer Surveys: User Guide.* July 4, 2007.

European Council *The European Council – An Official Institution of the EU* {http://www.european-council.europa.eu/the-institution?lang=en}

European Union. {http://europa.eu}

Eurostat *Gross Fixed Capital Formation.* {http://circa.europa.eu/irc/dsis/nfaccount/info/data/esa95/en/een00137.htm}

Eurostat *National Accounts Frequently Asked Questions.* {http://epp.eurostat.ec.europa.eu/portal/page/portal/national_accounts/documents/FAQ_NA_1.pdf}

Eurostat *QNA Release Policy.* {http://epp.eurostat.ec.europa.eu/portal/page/portal/national_accounts/documents/quarterly_accounts/release%20policy%202013.pdf}

Eurostat *Principal European Economic Indicators: A Statistical Guide.* 2009.

Eurostat *Europe in Figures: Eurostat Yearbook 2011.*

Eurostat *Eurostat News Release: Flash Estimate for the Second Quarter of 2012*, August 14, 2012.

Eurostat *Eurostat News Release: Euro Area GDP Down by 0.2% and EU27 GDP Down by 0.1%*, September 6, 2012.

Eurostat *Eurostat News Release: Euro Area Annual Inflation Stable at 2.6%*, October 16, 2012.

The Federal Chancellor. {http://www.bundeskanzlerin.de/Webs/BKin/EN/Chancellory/Timeline_Federal_Chancellors_since_1949/timeline_federal_chancellors_since_1949_node.html;jsessionid=912F8CE25F586DD660DF5F32FED84BB3.s4t1}

Federal Electoral Law (Bundewahlgesetz). Translated into English by Inter Nationes {http://www.iuscomp.org/gla/statutes/BWG.htm#ToC19}

Federal Reserve Bank of New York *U.S. Foreign Exchange Intervention.* {http://www.newyorkfed.org/aboutthefed/fedpoint/fed44.html}

Fiscal Affairs Department and the Strategy, Policy, and Review Department. *Modernizing the Framework for Fiscal Policy and Public Debt Sustainability Analysis.* International Monetary Fund, August 5, 2011.

Fischer, Bjorn, Lenza, Michele, Pill, Huw and Reichlin, Lucrezia *Money and Monetary Policy: The ECB Experience 1999–2006.* Preliminary Draft, November 6, 2006.

La Fonction de Premier Ministre. Portail du Gouvernement, La République Française. {http://www.gouvernement.fr/print/premier-ministre/la-fonction-de-premier-ministre}

French Embassy in the United Kingdom *Elections 2012: A User's Guide.* {http://www.ambafrance-uk.org/IMG/pdf/kit_election_2012_EN.pdf}

Friedman, Milton "The Case for Flexible Exchange Rates" in *Essays in Positive Economics.* Chicago: The University of Chicago Press, 1953.

Friedman, Milton *A Program for Monetary Stability.* New York: Fordham University Press, 1960.

Friedman, Milton "Should There Be an Independent Monetary Authority?" in *In Search of a Monetary Constitution.* Edited by Leland B. Yeager. Cambridge, Mass.: Harvard University Press, 1962.

Friedman, Milton *The Counter-Revolution in Monetary Theory.* London: Published for the Wincott Foundation by the Institute of Economic Affairs, 1970.

Friedman, Milton *Inflation and Unemployment.* Nobel Memorial Lecture, December 13, 1976.

Garcia, Juan Angel and Van Rixtel, Adrian "Inflation-Linked Bonds from a Central Bank Perspective." ECB Occasional Paper Series, No. 62. Frankfurt: European Central Bank, June 2007.

Garcia, Juan Angel and Werner, Thomas "Inflation Risks and Inflation Risk Premia." ECB Working Paper Series, No. 1162. Frankfurt: European Central Bank, March 2010.

"German Court Overturns 5 Percent Hurdle." *Spiegel Online*, September 11, 2011. {http://www.spiegel.de/international/germany/european-elections-german-court-overturns-5-percent-hurdle-a-796774.html}

German Missions in the United States "Short-Time Work of 'Kurzarbeit': Frequently Asked Questions." {http://www.germany.info/Vertretung/usa/en/07__Climate__Business__Science/02__Bus__w__Germany/FAQ/FAQ__ShortTimeWork.html}

Giannone, Domenico, Lenza, Michele and Reichlin, Lucrezia "Business Cycles in the Euro Area." Working Papers Series, No. 1010. Frankfurt: European Central Bank, February 2009.

Giannone, Domenico, Lenza, Michele and Reichlin, Lucrezia "Money, Credit, Monetary Policy and the Business Cycle in the Euro Area." CEPR Discussion Paper 8944. Centre for Economic Policy Research, September 24, 2009.

Gjedrem, Svein *Making Use of the Central Bank*. Speech at the Norges Bank Symposium "What is a Useful Central Bank?", November 17, 2010.

Goldrian, Georg (Editor) *Handbook of Survey-Based Business Cycle Analysis*. Cheltenham: Edward Elgar Publishing Limited, 2007.

Goldrian, Georg "A Leading Indicator Composed of Survey Data: Appropriate Construction and Prognostic Significance." *Handbook of Survey-Based Business Cycle Analysis*. Cheltenham: Edward Elgar Publishing Limited, 2007.

Greenspan, Alan *Risk and Uncertainty in Monetary Policy*. Remarks at the meetings of the American Economic Association, San Diego, California, January 3, 2004.

Greider, William *Secrets of the Temple*. New York: Simon & Schuster, 1987.

Hall, Stephen G., Swamy, P.A.V.B. and Tavlas, George S. "Milton Friedman, the Demand for Money, and the ECB's Monetary Policy Strategy." *Federal Reserve Bank of St. Louis Review*. Federal Reserve Bank of St. Louis, May/June 2012.

Hamilton, Scott "King Seen Writing U.K. Inflation Letter as 3% Overshoot Persists." Bloomberg News, May 18, 2012.

Harris, Ethan *Ben Bernanke's Fed: The Federal Reserve After Greenspan*. Boston: Harvard Business Press, 2008.

Harris, Ethan "The Opposite of 'Stagflation'." *The Market Economist*. Bank of America–Merrill Lynch, September 18, 2009.

Hervé, Karine, Pain, Nigel, Richardson, Pete, Sédillot, Franck and Beffy, Pierre-Olivier. "The OECD's New Global Model", *OECD Economics Department Working Papers*, No. 768, OECD Publishing, 2010. {http://dx.doi.org/10.1787/5kmftp85kr8p-en}

Hoover, Kevin D. *The Concise Encyclopaedia of Economics: Phillips Curve*. Library of Economics and Liberty. {http://www.econlib.org/library/Enc/PhillipsCurve.html}

Hott, Christian, Kunkel, André and Nerb, Gernot "The Accuracy of Turning Point Predictions with the Ifo Business Climate." *Handbook of Survey-Based Business Cycle Analysis*. Cheltenham: Edward Elgar Publishing Limited, 2007.

Ifo Institute *Ifo Business Climate Germany: Results of the Ifo Business Survey for August 2012*. August 27, 2012.

International Monetary Fund {http://www.imf.org/external/index.htm}

International Monetary Fund *Balance of Payments Manual*. November 16, 2005.

International Monetary Fund *Greece: IMF Country Report No. 12/57: Request for Extended Arrangement Under the Extended Fund Facility – Staff Report*. March 2012.

International Monetary Fund "Are We Underestimating Short-Term Fiscal Multipliers?" *World Economic Outlook: Coping with High Debt and Sluggish Growth*, October 2012.

International Monetary Fund *Fiscal Monitor. Taking Stock: A Progress Report on Fiscal Adjustment*. October 2012.

International Monetary Fund "Public Debt Overhang and Private Sector Performance." *World Economic Outlook: Hopes, Realities and Risks*, April 2013.

ISM Report on Business Frequently Asked Questions. "What is a Diffusion Index?" {http://www.ism.ws/ISMReport/content.cfm?ItemNumber=10706}

Issing, Otmar *The ECB's Monetary Policy Strategy: Why Did We Choose a Two Pillar Approach?* Contribution to: The Role of Money: Money and Monetary Policy in the Twenty-First Century, Fourth ECB Central Banking Conference, Frankfurt, Germany, November 10, 2006.

Issing, Otmar *The Birth of the Euro*. Cambridge: Cambridge University Press, 2008.

Janssen, Norbert "Measures of M4 and M4 Lending Excluding Intermediate Other Financial Corporations." *Monetary & Financial Statistics*, Bank of England, May 2009.

Jeffries, Ian *Socialist Economies and the Transition to the Market*. London: Routledge, 1993.

Joyce, Michael, Tong, Matthew and Woods, Robert "The United Kingdom's Quantitative Easing Policy: Design, Operation and Impact." *Quarterly Bulletin*, Bank of England, Third Quarter, 2011. {http://www.bankofengland.co.uk/publications/Documents/quarterlybulletin/qb1103.pdf}

Kang, Mingyi *Leading and Lagging Relationships in International Business Cycles*. University of Minnesota, January 1, 2010.

Kapetanios, George, Mumtaz, Haroon, Stevens, Ibrahim and Theodoridis, Konstantinos *Assessing the Economy-Wide Effects of Quantitative Easing*. Working Paper No. 443. Bank of England, January 2012.

Kenen, Peter B. "The Theory of Optimum Currency Areas: An Eclectic View" in *Monetary Problems of the International Economy*. Edited by Robert A. Mundell and Alexander K. Swoboda. Chicago: The University of Chicago Press, 1969.

Keynes, John Maynard *Essays in Persuasion*. London: Macmillan and Co., Limited, 1931.

King, Mervyn "Employment Policy Institute's Fourth Annual Lecture." Bank of England, December 1, 1998. {http://www.bankofengland.co.uk/publications/Pages/speeches/1998/speech29.aspx}

King, Mervyn "The MPC Ten Years On." Speech to the Society of Business Economists, May 2, 2007. {http://www.bankofengland.co.uk/publications/Documents/speeches/2007/speech309.pdf}

King, Mervyn "Letter from the Governor to the Chancellor." Bank of England, February 13, 2012. {http://www.bankofengland.co.uk/monetarypolicy/Documents/pdf/cpiletter120214.pdf}

KOF Swiss Economic Institute "*KOF Economic Barometer*" {http://www.kof.ethz.ch/en/indicators/economic-barometer/}

KOF Swiss Economic Institute *The KOF Economic Barometer: Design and Structure of the KOF Economic Barometer*. {http://www.kof.ethz.ch/static_media/filer_public/2012/09/16/konjunkturbarometer_methodik_en_1.pdf}

Köhler, Matthias and Schmidt, Sandra *ZEW Financial Market Survey*. Zentrum für Europäische Wirtschaftsforschung. {http://www.zew.de/en/publikationen/Kurzinfo_English.pdf}

Kran, Lars-Christian and Owre, Grete "Norges Bank's System for Managing Interest Rates." *Economic Bulletin*. Norges Bank, Q2 2001.

Krugman, Paul "Who Was Milton Friedman?" *The New York Review of Books*, February 15, 2007.

Krugman, Paul "Can Europe be Saved?" *The New York Times*, January 15, 2011.

Krugman, Paul "An Impeccable Disaster." *The New York Times*, September 12, 2011.

Krugman, Paul "Ireland Triumphs!" *The New York Times*, September 30, 2011.

Krugman, Paul "Revenge of Optimum Currency Area." *The New York Times*, June 24, 2012 and Mayer, 2012.

Krugman, Paul "Destructive Responsibility." *The New York Times*, November 30, 2012.

Krugman, Paul *End This Depression Now*. New York: W.W. Norton & Company Ltd., 2012.

Krugman, Paul and Obstfeld, Maurice *International Economics: Theory and Policy*, fourth edition. New York: Addison-Wesley, 1997.

Kumar, Manmohan S. and Woo, Jaejoon *Public Debt and Growth*. IMF Working Paper 10/174. International Monetary Fund, July 2010.

Labour Party *History of the Labour Party*. {http://www.labour.org.uk/history_of_the_labour_party2}

Lee, Jaewoo, Milesi-Ferretti, Gian Maria, Ostry, Jonathan, Prati, Alessandro and Ricci, Luca Antonio *Exchange Rate Assessments: CGER Methodologies*. International Monetary Fund, 2008.

Lee, Peter *UK National Accounts – A Short Guide*. Office for National Statistics, August 2012.

Liberal Democrat History Group *Time Periods: 2010*–{http://www.liberalhistory.org.uk/sub_approach.php?sub_approach_id=27}

Lindlbauer, Jürg "Evaluation and Development of Composite Leading Indicators Based on Harmonised Business and Consumer Surveys." *Handbook of Survey-Based Business Cycle Analysis*. Cheltenham: Edward Elgar Publishing Limited, 2007.

Malkin, Israel and Nechio, Fernanda "U.S. and Euro-Area Monetary Policy by Regions." *Federal Reserve Bank of San Francisco Economic Letter*. Federal Reserve Bank of San Francisco, February 27, 2012.

Mangasarian, Leon "How Germany's Election System Works: What to Watch For Tomorrow." Bloomberg News, September 25, 2009.

Mankiw, N. Gregory *Principles of Economics*, sixth edition. Mason, OH: South-Western Cengage Learning, 2012.

Markit *Markit Economics: About PMI Data*. {http://www.markiteconomics.com/Survey/Page.mvc/AboutPMIData}

Markit *Markit Economics: PMI Data Coverage*. {http://www.markiteconomics.com/Survey/Page.mvc/PMIDataCoverage}

Markit *News Release: Markit/CIPS UK Manufacturing PMI*. June 1, 2012.

Markit *News Release: Markit Eurozone Composite PMI – Final Data*. August 3, 2012.

Marsh, David *The Most Powerful Bank: Inside Germany's Bundesbank*. New York: Random House, 1992.

Martino, Antonio "Milton Friedman and the Euro." *Cato Journal*, Volume 28, No. 2, Spring/Summer 2008.

Mayer, Thomas "Euroland's Hidden Balance-of-Payments Crisis." Deutsche Bank, October 26, 2011.

Mayer, Thomas *Europe's Unfinished Currency: The Political Economics of the Euro*. London: Anthem Press, 2012.

Meier, Simone "Monetary Pillar May Hurt ECB Credibility, Saint Marc Tells FTP." Bloomberg News, May 3, 2007.

Menuet, Guillaume, Schmieding, Holger and Sharratt, Matthew *Eurozone Quarterly Economic Update: A Stronger Recovery*. Bank of America–Merrill Lynch, October 20, 2009.

Meyer, Laurence H. *A Term at the Fed*. New York: Harper Collins, 2006.

Mitlid, Kerstin and Vesterlund, Magnus "Steering Interest Rates in Monetary Policy – How Does it Work?" *Economic Review*. Sveriges Riksbank, 2001.

Mittnik, Stefan and Wohlrabe, Klaus "On the Methodology of Business Cycle Analysis" *Handbook of Survey-Based Business Cycle Analysis*. Cheltenham: Edward Elgar Publishing Limited, 2007.

Moec, Gilles *Euroland IP: Statistical Issues Matter*. Deutsche Bank, April 14, 2010.

Mortimer-Lee, Paul "ECB LTRO: It's QE, Jim, But Not as We Know It." *Market Mover*. BNP Paribas, January 12, 2012.

Münchau, Wolfgang "Why Europe's Officials Lose Sight of the Big Picture." *Financial Times*, October 17, 2011.

Mundell, Robert A. "A Theory of Optimum Currency Areas." *The American Economic Review*, Volume 51, No. 4, September 1961.

National Bureau of Economic Research *US Business Cycle Expansions and Contractions*. {http://www.nber.org/cycles.html}

Nechio, Fernanda "Monetary Policy When One Size Does Not Fit All." *Federal Reserve Bank of San Francisco Economic Letter*. Federal Reserve Bank of San Francisco, June 13, 2011.

Nielsen, Erik Comments made at The ECB and Its Watchers Conference, Center for Financial Studies, Frankfurt am Main, Germany, September 4, 2009. Video available at: {https://www.ifk-cfs.de/index.php?id=1608}

Nordbo, Einar W. *Staff Memo: CPIXE and Projections for Energy Prices. No. 7*. Norges Bank, 2008.

Norges Bank {http://www.norges-bank.no}

Norges Bank *Monetary Policy Report*, October 2012.

Norwegian Ministry of Finance *Market Value of the Government Pension Fund*. {http://www.regjeringen.no/en/dep/fin/Selected-topics/the-government-pension-fund/market-value-of-the-government-pension-f.html?id=699635}

Office for National Statistics *Statistical Bulletin: Consumer Price Indices, July 2012*. August 14, 2012.

Office for National Statistics *United Kingdom National Accounts: The Blue Book, 2012 Edition*. August 15, 2012.

Office for National Statistics *Information Paper: Quality and Methodology Information*. August 17, 2012.

Office for National Statistics *Statistical Bulletin: Labour Market Statistics, October 2012*. October 17, 2012.

O'Neill, Jim *Interview by Thomas Keene at FX12: The Bloomberg Summit*, October 16, 2012.

Organization for Economic Cooperation and Development. {http://www.oecd.org/}

Organization for Economic Cooperation and Development *Glossary of Statistical Terms: Gross National Income*. {http://stats.oecd.org/glossary/search.asp}

Organization for Economic Cooperation and Development *Quarterly National Accounts: Sources and Methods Used by OECD Member Countries*. OECD, 1996. {http://www.oecd.org/std/na/1909562.pdf}

Organization for Economic Cooperation and Development *OECD Economic Outlook*, 85. OECD, 2009.

Organization for Economic Cooperation and Development *Economic Policy Reforms 2011: Going For Growth*. OECD, 2011.

Organization for Economic Cooperation and Development *OECD Economic Outlook*, Volume 2012/1. OECD, 2012.

Orphanides, Athanasios *Taylor Rules*. Finance and Economics Discussion Series: 2007-18. Board of Governors of the Federal Reserve System, January 2007.

Orphanides, Athanasios "Monetary Policy Lessons from the Crisis." Working Paper 2010-1. Central Bank of Cyprus, May 2010.

Pattanaik, Swaha "ECB Must Reconsider M3 Role For Policy – BOF Official." Reuters, May 2, 2007.

Peersman, Gert and Smets, Frank "The Taylor Rule: A Useful Monetary Policy Benchmark for the Euro Area?" *International Finance,* Volume 2, No.1, 1999.

Plosser, Charles I. "The Benefits of Systematic Monetary Policy" Speech to National Association for Business Economics, Washington Economic Policy Conference. Federal Reserve Bank of Philadelphia, March 3, 2008.

Praet, Peter "Heterogeneity in a Monetary Union: What Have We Learned?" Speech at the conference "The ECB and Its Watchers XI", Center for Financial Studies, Frankfurt am Main, June 15, 2012.

Reinhart, Carmen M. and Rogoff, Kenneth S. "Growth in a Time of Debt." *American Economic Review Papers and Proceedings*. January 7, 2010.

Reinhart, Carmen M. and Rogoff, Kenneth S. "Too Much Debt Means the Economy Can't Grow." Bloomberg News, July 14, 2011.

Reinhart, Carmen M. and Rogoff, Kenneth S. "Debt, Growth and the Austerity Debate." *The New York Times*, April 25, 2013.

Reinhart, Carmen M. and Rogoff, Kenneth S. "Reinhart and Rogoff: Responding to Our Critics." *The New York Times*, April 25, 2013.

Reinhart, Carmen M., Reinhart, Vincent R. and Rogoff, Kenneth S. *Debt Overhangs: Past and Present*. Working Paper 18015, NBER Working Paper Series. National Bureau of Economic Research, April 2012.

Rich, Georg *Swiss Monetary Targeting 1974–1996: The Role of Internal Policy Analysis*. ECB Working Paper No. 236. Frankfurt: European Central Bank, June 2003.

Roberts, Russell *An Interview With Milton Friedman*. Library of Economics and Liberty, September 4. 2006. {http://www.econlib.org/library/Columns/y2006/Friedmantranscript.html}

Rogoff, Kenneth "The Global Fallout of a Eurozone Collapse." *Financial Times*, June 6, 2011.

Rosenberg, Michael R. *Financial Conditions Watch*. Bloomberg, October 26, 2011.

Roubini, Nouriel "Early Retirement for the Eurozone?" *Project Syndicate: A World of Ideas*, August 15, 2012. {http://www.project-syndicate.org/commentary/early-retirement-for-the-eurozone-by-nouriel-roubini}

Royal Institution of Chartered Surveyors *RICS UK Housing Market Survey, August 2012*. September 11, 2012.

Royal Swedish Academy of Sciences *Press Release*, October 13, 1999. {http://www.nobelprize.org/nobel_prizes/economics/laureates/1999/press.html}

Ruppert, Wolfgang "Business Survey in Manufacturing." *Handbook of Survey-Based Business Cycle Analysis*. Cheltenham: Edward Elgar Publishing Limited, 2007.

Scheller, Hanspeter K. *The European Central Bank: History, Role and Functions*. Frankfurt: European Central Bank, 2004.

Schindler, Martin, Spilimbergo, Antonio and Symansky, Steve *Fiscal Multipliers*. IMF Staff Position Note. International Monetary Fund, May 20, 2009.

Schmid, Peter "Monetary Targeting in Practice: The German Experience." Center for Financial Studies Working Paper No. 1999/03. Center for Financial Studies, March 1999.

Schmieding, Holger "Germany: The Sick Man of Europe?" *European Monitor*. Merrill Lynch, 1998.

Schmieding, Holger *Mind the Money: Could the Collapse in Real M1 Growth Indicate a Eurozone Recession Risk?* Bank of America, July 2, 2008.

Schmieding, Holger *Tough Love: The True Nature of the Euro Crisis*. Berenberg Bank, August 20, 2012.

Shearing, Matthew *Producing Flash Estimates of GDP: Recent Developments and the Experiences of Selected OECD Countries*. United Nations Economic Commission for Europe, 2003.

Silvia, Stephen J. "Keynes in Lederhosen: Assessing the German Response to the Financial Crisis." *AICGS Transatlantic Perspectives*. American Institute For Contemporary German Studies at Johns Hopkins University, June 2009.

Sinn, Hans-Werner *Can Germany Be Saved?: The Malaise of the World's First Welfare State*. Cambridge, Mass.: The MIT Press, 2007.

Sinn, Hans-Werner "Greece Probably Will, and Should, Leave the Euro Zone." *The Economist*, July 20, 2011. {http://www.economist.com/economics/by-invitation/contributors/Hans-Werner%20Sinn}

Sinn, Hans-Werner "A Crisis in Full Flight." *Project Syndicate: A World of Ideas*, April 25, 2012. {http://www.project-syndicate.org/commentary/a-crisis-in-full-flight}

Sinn, Hans-Werner and Wollmershäuser, Timo "Target Loans, Current Account Balances and Capital Flows: The ECB's Rescue Facility." *International Tax and Public Finance*, July 2012.

Stark, Jürgen "The ECB's Monetary Policy: Preserving Price Stability in Time of Financial Distress." Speech at the conference "The ECB and Its Watchers XI", Center for Financial Studies, Frankfurt am Main, September 4, 2009.

Stark, Jürgen Comments made at The ECB and Its Watchers Conference, Center for Financial Studies, Frankfurt am Main, Germany, September 4, 2009. Video available at: {https://www.ifk-cfs.de/index.php?id=1608}

Statistics Norway *Concepts and Definitions in National Accounts*. 2012. {http://www.ssb.no/english/subjects/09/01/terms/}

Sveriges Riksbank {http://www.riksbank.se}

Sveriges Riksbank "Forecasts and Interest Rate Decisions." {http://www.riksbank.se/en/Monetary-policy/Forecasts-and-interest-rate-decisions/}

Sveriges Riksbank *How is Inflation Measured?* {http://www.riksbank.se/en/Monetary-policy/Price-stability/How-is-inflation-measured-/}

Sveriges Riksbank *Press Release: The Riksbank to Phase Out the CPIX Inflation Measure.* June 9, 2008.

Sveriges Riksbank *Minutes of the Executive Board's Monetary Policy Meeting, No. 4.* September 16, 2009.

Sveriges Riksbank *Repo Rate Cut by 0.25 Percentage Points to 1.25 Percent.* September 6, 2012.

Swiss National Bank {http://www.snb.ch}

Swiss National Bank *The National Bank as a Joint-Stock Company.* {http://www.snb.ch/en/system/print/en/iabout/snb/org/id/snb_org_stock}

Swiss National Bank *The Swiss National Bank in Brief*, seventh edition. June 2012.

Taylor, John B. *Discretion Versus Policy Rules in Practice.* Carnegie – Rochester Conference Series on Public Policy 39, 195–214, 1993.

Taylor, John B. *Principles of Macroeconomics*, fifth edition. Boston: Houghton Mifflin Company, 2007.

Thatcher, Margaret *The Path to Power.* London: HarperCollins, 1995.

The Economist "Politicians in Proportion: How Germany, Seeking the Best of All Worlds, Fiddles With its Voting Rules." December 1, 2012.

Thwaites, Gregory and Wood, Rob "The Measurement of House Prices." *Quarterly Bulletin*. Bank of England, Spring 2003. {http://www.bankofengland.co.uk/publications/Documents/quarterlybulletin/qb0301.pdf}

Tilford, Simon "How to Save the Euro." *Centre for European Reform Essays.* Centre for European Reform, September 2010.

Tompson, W. *The Political Economy of Reform: Lessons from Pensions, Product Markets and Labour Markets in Ten OECD Countries*, OECD Publishing, 2009. {http://dx.doi.org/10.1787/9789264073111-en}

Treaty on European Union. {http://eur-lex.europa.eu/en/treaties/dat/11992M/htm/11992M.html}

Triami Media *What is Euribor?* {http://www.euribor-rates.eu/what-is-euribor.asp}

Trichet, Jean-Claude *Introductory Statement to the Press Conference (with Q&A).* Frankfurt: European Central Bank, April 7, 2011.

UK Debt Management Office *Gilt Market.* {http://www.dmo.gov.uk/index.aspx?page=gilts/indexlinked}

UK Parliament *What the Lords Does.* {http://www.parliament.uk/business/lords/work-of-the-house-of-lords/what-the-lords-does/}

Verdelhan, Adrien "Construction d'un indicateur des conditions monétaires pour la zone euro." *Bulletin de la Banque de France*, No. 58. La Banque de France, October 1998.

Webb, Alex "Bundesbank's Weidmann Has Considered Resignation, Bild Reports." Bloomberg News, August 31, 2012.

Weidmann, Jens "What is the Origin and Meaning of the Target2 Balances?" *Frankfurter Allgemeine Zeitung*, March 13, 2012. Posted in English on webpage of Deutsche Bundesbank.

"Where Do They Stand?: A Quick Guide to Germany's Political Parties." *Spiegel Online*. {http://www.spiegel.de/international/germany/where-do-they-stand-a-quick-guide-to-germany-s-political-parties-a-651388.html}

Yamarone, Richard *The Trader's Guide to Key Economic Indicators*. New York: Bloomberg Press, 2004.

ZEW *Financial Market Survey: Results October 2012*. {http://download.zew.de/e_10_2012_table.pdf}

ZEW *Indicator of Economic Sentiment: A Leading Indicator for the German Economy*. {http://www.zew.de/en/publikationen/Konjunkturerwartungen/konjunkturerwartungenberechnung.php3}

Index

Note: Italic page numbers denote figures, tables or boxes.

Abberger, Klaus 1, 50
average cost of debt 128, 129, *130*, 131

balance-of-payments crisis 105
Bank of England (BoE) 145
  inflation targeting 157, 158
  MPC 148–9, 150–1, 155, 158
  quantitative easing 153–5
base money (M0) 72, 113, *114*
Bernanke, Ben 36, 60–1, 70, 149
Blanchflower, David 88–9, 150–1
Blinder, Alan 2, 70
bond purchases, Germany 115–17
bonds, inflation-linked 76–8
broad money *see* M3 money supply growth
budget balances *130*, 131–2
Buiter, Willem 84, 112–13, 117
Bundesbank 22–3, 69, 71, 73, 84
  government bond purchases 115–17
  Target2 system 121–3
Bundesrat 140–1
Bundestag 137–8, 141
business climate index *see* Ifo Survey
business cycle clock 50–2
business cycles 16–19, 38–9

capital mobility 109–10, 111
Clegg, Nick 164–5
code words 86–7, 152
coincidental indicators
  industrial production 31–4
  PMI surveys 27–31
consumer price index (CPI) 24
  euro area 57–61, 88, 107
  Norway 175
  QE increasing 154
  Sweden 171, *172*
  U.K. 145–8, 157
  vs. GDP and PCE deflators 61–3
consumption 6–9
core inflation 59–60, 96, *106*
corridor systems 92–3, 152–3
Council of the European Union 101–2
currency markets, ECB intervention 93–5

De Grauwe, Paul 71, 89
debt-to-GDP ratio 117–20, 127–31
debt overhang 119
debt restructuring 118, 124
deflation 57, 78, 124, 126
deflators
  exchange rate 23–5
  GDP 61–2
  PCE 62–3
demographics 15
deposit rates 172, 173, 176

197

depreciation 5, 6
  of the euro 21, *22*
  exchange rate 43, 126
diffusion index 29, 44
Doyle, Peter, resignation letter 128–9
Draghi, Mario 61, 74–5, 84, 87, 99, 115
"Dutch disease" 177

East Germany 116–17
Ecofin 103
economic growth 8–9, 15, 52–6
Eichengreen, Barry 125
EUR LIBOR 37–8
Euribor 37–8, *93*
euro crisis 105
  departure from euro area 127
  fiscal consolidation 111–12
  government bond purchases 115–17
  measures of national solvency 117–20
  optimal currency area theory 109–11
  origins of 105–9
  quantitative and qualitative easing 112–15
  resolution of 123–7
  Target2 balances 121–3
  tools for debt sustainability analysis 127–32
Eurogroup 103–4
European Central Bank (ECB) 83–6
  intervention in currency markets 93–5
  mandate of 88–90
  monetary policy implementation 91–3
  survey of professional forecasters 78–80
  Taylor Rule 95–9
  traffic light system 86–7
  two-pillar strategy 90
European Commission (EC) 102–3
  survey of inflation expectations 80–1
European Council 104
European Parliament 102
exchange rate
  deflators 23–5
  East and West Germany 116–17
  ECB intervention 93–5
  effect on GDP 21–3
  fixed vs. flexible 105–7, 110, 125–6
  monetary conditions index 19
expectations *see* Ifo Survey; inflation expectations; ZEW Survey
expenditure method, GDP 5–10
exports 6, *7*, 8, *9*, 22–3

factor mobility 109–10
Federal Reserve
  focus on core inflation 60–1
  GDP deflator vs. CPI 61–2
  inflation measure 62–3
  "Long-Term Asset Purchases" 113, 114–15
  mandate 88
  monetary aggregates 70, 71–2
  press conferences 85
  role in international policy 95
  and the Taylor Rule 95, 98
  voting behavior 149–50
financial conditions index 35–8
fiscal consolidation programs 11–12
fiscal multipliers 112
fiscal transfers 110–11
Fisher, Irving 53
fixed assets 6
flexible exchange rate system 106, 110, 126
FOMC meetings, Fed 62–3, 150
forecasters' survey, ECB 78–80
foreign investment 120
France 143–4
  Banque de France 71, 123
  inflation-linked bonds 76, 77, 78
Friedman, Milton 19, 66–7, 68–9, 106, 126

Index

GDP *see* gross domestic product
Germany 133
   export activity 22–3
   labor market 133–7
   political institutions 137–9
   political parties 139–42
   real effective exchange rate 21–2, *108*
   surveys, ZEW and Ifo 39–52
   see also Bundesbank
gold standard 125
government bond purchases 115–17
government budget balances 132
Greece
   credit advanced to 121–2
   and origins of euro crisis 107–9
   price adjustments 124–5
Greenspan, Alan 98, 149, 150
gross domestic product (GDP) 5
   and the business cycle 16–19
   correlation with Swiss KOF 168–9
   effects of exchange rate on 21–3
   effects of monetary policy on 19–21
   exchange rate deflators 23–5
   expenditure approach 5–10
   income method 11
   and industrial production 31–4
   and loan growth 56
   monetary conditions index 19
   output method 10–11
   release schedule 12–15
   Sweden *172*
   trend growth 15
   in the U.K. 155–7
   versus GNP 11–12
gross national product (GNP) 11–12

harmonized index of consumer prices (HICP) 57–9, 61, 65, 77–8, *79*, 88
Hartz reforms 134–7
headline inflation 59–61
house market survey, U.K. 163
house price indices, U.K. 158–9, *161*, *162–3*

Ifo Survey 41, 44
   business cycle clock 50–2
   correlation with GDP 52
   correlation with ZEW Survey 39–40
   lead and trend 49–50
   questions 45–6, *47*
   supplementary questions 48
IMF 24, 98, 103, 112
   debt sustainability analysis 127–8
   Doyle resignation letter 128–9
   national solvency measures 117–19
   real effective exchange rate 19
imports 6, 8, 14, 19, 23, 62
income method, GDP calculation 11
indebtedness 117–20
industrial production 31–4, 50, *55*
inflation expectations 76
   market-based measures 76–8
   surveys 78–81
inflation measures 57
   inflation expectations 76–81
   labor costs 65–8
   money supply 68–76
   producer price index (PPI) 63–4
   retail price index (RPI) 157–8
   U.K. 157–8
   wage growth 158
   see also consumer price index (CPI)
inflation targeting
   Bank of England 145, 157, 158
   European Central Bank 67, 88
   Norges Bank, Norway 175
   Riksbank, Sweden 171
inflationary pressures 54, 60, 64, 65, 73, 97
interest payments 131
   exclusion from RPI 157–8
   as % of GDP, calculation *130*, 131
interest rates 19–22
   ECB "consensus" system 84–5
   ECB monetary policy 91–3
   ECB traffic light system 86–7
   impact of low 106–7

interest rates (*continued*)
  "purdah" period 86
  raising of 73, 87
  on short-term loans, Euribor and EUR LIBOR 37–8
"intermediate" money (M2) 72–3
"internal devaluation" 124
intervention in currency markets, ECB 93–5
inventories 6, 8–9, *10*, 31
investment spending 6, 8–9
Ireland 11–12, 106–9
Issing, Otmar 71, 86, 88, 94, 95–6
Italy 24–5

Japan 94–5, 119–20

k% rule, Friedman 69
Kang, Mingyi 38
Kenen, Peter 110, 111
Keynes, John Maynard 2, 124
King, Mervyn 2, 149, 150–1, 158
KOF Economic Barometer 168–70
Krugman, Paul 11, 60, 61, 89–90, 110, 112

labor costs 65–8
labor market 2, 38, 48
  Germany 133–7
labor mobility 109–10
Land Registry, U.K. 158, 159, 161, 162
leading indicators 1–2
  financial conditions index 35–8
  Ifo survey 41–52
  KOF, Switzerland 168–70
  M1 money supply growth 52–6
  U.S. business cycle 38–9
  ZEW survey 39–41
Lehman Brothers, bankruptcy of 61, 106–7
liabilities 72, 74, 113, 117, 121
Lindlbauer, Jürg 34
liquidity operations, ECB 115–17

loan growth 54–6, 74–6
loans, inter-bank 37–8

M0 (monetary base) 72, 113, *114*
M1 money supply growth 52–6
M2 money supply 69, 72–3
M3 money supply growth 73
  ECB's reference value for 73, 74
  failure as inflation indicator 71
  loan growth as counterpart to 54–6, 74–6
  ratio to M0, fall in 113, *114*
  vs. M1 money supply 54
M4 money supply growth 155
Maastricht Treaty 88, 93–4, 115
mandate, ECB 80, 88–90
Mankiw, Greg 61–2
Mayer, Thomas 110–11, 125–6
Merkel, Angela 116, 133, 137, 143
Meyer, Laurence 150
mobility, labor and capital 109–11
monetary aggregates 71–4
monetary base (M0) 72, 113, *114*
monetary conditions index 19
monetary policy 68–9
  ECB 61, 83–6, 88, 90–4, 117
  effects on GDP 19–21
  and financial conditions 36
  Norway 176
  Sweden 172–3
  Switzerland 167–8
  Taylor Rule 95–9, 106
  U.K. 146–52
  U.S. 62–3, 70
money multiplier 113
money supply 51–6, 68–76
mortgage lenders 159, *160*
MPC (Monetary Policy Committee)
  interest-rate decisions 148–9
  letter to the Chancellor 146–8
  meeting 151
  voting behavior 149
Mundell, Robert 109–10

Index

NAIRU 68, 97
narrow money (M1) 52–6, 72
National Assembly, France 143, 144
national solvency measures 117–20
natural rate of unemployment 97
NBER 16, *17–18*
NCBs (National Central Banks) 121, *123*
Nielsen, Erik 79–80
Nierhaus, Wolfgang 1, 50
nominal GDP 14, 19, 54, 61–2, 70, *155*
nominal growth 129–31
Norges Bank 175–7
Norway 175–7

OECD 19–22, 97–9
Office for National Statistics (ONS) 156, 157, 158, 159, 162
oil-price rises/shocks 62, 67, 77, 96–7
O'Neill, Jim 111, 116
Outright Monetary Transactions (OMTs) 115–16
optimal currency area theory 109–11
output method, GDP 10–11, *12*
"overhang mandates", Germany 138
overnight deposits 72
    ECB 91–2
    Riksbank 172, 173

PCE (personal consumption expenditures) deflator 62–3
pension fund, Norway 177
PMI (purchasing manager indices) 27–31
political institutions and parties
    Germany 137–41
    U.K. 164–5
population growth 15
Portugal 124–5
price adjustments 124–6
price stability 57, 58, 68, 69, *90*
    ECB's sole mandate 80, 88–90, 94, 97
    Swiss National Bank 167

producer price index (PPI) 63–4
purchasing manager indices (PMI) 27–31

qualitative easing 112–13
quantitative easing 112, 113
    by the BoE, U.K. 153–5
quantity theory of money 53–4

real effective exchange rate 19, 21, 23–5, 107, *108*
real GDP growth 30–1, 53, 54, 56, 74, 118, *130*
recession 8–9, 16, 38, 50–1, 61
"reference value", M3 growth 73, 74
refinancing operations, ECB 91–2, 106, 112–15
Reinhart, Carmen 118, 119, 127–8
repo (repurchase agreement) rate, Sweden 172
retail price index (RPI) 157–8
Rightmove index 159, *161, 163*
Riksbank, Sweden 171–3
risk premia, bonds 60, 77, 78
Rogoff, Kenneth 118, 119, 127–8
RPIX 157–8

Schmieding, Holger 60, 111
Schröder, Gerhard 133, 134–5, 137
"second-round effects" 65, 67
shocks, effects of 20, 22, 36, 38–9, 67
sight deposit rate, Norges Bank 176
Silvia, Steven J. 134
Sinn, Hans-Werner 121–2, 124–5
solvency of nations 117–20
Spain 106–9, 121–2
stability-oriented strategy, ECB 88–90
Stark, Jürgen 52, 59–60, 79, 81, 115
structural unemployment 97, *98*, 99
surveys
    Ifo 41, 44–52
    inflation expectations 78–81
    purchasing manager (PMI) 27–31

surveys (*continued*)
　U.K. housing market 163
　ZEW 39–41, *42–3*
sustainability of nation's debt 117–18, 120, 127–32
swaps 78
Sweden 171–3
Swiss National Bank (SNB) 167–8
Switzerland
　KOF leading indicator 168–70
　Swiss National Bank (SNB) 167–8

Target2 balances 121–3
Taylor Rule 95–9
Thatcher, Margaret 148–9
"three-times rule", business climate index 49–50
Thwaites, Gregory 158–9
tobacco, exclusion from HICP index 77–8
Tompson, William 135, 136–7
total budget balance *130*, 131
traffic light system, ECB 86–7
trend growth, GDP 15, 19, 20–1, 34, 74
trend, Ifo Survey 49–50
Trichet, Jean-Claude 61, 73, 86–7, 89, 111–12
two-pillar strategy, ECB 90

unemployment 66–8
　forecast, Sweden 172
　Hartz reforms, Germany 135–7
　rises in 108–9, 109, 124, 134, 135
　structural 97, 98, 99
unemployment gap 96–7, 106
United Kingdom (U.K.) 145
　Bank of England 145–53
　GDP estimates 155–7
　house prices 158–63
　inflation measures 157–8
　political institutions 164–5
　quantitative easing 153–5
United States (U.S.)
　business cycle 16, *17–18*, 38–9
　"misery index" 67
　Treasury FX decisions 94–5
　wage-price spiral 66
　see also Federal Reserve

value added
　industrial production index 32–3
　output method 10–11, 12

wage cuts 124, 125
wage growth 66, 67, 158
wage-price spirals 65–6
Weidmann, Jens 84–5, 115–16
Wollmershäuser, Timo 121, 122
Wood, Rob 158–9
World Economic Outlook (IMF) 128

Yamarone, Richard 51

ZEW Survey 39–41, *42–3*